Global Poverty, Ethics and Human Rights

Severe poverty is one of the greatest moral challenges of our times. But what place, if any, do ethical thinking and questions of global justice have in the policies and practice of international organisations? This book examines this question in depth, based on an analysis of the two major multilateral development organisations – the World Bank and the UNDP – and two specific initiatives where poverty and ethics or human rights have been explicitly in focus: in the Inter-American Development Bank and UNESCO.

The current development aid framework may be seen as seeking to make globalisation work for the poor; and multilateral organisations such as these are powerful global actors, whether by virtue of their financial resources, or in their role as global norm-setting bodies and as sources of hegemonic knowledge about poverty. Drawing on their backgrounds in political economy, ethics and sociology of knowledge, as well as their inside knowledge of some of the case studies, the authors show how, despite the rhetoric, issues of ethics and human rights have – for very varying reasons and in differing ways – been effectively prevented from impinging on actual practice.

Global Poverty, Ethics and Human Rights will be of interest to researchers and advanced students, as well as practitioners and activists, in the fields of international relations, development studies, and international political economy. It will also be of relevance for political philosophy, human rights, development ethics and applied ethics more generally.

Desmond McNeill is Research Professor, and former Director, at SUM (Centre for Development and the Environment), University of Oslo, Norway.

Asunción Lera St. Clair is Associate Professor and Scientific Director of the Comparative Research Programme on Poverty (CROP-ISSC), University of Bergen, Norway.

Rethinking Globalizations

Edited by Barry Gills, University of Newcastle, UK

This series is designed to break new ground in the literature on globalization and its academic and popular understanding. Rather than perpetuating or simply reacting to the economic understanding of globalization, this series seeks to capture the term and broaden its meaning to encompass a wide range of issues and disciplines and convey a sense of alternative possibilities for the future.

1 Whither Globalization?
The vortex of knowledge and globalization
James H. Mittelman

2 Globalization and Global History
Edited by Barry K. Gills and William R. Thompson

3 Rethinking Civilization
Communication and terror in the global village
Majid Tehranian

4 Globalization and Contestation
The new great counter-movement
Ronaldo Munck

5 Global Activism
Ruth Reitan

6 Globalization, the City and Civil Society in Pacific Asia
Edited by Mike Douglass, K.C. Ho and Giok Ling Ooi

7 Challenging Euro-America's Politics of Identity
The return of the native
Jorge Luis Andrade Fernandes

8 The Global Politics of Globalization
"Empire" vs "Cosmopolis"
Edited by Barry K. Gills

9 The Globalization of Environmental Crisis
Edited by Jan Oosthoek and Barry K. Gills

10 Globalization as Evolutionary Process
Modeling global change
Edited by Geroge Modelski, Tessaleno Devezas and William R. Thompson

11 The Political Economy of Global Security
War, future crises and changes in global governance
Heikki Patomäki

12 Cultures of Globalization
Coherence, hybridity, contestation
Edited by Kevin Archer, M. Martin Bosman, M. Mark Amen and Ella Schmidt

13 Globalization and the Global Politics of Justice
Edited by Barry K. Gills

14 Global Economy Contested
Power and conflict across the international division of labor
Edited by Marcus Taylor

15 Rethinking Insecurity, War and Violence
Beyond savage globalization?
Edited by Damian Grenfell and Paul James

16 Recognition and Redistribution
Beyond international development
Edited by Heloise Weber and Mark T. Berger

17 The Social Economy
Working alternatives in a globalizing era
Edited by Hasmet M. Uluorta

18 The Global Governance of Food
Edited by Sara R. Curran, April Linton, Abigail Cooke and Andrew Schrank

19 Global Poverty, Ethics and Human Rights
The role of multilateral organisations
Desmond McNeill and Asunción Lera St. Clair

Global Poverty, Ethics and Human Rights

The role of multilateral organisations

**Desmond McNeill and
Asunción Lera St. Clair**

LONDON AND NEW YORK

First published 2009
by Routledge
2 Park Square, Milton Park, Abingdon, Oxon OX14 4RN

Simultaneously published in the USA and Canada
by Routledge
270 Madison Avenue, New York, NY 10016

Routledge is an imprint of the Taylor & Francis Group, an informa business

© 2009 Desmond McNeill and Asunción Lera St. Clair

Typeset in Times New Roman by
Taylor & Francis Books
Printed and bound in Great Britain by
TJ International Ltd, Padstow, Cornwall

British Library Cataloguing in Publication Data
A catalogue record for this book is available from the British Library

Library of Congress Cataloging in Publication Data
McNeill, Desmond.
   Global poverty, ethics and human rights : the role of multilateral
organisations / Desmond McNeill and Asuncion St. Clair.
      p. cm. – (Rethinking globalizations ; 19)
   Includes bibliographical references and index.
   1. Economic assistance. 2. Non-governmental organizations. 3.
International organizations. 4. Social justice. I. St. Clair, Asuncion. II.
Title.
   HC60.M3626 2008
   362.5'526–dc22
   2008038493

ISBN 10: 0-415-44704-6 (hbk)
ISBN 10: 0-415-44594-9 (pbk)
ISBN 10: 0-203-88130-3 (ebk)

ISBN 13: 978-0-415-44704-1 (hbk)
ISBN 13: 978-0-415-44594-8 (pbk)
ISBN 13: 978-0-203-88130-9 (ebk)

Contents

Acknowledgements   viii
List of abbreviations   ix

1   Introduction   1

2   International organisations and the challenge of global poverty   10

3   Ethics, human rights and global justice   30

4   UNDP: the human development paradigm   63

5   The World Bank: the internal dynamics of a complex organisation   91

6   UNESCO: 'poverty as a violation of human rights'   113

7   The Inter-American Development Bank: 'social capital, ethics
    and development'   133

8   Conclusion   152

    Notes   155
    Bibliography   169
    Index   183

Acknowledgements

We owe a debt of gratitude to many individuals: friends and colleagues at SUM (the Centre for Development and the Environment, University of Oslo); the members of the reference group for this study – David Crocker, Des Gasper, Robert Archer and Thomas Pogge; audiences who made useful comments at various conferences, workshops and seminars at which we have presented our work, including our colleagues in the International Development Ethics Association (IDEA), and especially GARNET, the EU-funded Network of Excellence on Global Governance, Regionalisation and Regulation, section: North–South Development Issues and the Global Regulatory Framework.

We thank the Research Council of Norway for providing the funds for much of this study; and the Royal Norwegian Ministry of Foreign Affairs for engaging us in some of the activities described in this book.

We especially thank all those who gave us their valuable time in interviews, and spoke so openly and interestingly about their work. We regret that we have chosen not to name them – for reasons explained in the book. We thank also the United Nations Intellectual History Project, and especially Tom Weiss, for giving us access to their interview material and hosting us in New York.

We thank the editor of the series, Barry Gills, for encouragement to write this book; the editorial team at Routledge, Heidi Bagtazo, Amelia McLaurin, Paola Celli and Lucy Dunne; and Inge Tesdal for editorial assistance in finalising the manuscript.

We dedicate the book to our children: Tika Louise McNeill, and Thomas and Nicholas Lera St. Clair.

Abbreviations

ABCDE	Annual (World) Bank Conference on Development Economics
ADB	Asian Development Bank
ADG	Assistant-Director General
AI	Amnesty International
AIDS	Acquired Immune Deficiency Syndrome
BDP	Bureau of Development Policy (UNDP)
CEDAW	Convention on the Elimination of All Forms of Discrimination against Women
CELAM	Latin American Bishop's Conference
CGD	Center for Global Development
COMEST	Sub-Commission on the Ethics of the Information Society (UNESCO)
CROP	Comparative Research Programme on Poverty
DEC	Development Economics Vice-Presidency (World Bank)
DfID	Department for International Development (UK)
ECA	Economic Commission for Africa (United Nations)
ECLAC	Economic Commission for Latin America and the Caribbean (United Nations)
ECOSOC	Economic and Social Council (United Nations)
EGI	Ethical Globalization Initiative
FAO	Food and Agriculture Organization of the United Nations
GATT	General Agreement on Tariffs and Trade
GDN	Global Development Network
GNP	Gross National Product
HD	Human Development
HDCA	Human Development and Capability Association
HDI	Human Development Index
HDR	Human Development Report (UNDP)
HDRO	Human Development Report Office (UNDP)
HR	Human Rights
HRBA	Human rights-based approaches (to poverty)
HURITALK	Human rights talk
IDA	International Development Association

IDB	Inter-American Bank/Inter-American Development Bank
IDEA	International Development Ethics Association
IDRC	International Development Research Centre
IDS	Institute of Development Studies
IEG	Independent Evaluation Group (World Bank)
IFC	International Finance Corporation
ILO	International Labour Organization
IMF	International Monetary Fund
IO	International Organisations
IUCN	World Conservation Union/International Union for Conservation of Nature
WRI	World Resources Institute
LAC	Latin America and the Caribbean
MDG	Millennium Development Goals (United Nations)
MNC/TNC	Multinational Corporation/Transnational Corporation
NGO	Non-Governmental Organization
NIEO	New International Economic Order
NWICO	New World Information and Communication Order
ODC	Overseas Development Council
ODS	Office of Development Studies (UNDP)
OHCHR	Office of the High Commissioner for Human Rights
OXFAM	Oxford Committee for Famine Relief
PRSP	Poverty Reduction Strategy Paper
RAD	Research Alliance for Development
RwG	Redistribution with Growth
SAPRIN	Structural Adjustment Participatory Review Initiative
SDD	Social Development Department (World Bank)
SHS	Social and Human Sciences Sector (UNESCO)
SUM	Centre for Development and the Environment at the University of Oslo (Senter for Utvikling og Miljø)
SUNFED	Special United Nations Fund for Economic Development
UN	United Nations
UNCHR	United Nations Commission on Human Rights
UNCTAD	United Nations Conference on Trade and Development
UNDAF	United Nations Development Assistance Framework
UNDP	United Nations Development Programme
UNEP	United Nations Environment Programme
UNESCO	United Nations Educational Scientific and Cultural Organization
UNFPA	United Nations Population Fund
UNHCR	United Nations High Commissioner for Refugees
UNICEF	United Nations Children's Fund
UNIHP	United Nations Intellectual History Project
UNRISD	United Nations Research Institute for Social Development
UNU/WIDER	United Nations University – World Institute for Development EconomicsResearch

WB	World Bank
WBI	World Bank Institute
WCCD	World Commission on Culture and Development
WDR	World Development Report (World Bank)
WTO	World Trade Organization
WWII	World War II

1　Introduction

The United Nations Millennium Declaration begins with a statement of 'values and principles':

> 1. We, heads of State and Government, have gathered at United Nations Headquarters in New York from 6 to 8 September 2000, at the dawn of a new millennium, to reaffirm our faith in the Organization and its Charter as indispensable foundations of a more peaceful, prosperous and just world.
> 2. We recognize that, in addition to our separate responsibilities to our individual societies, we have a collective responsibility to uphold the principles of human dignity, equality and equity at the global level. As leaders we have a duty therefore to all the world's people, especially the most vulnerable and, in particular, the children of the world, to whom the future belongs.

What does this statement imply – in theory and in practice? Are these merely fine words, or can the very worthy intention of achieving 'a more just world' be realised? The language of justice and solidarity continues throughout the Millennium Declaration. For example: 'Global challenges must be managed in a way that distributes the costs and burdens fairly in accordance with basic principles of equity and social justice. Those who suffer or who benefit least deserve help from those who benefit most.' This reaffirmation of the principles on which the United Nations was founded is, in the declaration, explicitly placed in the context of globalisation – a significantly different situation to that of half a century earlier when the UN Charter was signed.

This book is concerned with the issue of global justice, and more specifically with the role of international organisations in responding to this challenge. There is in the world today no 'global state' or 'global government'; but international organisations such as the World Bank and the UNDP are the nearest thing we have. How are they responding to this challenge? Do they perceive their role as promoting global justice? They may be adopting the discourse of ethics and human rights that this declaration implies; but what does this imply for their policies? To address these questions requires insights from international relations, sociology of knowledge and applied ethics. These are the theoretical perspectives that we bring to bear. And in empirical terms, we explore the question by reference to four specific case studies. Two of these, though relatively modest, are relevant because they very explicitly relate to our central concern: one is the 'Poverty as a Human Rights Violation' initiative of UNESCO, the other is the 'Initiative on Social Capital, Ethics and Development' of the Inter-American Development Bank (IDB). Neither has been particularly successful; and it is revealing to examine why this is the case. But in order to gain a more generalised, systemic understanding of the challenge facing multilateral organisations we start by analysing the experience of the two major global development organisations – the World Bank and the UNDP (United Nations Development Programme) – in dealing with the language of ethics and human rights. We seek thereby to establish a theoretical framework for better understanding the forces, both external and internal, that shape these multilateral institutions and determine how they respond to the ethical challenge of promoting global justice.

One important influence on multilateral organisations is ideas, and their significance has been noted especially in recent years, with the World Bank and UNDP, in particular, emphasising their role as knowledge-brokers. Because of their continuing search for greater financial support, another recent phenomenon affecting multilateral organisations has been their encouragement of public–private partnerships. These two influences on the multilateral system – ideas and material resources – are explored in our earlier works (Bøås and McNeill 2004; Bull and McNeill 2007). The present book represents, in a sense, the completion of a trilogy, dealing, as it does, with a third and often underrated aspect of multilateral organisations – the moral dimension.

Ethics, global justice and the dynamics of multilateral organisations

In recent years, poverty reduction has increasingly been expressed as an ethical issue in the development 'discourse'. And here must be noted the huge influence of the economist-philosopher Amartya Sen, who has become an iconic figure – rarely unquoted in any speech, book or article where the words 'ethics' and 'development' appear together. Although these topics may seem novel to some development researchers and policy-makers, we argue in Chapter 3 that it is more accurate to say that these issues are now *back* on the agenda, reflecting a renewed concern for justice and international responsibilities – within the context of globalisation. But the ways in which multilateral organisations have approached the issues of ethics and global justice, and incorporated – or in some cases avoided – ethical language in their policy documents vary significantly. In this book, we use detailed empirical case studies to explore how ethical analyses of poverty and development are situated within the context of producing knowledge about poverty and its causes. Ethical analyses and human rights perspectives on poverty cannot be seen as disembedded from the world of actual practice and the political processes to which knowledge is subject within multilateral organisations.

In order to understand what might be called the political economy of morality, we introduce the concept of moral authority, arguing that multilateral organisations derive moral authority from being seen to promote the well-being of people of the world, and that this is an important resource for them, in justifying their existence, and maintaining their position in the multilateral system. But our case studies show that to enter the world of moral discourse, and adopt the language of ethics and human rights, constitutes a challenge to these institutions, and to global power relations. In this book we explore the different ways in which this plays out in each institution, and seek to understand these differences by examining the dynamics of multilateral organisations engaged in the common endeavour of poverty reduction.

It is necessary, but far from sufficient, to take account of their differing mandates. Each organisation has its own 'culture', developed over many years in response to both internal and external pressures. But, as we demonstrate, although an organisation can gain credibility by emphasising its moral purpose, to explicitly address ethical issues can also put it at risk. The power of a multilateral organisation derives from factors such as its financial resources, the expertise of its staff, and its relations with collaborating governments. But these, we show, are not easily combined with an emphasis on ethics and human rights; and organisations such as those we study here are therefore faced with a number of challenges.

One is neutrality. Multilateral organisations are created by, and answerable to, governments – many of which are authoritarian and/or corrupt. It is difficult for a multilateral organisation to seriously address the ethical challenge of poverty while also cooperating with a government which manifestly does not promote the well-being of its people. UNDP derives considerable moral authority from its being closely associated with the 'human development' paradigm. But if it allows its decisions to be governed by corrupt and authoritarian states – whether through their place on the executive board or control over UNDP's activities within their national boundaries – this authority is of little use.

A second challenge is accountability. The more powerful a multilateral organisation is, the more it can be held responsible for failing to reduce poverty – or even for exacerbating it. (In some poor countries, foreign aid accounts for the major part of the investment budget.) One way of increasing moral authority is to allow oneself to be held accountable by those one is meant to serve. World poverty is the result of the complex interaction of many forces at global, national and local levels. Multilateral and bilateral development agencies are responsible only in part for this situation; and many different ones are involved, so that it is difficult to trace the individual responsibility of each of them. But to the extent that one of them predominates – through its financial resources and economic expertise – it risks being held responsible for the dire conditions of many millions of poor people; thereby reducing its moral authority. In poor countries, a major international agency may exert considerable influence over the macro-economic policies of a government as well as financing massive projects which affect the well-being of thousands or even millions of people. From the critics of globalisation it is generally the World Bank that gets most blame in this regard.

International development organisations share a moral purpose: the reduction of poverty. And their leaders are accustomed to declaring their lofty goals when making speeches at international fora, and often emphasise the moral imperative that motivates their work. Yet within these organisations ethical debate is muted. In this book we ask: why is this so? In broad terms, the answer lies in the interplay between politics and ethics, and our investigation takes us into a range of different disciplines – most notably international relations and philosophy. In recent years, increasing globalisation has led to concern among theorists of international relations about issues of global justice; and political scientists have addressed questions of the legitimacy and authority of global actors other than nation-states, including multilateral organisations. The work of Amartya Sen, in particular, has drawn attention to the ethical challenge of global poverty; and other philosophers, notably Thomas Pogge, have focused especially on the role of global institutions. Where John Rawls addressed ethical issues within the confines of a bounded community or nation, Pogge has extended our gaze to the international economic system and the role of international organisations. But, as we elaborate in detail in Chapter 3, there is a long tradition not only among researchers, but also activists and theologians, addressing issues of ethics, justice and human rights in relation to the poor. In this book we draw on these rich sources in addition to political science and philosophy. One of the major reasons why ethics and human rights have entered the agenda is pressure from NGOs, which have been increasingly vocal in their criticisms of the Bretton Woods institutions in particular, and the global economic and political system in general. We will not be making many specific references to their publications, but they are becoming a significant source of critical, and often well-informed, comment.

An important manifestation of the concern with global justice has been the increasing use of the language of human rights; even the claim, explored in this book, that poverty is a violation of human rights. But the practical impact of such a claim is limited by the absence of any global equivalent of the state. All of us, we are told, are 'citizens of the world'. But what does this actually mean, if there exist only nations and no super-ordinate body? The nearest thing we have, it seems, are the various multilateral organisations, such as those studied in this book – though some would argue the merits of an 'alternative' body such as the World Social Forum.

It is widely agreed that rich, privileged people in the world have some moral obligation to improve the well-being of poor, disadvantaged people – wherever they may reside. This sentiment seems to have gained strength over time, with the burgeoning of cosmopolitanism. Perhaps there is a parallel here with the increasing acknowledgement, a century or two ago, of the same sentiment with regard to the citizens of a single country. This sense of duty towards people of other nations is the primary rationale for foreign aid. (There are, of course, other – more self-interested – reasons for providing development assistance. See, for example, Martinussen and Engberg-Pedersen 2003.) But aid has turned out to be problematic in practice. The business of aid has, from the start, been state-based, and a complex machinery has been constructed to link the rich person and the poor person – separated as they are by national boundaries. In the case of multilateral development assistance, this machinery involves three parties: the government of the rich person, the government of the poor person, and an international organisation. (Largely in reaction against this situation, NGOs have played an increasingly important role – a role that was played by religious bodies a century ago. These NGOs tend to bypass the state, both in the rich and the poor country; but not entirely – rich countries provide much of the NGOs' funding, and the states in poor countries often seek to control the activities of NGOs.) The relationship between rich and poor, in different countries, is thus a complex mix of morality and politics; and the moral responsibility of the rich to the poor is mediated through a plurality of institutions. Does the existence of multilateral organisations resolve or compound this ethical dilemma? Does it promote or hinder a cosmopolitan approach, wherein the moral responsibilities of the rich of the world towards the poor can be effectively exercised? And does the language and practice of human rights help? International human rights law assigns rights to the individual, but assigns responsibilities to the person's state, not to some international body. But what is the alternative: direct intervention, transgressing national sovereignty; or indirect intervention, imposing conditionality? To what extent can and should international organisations 'cut out the state'? These are some of the issues that confront multilateral organisations such as the four which we examine in this book.

The case studies

The World Bank is the most powerful international development organisation. Although its leaders may adopt the rhetoric of noble purpose, the organisation is in fact rather cautious about taking on the language of ethics and rights. We argue that it is precisely because of its financial muscle and its economic expertise that this is so – basing our argument mainly on an analysis of the process of producing the World Bank's *World Development Report 2006* on equity and development, and the organisation's recent engagement with human rights issues.

By contrast, the UNDP has much less clout. Through its promotion of the concept of human development, it has gained some moral authority, but it is constrained by its need to work so closely with national governments – many of them quite resistant to both the language and practice of justice for their citizens. We show how the legitimacy that the UNDP gains by virtue of its close relationship with partner countries acts as a powerful limitation on its ability to exert influence – especially within the field of human rights.

In addition to examining these – the two most important 'global' development organisations – we also include in this book case studies of two less studied organisations, which we have chosen because each of them has taken an initiative explicitly related to ethics and/or human rights. In UNESCO, we examine the fortunes of the project, 'Poverty as a Human Rights Violation'. This was an attempt to involve philosophers, lawyers and economists in a serious debate over the ethics of extreme poverty, but it was severely hampered by UNESCO itself – being regarded as unduly controversial. In the IDB, we examine the 'Initiative on Social Capital, Ethics and Development', which was initiated and supported by the President of the organisation. In this case, the limitations of the initiative lay largely in the weakness of its conceptual foundations; and although it attracted considerable interest in the region, it had negligible impact within the IDB itself and has now virtually come to an end.

Our four case studies thus show how, in very different ways, global organisations established to enhance the well-being of people of the world, regardless of national boundaries, are hindered from addressing their work in ethical terms. To understand the reasons for this, it is necessary to take a step back and examine the fundamentals of development assistance. The phenomenon with which we are concerned is global justice.[1] Justice may be seen in terms of relations between persons, or between groups of persons. When the issue is global justice, this distinction becomes particularly significant, especially when global justice is cast more narrowly within the context of foreign aid. Stripped to the essentials, foreign aid involves people in rich countries providing material assistance to people in poor countries. To simplify, one may refer to these as 'rich people' giving to 'poor people'.[2]

In order to arrange for the transfer of aid from rich people to poor people, a complex organisational structure is necessary; but that which has been built up is very far from ideal. Let us briefly examine the structure that exists today.[3]

Rich people (mostly) pay taxes, part of which is used for foreign aid. And they vote for governments which favour foreign aid. The government of the rich country transfers funds to the government of the poor country (either through bilateral channels, a multilateral agency or an NGO), which, ideally, then uses the money to promote the well-being of its people. The administrative complexity of the structure leads to commensurate complexity in the moral obligations between the entities concerned. In principle, the requirements of global justice assign rights to the poor, and impose obligations on the rich. In practice, in the case of multilateral development assistance, these rights and obligations are mediated through three institutions: the donor government, the international organisation, and the recipient government. Responsibility is, under these circumstances, very readily dissipated.

The revamping of the Universal Declaration of Human Rights, and recent efforts to mainstream across the whole UN system a unified view of first- and second-generation rights, have transformed human rights into the global ethic of our secular age. And the Millennium Development Declaration, and the accompanying Millennium Development Goals (MDGs), may be seen as the nearest thing we have to a statement of global moral obligations. But these rights and obligations are expressed almost entirely in relation to national states.

In this book we explore some of the hindrances to a truly global moral order – to global justice – making use of the detailed knowledge we have gained through working with the chosen organisations and, in several cases, with the specific initiatives examined. Why cannot organisations with global scope and a global mandate – such as the World Bank and the UNDP – more explicitly act, and be proud to act, as promoters of global justice? One major reason we find is the structure of these global organisations, and more specifically the role of national governments within them. There are two sides to the coin of global justice: justice between nations, and justice within nations. While poor countries emphasise the importance of the former; rich countries emphasise the importance of the latter. The result is often a sort of stalemate, although this plays out rather differently between different organisations.

As we describe, there is considerable variation in the 'culture' of these different international organisations; but many of their staff are highly motivated – seeking, through their work, to make a contribution to development and the reduction of world poverty. Yet they are often frustrated, finding it hard to translate the moral purpose which justifies the existence of their organisation into practical action – linking the 'why' and 'how' of the development task. Yet their frustration, and implicit criticism, is seldom publicly expressed. Perhaps it should be; perhaps staff should be allowed some 'ethical space' within which to voice their views. Multilateral development organisations have a moral purpose, and they derive authority from this purpose. But their efforts are often thwarted by the governments of the people they are meant to assist: whether by their representatives that sit as directors on the boards of governors of the organisations, or by government officials who resist (overtly or covertly) efforts to ensure that the assistance provided reaches those in greatest need. As employees of a 'global' institution, the staff – from the President or Administrator on down – should, we suggest, feel a responsibility to their global fellow-citizens. If this provokes them to speak out against the 'owners' of the institution then this is something which we, as fellow global citizens, should welcome and support. Such, however, is the nature of these organisations that this is the exception rather than the rule, and is seen as a transgression rather than fulfilment of their duties and loyalties. In the rest of this book we seek to understand better how this situation has come about: why, when it comes to practice rather than rhetoric, the language of ethics proves unsuited to multilateral development organisations, and the demands of universal human rights are muted.

Observant participation

The material we use in this book is based largely on written sources, and on interviews with people in, or very close to, the organisations concerned. But we have also learned much from being involved, to varying extents, in most of the activities which we take as our empirical case studies. In the case of the World Bank (Chapter 5), we interacted on a number of occasions with members of the team preparing the *World Development Report 2006*; and, on behalf of the Norwegian Ministry of Foreign Affairs, were involved in efforts by the Nordic countries to promote a human rights agenda in the Bank. In the case of the IDB (Chapter 7), we were engaged by the ministry to collaborate with the team working on the 'social capital, ethics and development' initiative, supporting their efforts and presenting papers at their conferences. Our involvement in the UNESCO case (Chapter 6) was much more limited, but here too we had access to some information by virtue of meetings attended. The UNDP is an organisation that we both know quite well from earlier work, but here we have not had privileged access.

The approach that we have adopted under these circumstances we refer to as 'observant participation' – to distinguish it from the more well-established 'participant observation' of anthropologists, while making the point that we are not complete outsiders. Researchers working on development organisations are increasingly finding themselves in a similar situation, and it raises both ethical and methodological questions.[4] The ethical question is whether we have abused our position vis-à-vis either those in the organisations concerned with whom we have interacted or the Norwegian Ministry of Foreign Affairs.[5] And there are two methodological questions: one is whether our interpretation is biased by our 'insider' position; the other is whether we have ourselves influenced the situation we are trying to understand. What is clear is that had it not been for our privileged position, the opportunity to participate so actively (and possibly even exert influence) would have been absent.

As regards the ethical issue, we would note that at the meetings that we have attended it has been clear that we are researchers, not government employees. But we have clearly benefited from being associated with the Norwegian Ministry of Foreign Affairs, and this places us in a dilemma when it comes to the use of the material obtained, and more specifically to the use of quotations. In this book, we have chosen to resolve this by giving direct quotations only from interviews that we have carried out as an explicit part of the research for this book, never from remarks made outside an interview situation. The next question concerns attribution. This is problematic not only because some of those we interviewed were quite outspoken, but also because they may have been more outspoken precisely because they looked on us as 'insiders', even if we were in a formal interview situation. Somewhat reluctantly, we have resolved this by not naming any of those interviewed – making reference, when necessary, only in broad terms, e.g. to 'a senior staff member'. This is regrettable, since we were fortunate to be able to interview some very senior staff, but on balance we decided this was the best course to follow. (In principle, we could have adopted a different rule in the case of UNDP, where we did not have 'insider access', but we felt this would be inconsistent with the rest of the book. As a result, however, our use of direct but not directly attributed quotations is greatest in the UNDP chapter.)

The methodological challenges of 'observant participation' are less serious, but still deserve mention. As partial 'insiders' we are certainly not unbiased; but no commentator can be, and we believe that our position has allowed us to see what someone further removed could not. Whether this gives us a more 'correct' or 'true' understanding of events is for others to judge; but our views are not thereby invalidated. On the second methodological issue, we do have reason to believe that we had some minor influence – for example on the process of producing WDR 2006 – but it would be foolish to exaggerate our importance. In this case, although our involvement might have marginally modified the final version of the report, it was certainly surely not sufficient to change the conclusions that we have drawn in this book.

Although adopting a broadly uniform approach to the study as a whole, we have not found it appropriate to impose a common structure in the presentation of the four case studies. In part this is because the nature and extent of our own involvement has varied; but also because of our differing personal perspectives and disciplines. Each chapter may therefore be read independently, although there are also many interesting insights to be derived from a comparison between them.

We have also brought to the analysis our own normative position, and it is perhaps appropriate to state this explicitly. We believe that the existence of international institutions renders it possible for individuals to respond to the intuitive demands of global justice; something which, in the absence of such institutions, would for practical reasons be impossible. And because this is possible, it is also, we believe, a moral duty. International organisations are what we call 'response-able'; they are particularly well placed to act by virtue of the powers that the people of the world have given them: the economic resources and expertise that enable them to change the world, and the political legitimacy they enjoy by virtue of their mandates.

In addressing the moral dimensions of multilateral organisations, this book is an exploration and reflection about the difficulties and complexities of bringing development ethics and global justice home – so to speak – as part of the normal functioning of multilateral organisations. As such, it aims to contribute to a sociological understanding of the field of development ethics and to complement our earlier work on the interrelations between knowledge production, politics and ethics (St. Clair 2006a, 2006b, 2007; McNeill 2004, 2007b). At the same time, the book aims to provide insights that may allow the opening of 'an ethical space'; the possibility of ethical analysis and reflection within multilateral organisations entrusted with fighting poverty. Our own normative position is that precisely because of their mandates, capacities and resources, organisations whose explicit purpose is to ameliorate poverty have not merely a formal but also a *moral* responsibility to do so. They are response-able to protect people from the scourge of poverty.

2 International organisations and the challenge of global poverty

Introduction

Many people living in rich countries today regard the existence of extreme poverty in poor countries as an affront to justice. But it is implausible, we suggest, to claim that each of these individuals is morally responsible for this extreme poverty – unless one also includes international organisations in the picture. International *development* organisations, such as World Bank and UNDP, are important because they are mandated to ameliorate conditions of extreme poverty; and international organisations of various kinds, such as WTO and the IMF (and also, again, the World Bank), may implement rules which, in practice, contribute to the conditions of extreme poverty. For these reasons, such organisations have a very real responsibility; and the responsibility of their staff and the 'non-poor' inhabitants of the world is to ensure that the organisations successfully achieve their task.

The existence of international institutions, then, renders it possible for individuals to respond to the intuitive demands of global justice; something which, in the absence of such institutions, would for practical reasons be impossible. By contrast with individuals, international organisations are thus 'response-able'; they are particularly well placed to act by virtue of the powers that we, the people of the world, have given them: the economic resources and the expertise that enable them to change the world, and the political legitimacy they enjoy by virtue of their mandates.

In this book, however, we shall show how these same powers have constrained them from behaving as moral agents; how the various organisations we examine have, for very differing reasons, been hesitant to embrace the discourse of ethics and human rights. The reasons for this are complex and varied, as we shall show. But a major constraint has been the actions of states; both those that created them (in the idealistic period after World War II) and the newly independent states which later joined, and claimed that – in contrast to the imperial powers that had once ruled them – they would act in the best interests of their people.[1] For this reason we shall argue, more controversially, that not only do these international organisations have a responsibility to ameliorate poverty, they also have a responsibility to rise above the states that created them – should this be necessary in order to achieve their purpose.

In this chapter, we set out a framework for analysing the situation facing multilateral organisations, and summarize some of the findings from the four case studies (presented in detail in Chapters 4 to 7) in terms of this framework.

The analytical framework

Four factors are crucial in determining the scope for action of multilateral organisations:

- their clout (mainly financial);
- their expertise (especially economic);
- their political legitimacy (delegated authority from states);
- their moral authority.

These factors may be seen as sources of power, legitimacy and authority; as different dimensions of the comparative advantage of these organisations vis-à-vis others; or even as expressions of their institutional identity. We find them instructive in our efforts to compare the strengths and weaknesses of the organisations under study, and the dilemmas that they face in addressing ethical issues. They help us to understand the varying and ambivalent attitudes and practices regarding ethics and human rights of the different organisations. The nature and significance for our research of these four factors became clear in the course of collecting empirical material in our case studies. This was perhaps most marked in our interviews relating to UNDP, an organisation which, by virtue of its broad and challenging mandate, is especially concerned with defining its place in the multilateral system, largely in contradistinction to the World Bank. The considerable power of the World Bank, relative to other development organisations, is very widely acknowledged; but this is also regarded by many as weakening its legitimacy. To put it simply, the World Bank is seen by its critics as using its financial clout and economic expertise to enforce policies and promote projects which do not benefit the poor. The UNDP benefits to the extent that it is contrasted to the World Bank; and the legitimacy that it derives from this is nowhere more evident than in the UNDP's association with the human development paradigm. This, we suggest, gives the organisation significant moral authority.

Of the four factors we have identified, it is this, 'moral authority', that is the most nebulous. And it is least well-established in the international relations literature, although the term has occasionally appeared in recent works.[2] (Note that our conception of moral authority is significantly different from that which is standard among philosophers; this book draws on both philosophy and political science, but the terminology of the two disciplines is not always consistent.) Of particular relevance to our analysis is an article by Rodney Hall relating to feudal Europe, which 'advances the argument that transnational moral authority is employed as a power resource to influence transnational outcomes and that it was employed as such in the presovereign system of feudal Europe' (Hall 1997: 591).[3] We shall argue that moral authority is a power resource today – albeit in a very different context. We suggest that the role of the church in the Middle Ages is in the West today occupied by 'civil society': a humanistic source of moral authority, represented by 'the people'.

An excellent example of the sort of organisation which enjoys such moral authority is Amnesty International. Can international organisations also draw on such moral authority – the authority that comes from representing the common good, the interests of the poor? Development organisations, like World Bank and UNDP, have a moral purpose: the reduction of poverty. This, in principle, gives them moral authority. However:

- in view of the heavy criticism that some, especially the World Bank, have received in recent years, it is clear that it is not enough simply to have stated good intentions;
- to the extent that international organisations (IOs) compete for resources and influence, what matters is how each IO performs relatively to the others.

In the field of international relations, it is rather unusual to find reference to moral authority. This is certainly the case with regard to the 'realist' school.[4] Realists see international relations as essentially competitive, even conflictual, with each state serving to maximise its own interest; and they emphasise mainly military and economic power. For realists, to simplify somewhat, an international organisation is simply a forum where the competing interests of states are brought together, not an autonomous body in any significant sense. Morality finds no place in such a theory, and international organisations rather little. There are, of course, numerous alternative theories in international relations, ranging to the opposite extreme of social constructivism.[5] It is not necessary to go fully to this other extreme to find acceptance for the claim among political scientists that ideas and norms – if not explicitly morality – are also important determinants of state action. It is also widely recognised, outside of realist theory, that states are not the only important actors. This is now particularly recognised in the context of globalisation, which, to quote Kahler and Lake, 'drains political authority from nation-states'. Governance, as they put it 'migrates down to newly empowered regions, provinces and municipalities; up to supranational organizations; and laterally to such private actors as multinational firms and transnational organizations (NGOs)' (Kahler and Lake 2003: 1).

Multilateralism and globalisation[6]

Most of the recent academic discussion on multilateralism has focused on security, and much of the debate has been concerned with the role of the

United States; development has not been a central issue. In the literature on multilateral organisations, our concern in this book, John Ruggie is a major figure. His famous definition of multilateralism is 'an institutional form that coordinates relations among three or more states on the basis of generalized principles of conduct' (Ruggie 1993:11). Based on the work of Karl Polanyi (1944), he describes the post-war international economic order as a system of 'embedded liberalism'. This, he says,

> rested on a grand domestic bargain: societies were asked to embrace the change and dislocation attending international liberalization, but the state promised to cushion those effects by means of its newly acquired domestic economic and social policy roles.
>
> (Ruggie 1997: 5)

Ruggie rejected the argument of orthodox liberals that many problems of the post-war regime emerged out of the inconsistent application of liberal norms; rather this was inherent in the 'embedded liberal compromise':

> [T]hat a multilateral order gained acceptance reflected the extraordinary power and perseverance of the United States. But that multilateralism and the quest for domestic stability were coupled and even conditioned by one another reflected the shared legitimacy of a set of social objectives to which the industrial world had moved, unevenly but 'as a single entity'.
>
> (Ruggie 1982: 398)

But, as Ruggie himself notes, the benefits of embedded liberalism were never fully extended to developing countries, since they were exposed to the demands of openness towards international markets but ill equipped to provide buffers against the negative effects. This resulted in various attempts at forging a compromise at the international level. Whether or not one accepts Ruggie's model,[7] it appears that embedded liberalism has been gradually undermined by a combination of factors: the introduction of neo-liberal policies at the domestic level; economic globalisation that has increased the speed and volume of flows of goods, money, knowledge and information across the world; and the related rise of transnational actors, not least major transnational companies (see Bull and McNeill 2007). The weakening of state protection of vulnerable sectors, and the reduced ability of states to absorb surplus labour, have led to increased inequality across the globe.

At the same time, the multilateral system is less willing, and less able, to exert control over powerful economic actors; the market-augmenting institutions of the multilateral system – such as the World Trade Organisation (WTO) and the International Monetary Fund (IMF) – are still strong, in spite of periodical crises. (The IMF has, in recent years, become less powerful than in the 'heyday' of structural adjustment, and some – such as Woods 2006 – are forecasting its demise.) Certainly the WTO is in many respects stronger than its predecessor, the General Agreement on Tariffs and Trade (GATT). At the same time, parts of the multilateral system that have attempted to regulate global capitalism have been weakened.

Moral authority

Few theorists of international relations have devoted attention to moral questions in relation to states, and even fewer in relation to international organisations. But if, as we claim, moral authority can be a source of power, then it certainly merits attention by political scientists.[8] To the limited extent that moral authority has been studied, it has been mainly with regard to the behaviour of states rather than international organisations. And to the extent that it has been debated with regard to international organisations, this has been mainly in relation to humanitarian issues, narrowly defined; not issues of global poverty.

Barnett and Finnemore, who have contributed greatly to the limited body of work on this topic, use the term 'moral authority' to supplement forms of authority that are better established in the international relations literature (Barnett and Finnemore 2004: 25). In *Rules for the World: International Organizations in Global Politics*, they analyse the power, legitimacy and authority of international organisations such as the International Monetary Fund and the United Nations High Commission for Refugees (UNHCR). Here, they make the standard distinction between the substantive legitimacy of organisations ('whether they are reasonably successful at pursuing goals that are consistent with the values of the broader community'), and their procedural legitimacy (that 'their procedures are viewed as proper and correct'). (Barnett and Finnemore 2004: 166). In analysing the authority of international organisations they focus particularly on rational-legal authority, which, they state, referring to Max Weber, derives from their being bureaucracies, whose authority 'is invested in legalities, procedures, and rules and thus rendered impersonal' (2004: 21). Their 'rational-legal authority' thus corresponds, we suggest, to their 'procedural legitimacy'. What is interesting for our purpose is that they sub-divide rational-legal authority into three sub-broad categories: delegation, morality and expertise, which they refer to as 'providing content to the overall form – rational-legal authority'. In summary, the different sources of power of IOs that they identify correspond fairly well to the four that we have identified, including moral authority.[9]

Moral authority, they say, derives from the organisations representing the world community's interest as opposed to national interests: here, notions of neutrality, impartiality and objectivity come into play. 'IOs are supposed to be more moral (ergo more authoritative) in battles with governments because *they represent the community against self-seekers*' (2004: 23, italics added).

Another relevant theorist to cite is Risse: 'Take the UN and its organizations. These IOs gain their legitimacy because they claim to be oriented toward the world's common good rather than to the egoistic interests of the principals to whom they are internally accountable' (Risse 2004: 11). 'Compared to states, IOs, and MNCs', he argues,

> NGOs lack material resources. All they have to wield influence in world politics is moral authority and expert knowledge in their respective issue-area of concern. (I)NGOs' moral authority, however, is directly linked to claims that they represent the common good in global affairs as well as the 'voices of the weak and powerless'.
>
> (Risse 2004: 13)

He quotes Willetts (1996), who refers to NGOs as the 'conscience of the world'.[10]

More generally, this discussion relates to the concept of 'soft power' in international relations, associated most notably with Nye, and of especial relevance in recent years in the context of US foreign policy and attitudes to multilateralism. Nye too makes reference to the power of NGOs: 'Many nongovernmental organizations claim to act as a "global conscience" representing broad public interests beyond the purview of individual states' (Nye 2004: 90).

In summary, it appears that within international relations theory, and more specifically the study of IOs, the significance of moral authority is beginning to be recognised. Before proceeding, we shall, against this background, clarify more precisely the meaning we attach to the four forms of authority we wish to distinguish. We find it helpful to begin by quoting at greater length from Hall's paper on moral authority.[11]

> The crown, and later its state, was to compete effectively with the Church for this moral authority as the Middle Ages waned. The absolutist state would ultimately wrest this authority from the Church, uniting temporal and sacral authority in the person of the absolute monarch. ... More recently, the moral authority of the monarch, sacred in his person, has been transferred to 'the people'. ... political leaders have found it useful to invoke the moral authority they derive from speaking and acting in the name of their 'people' and have exercised it nationally rather than transnationally.
>
> (Hall 1997: 619)

Thus, Hall describes two parallel and interrelated processes. While temporal authority gradually shifted from the crown to the state, moral authority shifted first from the church to the crown, and subsequently to political leaders – speaking and acting in the name of their 'people'. Hall asserts that this was exercised only at national level; while we are suggesting that international organisations (and NGOs) now seek to exercise moral authority transnationally. To clarify what we mean by the moral authority of international organisations, we need to define it in relation to the other three, better established, sources of power.

The first that we identify, briefly termed 'clout', we use to refer to power in financial/economic terms: the extent to which the organisation in question can use its 'muscle' to bring about change. (The 'clout' that derives from financial/economic power is intimately linked with economic expertise, and hence bound up with the next factor listed.) Although this is an important factor distinguishing the World Bank from, say, the UNDP, it should also be noted that the ability of multilateral organisations to influence the actions of states – e.g. through structural adjustment programmes – is more limited than critics often claim. Several commentators have questioned whether the multilateral organisations can really be said to have made countries do what they otherwise would not (Mosley *et al.* 1991; Killick *et al.* 1998; Bull 2005; Easterly 2006).

The second factor we identify is expertise. The significance of knowledge and expertise as a source of authority within the multilateral system has long been acknowledged (E. Haas 1990; P. Haas 1989, 1992), and there has been an upsurge of research on the topic in recent years (Stone 2000; Wade 2002; Bøås and McNeill 2003; Stone and Maxwell 2004), perhaps because the construction of expertise-based authority has been a conscious strategy of several multilateral institutions, particularly the World Bank, which since 1996 has attempted to purvey the image of being a 'knowledge bank' (ref. Wolfensohn's speech at the Bank's annual meeting that year). What is considered knowledge and expertise, however, is highly contested; particularly, perhaps in the field of development (Stone 2000; Bøås and McNeill 2004; Keeley and Scoones 2003; King and McGrath 2004; Mosse forthcoming a; St. Clair 2006b). And expertise can be used as a powerful instrument for 'framing' debate, exercising a Gramscian hegemony over the discourse:

> Powerful states (notably the USA), powerful organizations (such as the IMF) and even, perhaps, powerful disciplines (economics) exercise their power largely by framing: which serves to limit the power of potentially radical ideas to achieve change. A successful framing exercise will both cause an issue to be seen by those who matter, and ensure that they see it in a specific way. And this is achieved with the minimum of conflict or pressure. For the ideas appear to be 'natural' and 'common sense'.
>
> (Bøås and McNeill 2004: 220)

What kind of expertise counts? International development organisations have treated poverty as primarily an economic phenomenon, with the emphasis placed on economic growth. Despite resistance from many critics, it is economics that has been the dominant discipline in terms of the power to set and frame the development agenda. Although we choose to define the term 'expertise' to refer to all potentially relevant types of expertise, such as engineering, anthropology and law, it is clear that it is economic expertise that is the major source of power.

Political legitimacy (delegated authority from states) is the third category that we distinguish. One might suggest that this should refer to the actual (or perceived) responsiveness of the institution with regard to the interests of the poor – who make up the greater part of the world's community. But we interpret it in formal terms, to refer to the system of governance of the organisation. Traditionally, the legitimacy of a multilateral organisation rests on its democratic governing structure and its legal dependence on legitimate states. In the case of United Nations organisations, the governance structure was designed to partially correct the discrepancy of power between the large and powerful countries and the smaller, less powerful ones. The formal-legal legitimacy of the multilateral system is thus based on a traditional view of the distinction between the domestic and the international sphere in international politics. Following a Weberian logic, the state – defined by its monopoly of the legitimate use of physical force within a given territory – is the exclusive locus of legitimacy in international politics. According to this view, the multilateral organisations are legitimate because they were established by legitimate states, and are run according to rules made and interpreted by legitimate states. The international bureaucracies of the multilateral organisations are, according to this view, little more than formal implementing agencies for the collective decisions of states. (Mouritzen 1991, quoted in Jönsson 1995: 5, describes the international bureaucracies as the 'twining plants of international cooperation': they are too weak to keep upright without support; they look beautiful and often serve to hide ugly walls, and they are almost impossible to get rid of. According to this view, should these 'twining plants' ever gain any real influence this would pose a threat to the legitimacy of the organisation.)

Multilateral development organisations are, by their constitutions, required to be representative both of the richer countries, which provide most of the funds, and the poorer countries that are the recipients of such funds; but these two groups of countries sometimes have contradictory interests. And more importantly, in the context of this chapter, the states of poor countries often do not represent the interests of 'their' poor. This remains one of the major challenges of development assistance. A multilateral organisation may be very 'democratic' in its governance – with each state, weak or powerful, having an equal voice; but many of the states that make up that organisation may be very undemocratic, with little interest in promoting the well-being of the poor – the stated aim of the organisation concerned. We define 'political legitimacy' in a narrow, formal sense, to refer to whether the organisation concerned, in taking its decisions, gives voice to the *states* that compose it. Whether this results in decisions intended to favour the poor is indeterminate. But this question is, of course, very relevant in relation to our fourth and last category, moral authority.

What is moral authority, and how may one assess its extent? When applied to international organisations, we define it as the authority which derives from being seen to promote the common good. For the purposes of this chapter, which is concerned specifically with international development organisations,[12] we define moral authority more specifically as the authority which derives from being seen to promote the well-being of the poor.[13] Note that we do not define it as actually promoting the well-being of the poor. This is not only because such a judgement is notoriously difficult to make; rather, it is in order to make clearer the distinction between moral and other forms of authority.

To clarify the distinction between our four analytical terms, and to illustrate how this framework may be applied, consider two very different organisations, the International Monetary Fund and Amnesty International (AI). These are not among those that we are studying, but chosen because they well exemplify how the framework may be applied.[14]

IMF scores high with respect to clout and expertise,[15] but low on political legitimacy. (Developing countries have a relatively limited voting power in the board, where votes are linked to paid-in capital; and IMF is not well known for canvassing the opinion of borrowing countries, or the poor in those countries.) As regards moral authority, the IMF is often accused of defending the views of the rich and of finance capital at the expense of the interests of the poor.[16]

Amnesty International scores low with respect to clout, and, perhaps, expertise. The latter judgement depends, of course, on what sort of expertise is valued, and what constitutes expertise. Clearly AI lacks economic expertise, but the reputation of the organisation for well informed and objective information is an enormously important asset. Yet it is relevant to refer here to the substantial internal debate within the organisation, questioning the need for a research department (Hopgood 2006).

Amnesty International clearly scores high on moral authority. This is not only because the cause which it stands for (defending human rights and the integrity and dignity of people unfairly treated) is highly respected as morally worthy, but because AI is widely regarded as achieving its purpose. It is more problematic to assess Amnesty International's political legitimacy, as we have defined it. The organisation has established legitimacy over many years by representing in an impartial way the interests of those unfairly treated – prisoners of conscience (AI has moved also to other issues, such as violence against women). But it is not composed of states, and certainly does not represent them in a formal sense; indeed its aim is largely to give voice to individuals against states.

These two organisations – IMF and AI – exemplify extremes. The organisations we are studying fall somewhere in between; and a dilemma for all of them, we shall argue, is whether it is desirable, and possible, to shift – in one or the other direction. The significance of each of the four sources of authority varies between international organisations, and thus different sorts of dilemmas confront them as they develop and present their ideas and policies. In the following discussion we shall focus solely on the World Bank and UNDP; but in drawing conclusions we shall refer also to our other two cases – UNESCO and IDB.

The World Bank and UNDP compared

We will now briefly summarise how the World Bank and UNDP compare in relation to the four sources of power that we have identified. In each case, one may ask: on what basis do we make our judgement? In the case of the first three sources of power – clout, expertise and political legitimacy – we base it primarily on the assessment of others, backed up, where possible, by objective indicators. In some cases, the assessment of the organisation itself may also be relevant. With regard to moral authority, the basis of assessment is more problematic, as we shall discuss.

Clout

As noted, this refers to clout in financial/economic terms: the extent to which the organisation in question has 'muscle' which it can use to bring about change. There is widespread consensus – also among critics – that the World Bank has much greater clout than the UNDP. This clout relates both to impact on the ground – financing the building of roads, hospitals and irrigation schemes – and to impact on policy, at national and international levels. With regard to the former, a simple and valid indicator is the total annual budget of the two organisations. That of the World Bank is several times that of UNDP. (In the case of the World Bank, these funds are used both for investment projects and other purposes, such as technical assistance. In the case of UNDP, a relatively smaller share is used for investment purposes.) This gives it 'clout' in a direct sense, in relation to activities in its client countries. In addition, and perhaps even more important, is the power that the World Bank exerts over national and international policies – especially those of poor countries. This derives from its influence over the provision of loans and grants by others – multilateral and bilateral agencies, and international banks – and also the technical assistance and training that it provides to poor countries, often linked to its loans. (This clout has been derived in part from the World Bank's working in close collaboration with the IMF, especially during the heyday of structural adjustment.)

In addition, the World Bank exerts some influence over the international rules of the game; it participates actively, and with considerable authority, in global fora where these issues are discussed; for example concerning international trade or debt. The UNDP also participates in such fora, both national and international, but exerts considerably less influence. (In each case it is important conceptually, though rather difficult in practice, to distinguish between 'clout' and expertise, since the influence that money buys is closely linked with the expertise that determines how this influence is used.) It is not easy to provide quantitative indicators, but there is no doubt that the World Bank wields far more influence, for better or worse, than the UNDP; as those that we interviewed in UNDP also conceded. Ideally, of course, 'getting something done' in a country is achieved not by forcing a weak government to acquiesce but by providing requested support in a shared enterprise. And clout, as here defined, may be associated with such positive features as professionalism and efficiency, or with such negative features as bullying and infringement of sovereignty. We have here chosen to define it in a sense which allows for both. The UNDP is widely regarded as less professional and efficient than the World Bank; but also less inclined to push states around.

Expertise

There is no doubt that among international development organisations it is economic expertise that carries most weight. But we may briefly note some of the other types of expertise which are relevant for our concerns in this book. First, 'social' expertise. This may, in principle, be technocratic, 'top-down' expertise, which promotes the use of indicators, impact assessments, etc., or a participatory perspective which favours 'bottom-up' approaches. In practice, especially in the World Bank, the former tends to predominate; even so, they have less power than economists, as is evident from the number of them among the staff and the size of their budgets. Political science expertise is almost entirely absent – certainly in any formal sense. Power and politics have, especially since 1990, been more explicitly discussed in the WB (and perhaps to a lesser extent in UNDP); but here also an economic perspective has been influential – with the debate dominated by rational choice and the new institutional economics.[17] Philosophy and ethics have been even less in evidence in WB (notwithstanding the former existence of a Senior Advisor on Human Rights, and a small department concerned with inter-faith dialogue; see Chapter 5). In UNDP the situation is similar, although philosophy perhaps has a more significant status, as discussed in Chapter 4. Other types of expertise – such as soil science, engineering – are of course very important, and are well represented in both WB and UNDP. But they are less relevant for our purposes in this book.

For comparing the economic expertise of the two organisations, the total number of trained economists, and their level of education, provide appropriate indicators, and here the WB scores much higher. Indeed, it sees its reputation as based largely on the claim that it has more economic expertise than any other IO. Our interviews confirmed that UNDP staff acknowledge this claim; here, there are also many economists, but their dominance is far less; and attitudes towards economics are more ambivalent than at the World Bank.

Within the discipline of economics, what sort of expertise carries weight? In most international organisations, and certainly the World Bank, it is mainstream economics that is dominant. Economists in international organisations are usually, though not invariably, in the neo-liberal tradition; but even those who are not, do tend to adopt an economistic perspective – in the sense that they favour quantitative methods, and a methodological individualist approach to the explanation of socio-economic phenomena. Economics is, in this sense, a powerful 'way of seeing', whether or not it is linked with neo-liberal views. Economics is ill equipped to deal with ethical issues. As a discipline, it prides itself on being value-neutral. Although this is clearly not the case, it means that economists are not accustomed to dealing with such matters. If the World Bank wishes to impress other economists, in the dominant mainstream, it is required to adopt an economistic approach. (This is unlikely to impress – indeed may well provoke – non-economists. Those who are critical of the World Bank are often also critical of economics, or at least the dominant strain of it.) In the case of the World Bank, as discussed in Chapter 5, a powerful self-reinforcing process operates, whereby expertise is judged by others with the same mindset. World Bank documents are assessed mainly by academic economists in the same tradition, or by senior bureaucrats or ministers of finance in developing countries, many of whom have been trained in the same tradition and/or attended courses at the World Bank Institute.

Delegated authority

International organisations derive authority by virtue of the fact that this is delegated to them by the states that create and maintain them. But they vary in terms of their governance structures. For the purposes of this analysis, partly in order to maintain a clear distinction between delegated authority and moral authority, we have, as noted, defined the former in clear (and perhaps rather formalistic) terms: the extent to which an international organisation is representative of the states that compose it – a standard criterion for assessing the legitimacy of delegated authority. Here the World Bank scores badly, since its governance is based on 'one dollar, one vote', rather than 'one country, one vote' as in the UNDP; and one single country, the USA, has very considerable power. It may be argued that 'one country, one vote', however, is also undemocratic, since China and India have no more voting power than countries with one thousandth of their population; but this is at least a random bias rather than one that clearly favours the rich.

But the views of the states that make up IOs are not only expressed in meetings of their boards. UNDP draws significant power from its being – in the words of Craig Murphy in his recent history of the organisation – 'the development programme *of* the developing countries, the intergovernmental organization most trusted by governments in the developing world because it was the most responsive to them' (Murphy 2006: 8). By comparison with WB, UNDP is much more strongly in evidence at country level, in the person of the UNDP Resident Coordinator. The Coordinator on the one hand enjoys a high degree of autonomy from New York, and on the other is very much concerned to ensure that the UNDP's in-country programme of activities is determined by the government of the country. By contrast, the

WB – its President and staff – exercises a greater degree of autonomy from the states that compose it.

Moral authority

Hall, quoted above, writes of political leaders 'invok(ing) the moral authority they derive from speaking and acting in the name of their "people"'. But international organisations do not have 'their people' in a directly comparable sense. They have 'their states' (which do not necessarily speak and act in the name of their people); and they have the intended beneficiaries of the projects, programmes and policies that the organisations support. One might say that the World Bank, for example, is formally accountable to its board, but morally accountable to the poor of the world. To quote President Wolfowitz's address at the Bank's annual meeting in September 2005:

> Whether investing in education, health, infrastructure, agriculture, or the environment, we in the World Bank must be sure that we deliver results. And by results, let us be clear. We mean results that have a real impact on the daily lives of the poor. *We stand accountable to them.*
>
> (Wolfowitz 2005, italics added)

It is for these reasons that we define moral authority slightly differently from Hall: as the authority which derives from being seen to promote the well-being of the poor. It thus refers to reputation – dependent on the perception of others. The question therefore arises: Whose perception? Whose judgement? We suggest that the dominant moral arbiters today are the international NGOs. Certainly it matters what other international organisations and bilateral donors think. And the opinions of commentators from the world of research and the media also count. But, especially in the last 10–15 years, international NGOs have claimed, and successfully occupied, a privileged place in judging international organisations. This status is closely linked, of course, to the political role that NGOs have played in recent years. This can be traced back at least to their criticisms of the World Bank's environment activities in the late 1980s (Bøås and McNeill 2004). More recent, and more significant, are the anti-globalisation campaigns, and the attacks on the World Bank, IMF and WTO. In putting the Bretton Woods institutions on the defensive, the NGOs also bolstered their own moral authority. Some would say that Wolfensohn encouraged this process by inviting NGOs into a dialogue with the World Bank at an early stage in his presidency. We suggest that few would grant the WB much moral authority, at least by comparison with other development organisations.[18] UNDP sometimes makes such claims, if only implicitly; the validity of the UNDP's claim to moral authority is based largely on its annual Human Development Reports and the associated concept of human development, as we shall argue below (see also McNeill 2007a; St. Clair 2003).

Combining sources of power: an analysis of the dilemma

We have identified four sources of power for IOs. Ideally, perhaps, the World Bank and UNDP might wish to draw on all of these. But, as we shall show, they are not easily combined; choices are made – whether explicitly or by default.[19] This applies most especially to that which is in focus in this chapter, namely moral authority, which cannot easily be reconciled with the other forms of power. We shall here explore how this dilemma is addressed by WB and UNDP, taking each of the first three sources of power in turn.

Moral authority and clout

This is a dilemma for the World Bank rather than UNDP: should they even seek moral authority? In discussing 'clout', it is appropriate to distinguish between influence over the 'international rules of the game', over national policies in poor countries, and over investment projects. With regard to the 'international rules of the game', the World Bank, although clearly exercising some influence, would claim that it in practice bears little responsibility. (One may also note that, especially in recent years, WB senior staff and its flagship publication the *World Development Report*, have been quite outspoken against trade restrictions and subsidies in Western countries.) More challenging have been the many criticisms of its structural adjustment programmes and the major investment projects it has financed, especially those involving involuntary resettlement. The WB has established a number of different accountability mechanisms, with varying success (as judged either by the Bank or its critics). It certainly claims that it uses its resources to promote the well-being of the poor. In order, however, to convince others – and especially its critics – that this is the case, it needs to 'put itself in the dock' of public opinion: a hazardous enterprise for several reasons. One is that in theory, and to a large extent also in practice, it is the responsibility of its client countries how the funds provided are used. Second, all interventions will have some negative as well as positive impacts. Third, it is unclear who represents 'public opinion'. This role is in practice largely occupied by international NGOs, many of which depend for their credibility on being consistently critical of the World Bank; those that engage in dialogue with the World Bank being often regarded with suspicion. Some may wonder whether the World Bank should even go down the road of seeking moral authority. Why not emulate the IMF, for example? (Although this organisation, too, has in recent years been following in the steps of the World Bank to a limited extent.) Some believe that President Wolfensohn went too far in seeking the approval of NGOs.

To summarise this brief account: there is indeed a dilemma in seeking to combine moral authority and clout, and this is well demonstrated by the experience of the World Bank in recent years.

Moral authority and expertise

Here, too, the dilemma is primarily one for the World Bank. The economic expertise of the organisation is a double-edged sword. The Bank derives authority from the fact that it has very considerable expertise, particularly in economics. But if it uses this expertise in such a way as to reduce, or simply fail to improve, the well-being of the poor, it thereby loses moral authority. (For discussion of the professional responsibility of economists in the World Bank and IMF, see Stiglitz 2002; McNeill 2007b.)

Criticism of the economic expertise of the World Bank (from those other than their peers[20]) can take various forms. The most extreme is that the staff knowingly and intentionally pursue and advocate economic policies that promote the interests of the rich at the expense of the poor. More moderate views include the claim that they have merely been misguided (for example, in their advice in recent financial crises), that they are unduly neo-liberal, or unduly 'economistic'. Many in the World Bank (and certainly most of the economists) firmly believe in the merits of the discipline that they practice; not only by virtue of its obvious relevance to the issue of poverty, but – more controversially – because of its claimed analytical rigour by comparison with other social sciences. Although opinions vary within the World Bank, at an institutional level the organisation has discouraged dissent regarding what is and is not good economics. High-profile examples include Joseph Stiglitz and Ravi Kanbur (2001), but others less well-known have certainly experienced this also. It has allowed some (rather limited) space to other social sciences. But the dominant view in the WB is that its greatest asset is still its economic expertise. The organisation would be very reluctant to put this at risk.

UNDP recognises that, relative to WB, it has very limited expertise – at least in the economic domain. To this extent it therefore does not face the same dilemma. But it does wish to be seen as a competent organisation with well qualified staff. And in this situation, it needs to decide to what extent, and on what terms, it should seek to compete with the World Bank. Should it argue in terms of 'good' (i.e. mainstream) economics; or promote an alternative economics (held in low regard by the mainstream); or seek more radically to change the discourse, downplaying the importance of economics as a discipline? Evidence of all three strategies may be found – often linked to the concept of human development and UNDP's flagship document, the *Human Development Report*. Loosely associated with the UNDP are the *Journal of Human Development* and the Human Development and Capability Association (HD-CA). The former promotes 'economics as if people mattered', while the latter encourages interdisciplinary research, drawing on several different disciplines. The concept of human development, and the associated Human Development Index, have proved to be very powerful – thanks, in part, to the intellectual status provided by the support of Amartya Sen and others.

Human development may be seen as drawing on philosophical as well as economic expertise. This raises the question, discussed briefly above, of how important, in terms of the organisation's power, is expertise in the 'non-economic social sciences'. (We deliberately adopt this somewhat provocative terminology because it is widely used by the World Bank and to some extent by others. It is provocative because it could be taken to imply that economics is of equal importance as all other social sciences combined; or even more important, since others are defined in relation to economics. It is true that within development studies there has for decades been a rift between economics and others, and, as we assert, economics is in practice extremely powerful.) In Chapters 4 and 5, we compare the challenges faced by UNDP and World Bank in seeking to combine moral authority with economic expertise, and find that this is a problem mainly for the latter organisation.

Moral authority and political legitimacy

We have defined 'political legitimacy' in a narrow, formal sense, to refer to whether the organisation concerned, in taking its decisions, gives voice to the states that compose it. Combining this source of power with moral authority is a greater challenge for UNDP than for the World Bank. In order to explicate the problem, we find it useful to examine it in terms of what might be called the 'composite legitimacy' of an IO: the combined outcome of two factors – the extent to which the IO gives voice to the states that compose it (loosely referred to as 'democracy in the international organisation') and the extent to which the relevant state gives voice to its citizens (loosely referred to as 'democracy in the state'). From the point of view of 'the poor' in poor countries, the merits of alternative combinations may be compared, as shown in Table 2.1 below.

Clearly the preferred combination is a democratic international organisation and a democratic state: the combined 'high' score in the top left hand corner of the matrix. But the ranking thereafter may be disputed. Is it good to have Zimbabwe chairing a human rights committee? Is the Congo under Mobutu a state that one would wish to exercise its voice in the World Bank, and be granted the power to determine how resources provided by IOs are to be used in its country? This is a dilemma for both WB and UNDP, but

Table 2.1 Comparing democracy in the international organisation and democracy in the state

		Democracy in international organisation	
		High	Low
Democracy in state	High		
	Low		

especially for the latter, since it prides itself on being 'the development programme *of* the developing countries' and working very much through the
national government.[21] Thus, the third dilemma identified is a problem more
for UNDP than World Bank: how can the organisation enjoy moral
authority while at the same time associating closely with corrupt and
authoritarian regimes which do not share its stated ideals?

How WB and UNDP respond to the dilemma

International organisations share a moral purpose in promoting the common
good, and they derive legitimacy and authority from this. But they also
compete with each other – for resources, status, influence, etc. In this situation,
they can draw on, and perhaps also promote, different types of authority, of
which we have distinguished four: clout, expertise, delegated authority and
moral authority. But, as we have shown, these are not easily combined, and
each organisation is faced with a dilemma. We have argued that it is not
straightforward to combine moral authority with other well established
sources of authority on which international organisations are accustomed to base
their power. How have the two organisations responded to this challenge?

The World Bank

The World Bank certainly does not wish to sacrifice either its clout or its
economic expertise in seeking to increase its moral authority; but it has, we
suggest, sought in a number of ways to respond to this dilemma.

One way is not only to seek to ensure that projects and policies do indeed
promote the well-being of the poor, but to be *seen* to be caring for the poor
in some more direct sense. This may be regarded simply as a technocratic
response; one that belongs rather to the category of 'expertise': economists
being supplemented by others, such as sociologists and anthropologists, in
the preparation of projects. But we are here thinking rather of initiatives such
as the *Voices of the Poor* study, which seeks to associate the Bank more
directly with its ultimate 'clients'.

Another alternative, briefly mentioned above, is to increase the transparency
and accountability of the World Bank. This is achieved both by entering into
dialogue with critics, especially NGOs, and by establishing formal procedures and processes: the Independent Evaluation Group, the Joint Inspection
Panel, the Extractive Industries Review, the World Commission on Dams,
the Structural Adjustment Participatory Review International Network, etc.

More relevant to our concerns in this chapter are the ways in which the
Bank may enter into the dangerous terrain of morality. One alternative is
simply for the senior staff, and especially the President, to make assertions
about the moral purpose of the organisation. President Wolfensohn gave
many such speeches, and President Wolfowitz continued the tradition (as
noted in the quotation above). This is not to say that such statements are

dishonest; but it is notable that explicitly ethical language seems mostly to be used only in speeches by very senior staff; not in policy documents. Indeed, an explicit discussion of ethical issues appears to be largely lacking within the Bank. There were a few minor initiatives under President Wolfensohn, as described in Chapter 5, but these have not been of any great significance. One may speculate as to the reason for this. One is the very nature of bureaucracy (exacerbated here by the dominant discipline of economics); a second is resistance from the Board. A more discouraging explanation is that the staff of this, and other development organisations, may avoid overt discussion of such issues because they perceive a huge and unbridgeable gap between aspirations and achievement.[22]

Another approach is to enter the human rights arena, which appears to hold the potential for responding more directly and perhaps more effectively to the needs of the poor. The World Bank has, in the past, been rather cautious concerning how far it addresses human rights issues and its own responsibilities, but there have been some significant changes in this regard in recent times.

Another possible way is to try and combine economic expertise with explicit discussion of ethical issues. The *World Development Report 2006* on 'Equity and Development' may be seen as a good example of this. But our detailed analysis of the product and the process of this report in Chapter 5 shows that the authors in practice find this a difficult exercise, and the practice of favouring standard economic approaches is hard to abandon. In that chapter we examine in some detail the situation facing the World Bank, concentrating particularly on the latter two issues: the interplay between ethics and economic expertise, and the World Bank and human rights.

UNDP

For the UNDP, the dilemma is very different. Its main problem, as noted, is how to enjoy the moral authority derived from its close association with the human development paradigm, while at the same time working closely with many governments which do not, in practice, adhere to these ideals. The concept of human development serves UNDP not only as the embodiment of an ethical position, but also a political shield for the protection of critical views; this applies to national or regional Human Development Reports, but also, for example, to other controversial reports – as described in Chapter 4. (The Human Development Report is not subject to approval by the Board, and does not present the official views of the Administrator – even though it is described as UNDP's flagship document.) Some of the other strategies referred to with regard to the World Bank apply also to the UNDP, including the Administrator making appropriate speeches.

UNDP's approach to human rights issues is also of relevance. Its involvement here is constrained by the existence of other UN agencies dealing with the same issue,[23] and by its decentralised mode of operation. The latter renders it rather inappropriate to promote 'global' policies on human rights – or indeed other issues apart from the most general. But UNDP does support 'HURITALK' (human rights talk), an email-based network which offers staff all over the world the opportunity to exchange knowledge and experience, and seek advice on specific questions. This is an example of what UNDP may be able to do within its rather severe constraints: cautious about an advocacy role, short on expertise, and with a heavily decentralised model, in which the country office, and the country itself, are largely autonomous.

In Chapter 4 we examine in some detail the situation facing the UNDP, concentrating particularly on the significance of the human development paradigm, and the dilemma of seeking to promote human rights concerns as just outlined.

UNESCO and IDB

UNESCO's 'Poverty as a Violation of Human Rights' initiative was promoted under the leadership of Pierre Sané, Assistant Director-General, and formerly head of Amnesty International. The project's aim was to promote and solicit research to build support for the idea that severe poverty is a violation of human rights – including the organisation of workshops at Harvard and All Souls College, Oxford. This case study shows how the initiative proved unduly radical for key figures in the organisation, which quite effectively resisted it. UNESCO is an intergovernmental bureaucracy entrusted with an intellectual, ethical role, and it is a challenge to navigate between the two very differing imperatives that this implies. It appears that UNESCO chose, in this instance, the more cautious approach. In doing so, it missed an opportunity to play a valuable moral and intellectual role, by continuing to promote an important debate inside and outside the UN system around the concepts of violation and abolition with all the implications that this change in language has, and to contribute to a substantive conceptual shift in global poverty studies.

The other case study relates to the 'Social Capital, Ethics and Development' initiative of the Inter-American Development Bank, which received strong support from IDB's former President Enrique Iglesias. This is a rare example of an international organisation focusing specifically on ethics. Since its inception in 1998, the initiative has been very broadly interpreted, including concerns for civic virtues, religious values, the role of education in building solidarity, etc. Although it attracted the involvement in Latin America of a considerable number of university researchers, of religious groups, and of voluntary organisations, the initiative has had little influence on other departments in the IDB. Staff tend to be wary, seeking clarification as to what a focus on ethics means for an international financial institution such as theirs. And the attempt to use social capital as a guiding concept has not resolved this dilemma. The new President of the IDB has shown little sign of promoting the initiative.

In brief, neither has been particularly successful. One might say that in the case of the IDB the initiative lacked a coherent central idea; while in the case of UNESCO the central idea was all too clear, and too challenging for the organisation to cope with.

Concluding remarks

International organisations derive moral authority from their claim to act for the common good; and more specifically to ameliorate poverty. But this authority is undermined to the extent that they fail to achieve their stated purpose. The reasons for such failure are, to some extent, beyond their power to control. But to the (very considerable) extent to which the reasons for such failure lie with the unwillingness of these institutions to act against the will of individual states – whether rich or poor – this cannot be regarded as an adequate excuse. The moral case is, we suggest, clear: international institutions should, when necessary, be willing to stand up against the states that compose them. We are well aware that this implies a considerable political challenge; and recognise that compromises will in practice be unavoidable. Our claim, however, is that the moral aspect of the issue is clear: international development organisations have a responsibility to relieve global poverty, not only because they have been explicitly given the mandate to do so, but because they (unlike individuals) have the resources – in terms of expertise, finances and political backing – to achieve this goal. And in recent years, as the discourse of development has become increasingly concerned with ethics and human rights, these organisations have sought to derive moral authority from their purpose. But, as our case studies show, the very resources which should enhance their moral authority have served, in differing ways, to limit their ability to exert such authority.

Our analysis shows that the ability of international organisations to fulfil their moral duty in ameliorating poverty is hindered by states – both rich and poor. Their engagement, especially in recent years, with a discourse of morality is one whose practical effects have proved easily controlled by self-interested states. We therefore suggest that international institutions should adopt a more proactive role – accepting a moral responsibility beyond that which states 'allow' them. This implies that they should exercise a greater degree of autonomy from states than has historically been the case.

In all four international organisations the tendency is to keep issues of ethics and human rights 'under the radar'. In the World Bank, they are allowed to surface only to the extent that they can be expressed in economic terms. In UNDP, they can be discussed so long as there is no possible hint of conditionality. In UNESCO critical debate was here virtually censored, while in the IDB it was almost wholly absent – despite considerable interest in ethical issues in the region. In Chapters 4 to 7 we examine these different cases in detail. Before doing so, however, we need to examine the context within which these organisations find themselves: to describe in historical terms when and how ethics and human rights came on to the development agenda.

3   Ethics, human rights and global justice

Introduction

Ethics and human rights are now high on the international development agenda. Although these topics may appear novel to some development researchers and policy-makers, we shall argue in this chapter that it is more accurate to say that these issues are now *back* on the agenda, reflecting a renewed concern for justice and international responsibilities within the context of globalisation. The United Nations organisations that were created in the aftermath of the Second World War were a manifestation of a powerful moral concern about the well-being of all citizens of the world; and still more explicit was the 1948 Declaration of Human Rights. As the colonised countries gained independence, the phenomenon we call 'development' became a sort of business: a specialised arena dominated by 'donor agencies' dealing with their 'recipients', and by professional development experts sharing an arcane language in which fundamental ethical issues were largely absent. In the early years of development assistance, to simplify considerably,[1] aid was largely a technical activity, involving the provision of technical assistance and investment funds for infrastructure projects. Soon, economists began to assume a dominant role, both in preparing national development plans and in the appraisal of development projects; they continue to retain this dominant position, but this too is based on technical expertise. For many years, 'the development business' was overshadowed by the Cold War which, paradoxically, created an intensely political context for the provision of aid funds while at the same time discouraging explicit mention of politics by development professionals (Ferguson 1994). The competition between East and West led also to a disassociation and even competition between civil and political rights on the one hand, and socio-economic rights on the other, which has further deepened the rift between the project of development and its moral foundations. It was not until the 1990s, and the fall of the Berlin Wall, that it became acceptable – and more recently de rigueur – for development organisations to address non-technical issues. But these were presented as questions of governance – corruption and public management; and the debate was primarily about conditions *within* poor countries. It has taken still longer for issues of global justice to become of central concern, including reflection on the role of advanced economies and their citizens. But following the signature of the Millennium Declaration (including also the Millennium Development Goals), with its renewed focus on the challenge of global poverty, one may legitimately claim that development is now again seen as an ethical issue – a question of global justice – calling for multilateral institutions to act not only as expert and efficient, but also responsible institutions in a moral sense. This renewed concern with global norms, however, comes at a time of neo-liberal economic globalisation. The commodification of most aspects of human life and the ethic of the market clash head-on with global morality, not only regarding extreme poverty but now also climate change. (It is abundantly clear that not only is this a hugely important global issue, but it is the poor who will suffer most severely.) Complex issues such as extreme poverty and climate change cannot be solved by nation-states or individual people; they require coordinated action at many levels, from local to global. To reconcile the many competing interests will require concern for solidarity and equity and also radical changes in the behaviour, values and attitudes of the non-poor.

But even if the 'development business' began only in the second half of the last century, the sorts of questions – of ethics and human rights – that need to be confronted go far back in history. What is new is the creation of development institutions; and with increased globalisation there is now a growing interest in the question of global responsibilities. We see the emergence amongst philosophers, social scientists and activists of a fast growing body of work on global justice, and an emergent concern with formulating a feasible and politically credible account of global responsibilities for global problems: how to achieve a fair globalisation, or alternative globalisations.

In this chapter, therefore, our purpose is to trace the progression from the origins of development ethics to today's concern with global ethics, universal human rights, global justice and responsibilities as they relate to poverty. Our primary focus is on ideas and authors that relate directly to the institutions and 'business' of development, complementing discussions about cosmopolitanism in international relations and globalisation studies. We seek also to reveal some significant underlying themes that may be omitted in standard debate in development bureaucracies when dealing with questions of ethics and human rights in their work: the place of religion and (sometimes radical) religious and spiritual ideas; a view of ethics as activism and social critique; the relationship between ethics and politics, and between ethics and economics.

The idea that extreme poverty, wherever it occurs, is an ethical challenge for all, a matter of global justice – this has existed for a long time. But the proponents of this view lacked the power to have their ideas acted upon; they were not viewed as 'experts' or legitimate sources of authority. Their ideas were therefore not 'embedded' in relevant organisations. But the time is now ripe to address such basic moral issues. Ethics is about self-reflection, about the possibility to envision and to realise alternative futures that are more fair to all. Global institutions have a key role to play in making ethically grounded choices. Although there is a tendency, especially in the literature on human rights, to place the burden of responsibility for achieving justice on nation-states, the more recent movements and scholarship on global justice and responsibilities for global issues such as poverty (and more recently climate change) are pointing to global institutions to use their power, expertise and political position to be the pioneers in promoting global justice. Our own normative position is that multilateral organisations are 'response-able': they are particularly well placed to act by virtue of the powers that we, the people of the world, have given them: the economic resources and expertise that enable them to change the world; and the political legitimacy they enjoy by virtue of their mandates. Rather than simply blaming these global actors for their mistakes, we argue for a forward looking construction of responsibility. Multilateral organisations are responsible for protecting people from poverty – but are they ready for the task?

From development ethics to global ethics

Among contemporary scholars of development ethics (Crocker 2008; Gasper 2004) it is common to take as a historical point of departure the writings of Marx and Gandhi; and one could no doubt trace the history of this field even further back, depending on one's definition of development. These two have the merit of relating, in their very different ways, to important strands which we wish to trace in this brief account – including not only politics and economics, but also spirituality and activism; but our focus is on 'the development era' – from World War II to the present. During this period the concerns of development researchers and policy-makers shifted from 'modernisation' to 'globalisation', and, we shall argue, from development ethics to global justice, incorporating concerns of global ethics and human rights.

Development ethics today is associated primarily with the capabilities approach (later named 'development as freedom') pioneered by Amartya Sen, and American philosopher Martha Nussbaum's own version of a capability ethic. The notion of capability was first used by Sen in the 1980s, in an effort to expand the dominant informational basis of development economics to also include concerns for the quality of life, well-being, agency, social justice, entitlements and rights and freedoms. The notion developed from his early work on famines (Sen 1981), where he argued that the cause of famines cannot be primarily explained by lack of food availability. Rather, it is important, he argued, to focus on the set of entitlements (rights and access) that people have to basic goods (e.g. food) and services (health). Thus, famines are caused by weak socio-economic structures, not necessarily by natural disasters, population growth, or weak agricultural systems.

In his capabilities approach, Sen focuses on what individuals like 'doing and being' and the freedoms that exist in society to enable them to achieve some of these doings and beings. Sen has elaborated the notion of 'functioning' to specify and differentiate between actions that people actually do or achieve (functionings), from the opportunities or freedoms to be and to do (capabilities). For example, the 'capability' to be well nourished is not the same as the functioning of being 'well nourished'. These two terms permit one to differentiate between a person who is on a hunger strike and a person suffering from a famine. He emphasises the Aristotelian tradition of 'human flourishing', according to which human beings have projects they wish to carry out and goals they want to achieve. Such goals and achievements should be taken as ends in themselves, that is, they are expressions of people's intrinsic value. Sen emphasises the intrinsic and instrumental importance of widening people's choices in order to live productive and creative lives according to their needs and interests; or, as he often phrases it, to focus on the lives that people have reasons to value (Sen 1985). In *Development as Freedom* (Sen 1999), Sen argues that capability is a kind of freedom, and that development must not be divorced from 'the lives that people can lead and the real freedoms they can enjoy'. Poverty is a kind of unfreedom, often determined by socio-economic conditions and structural causes. Freedoms have, for Sen, both an intrinsic and an instrumental aspect, yet these are inseparable. To remove unfreedoms involves seeking the ways in which people's agency is constrained.

In Martha Nussbaum's version, capabilities ought to be the basis for fundamental political principles and constitutional guarantees (Nussbaum 2001), and she views the core role of governments as *fundamental development actors* entrusted with endowing citizens with the required conditions for realising central human functionings. Moving away from the position of Amartya Sen, who has consistently refused to specify a particular set of capabilities, Nussbaum proposes a list of central human functional capabilities based on the political goals of liberalism. These, she claims, could be the object of an overlapping consensus among people with different conceptions of the good. Sen, and to a lesser extent Nussbaum, has been extremely influential, especially since the capabilities approach provides the intellectual basis of the human development concept, as espoused by the Human Development Report office in UNDP (as we shall further elaborate in Chapter 4). The terms 'capability' and 'capability poverty' are now widely used, and are of fundamental importance in the currently accepted view that poverty is multidimensional. But Sen is cautious in relation to political issues, such as the global responsibilities of the multilateral agencies themselves.

In order to better understand the place of ethical analysis in development, we believe it is important to look also at several other sources, whether earlier in time or different in scope from the capabilities approach. Development ethics has been the subject of a hybrid group of scholars who, following the inspiration of Denis Goulet (whose work we discuss below) have addressed the ethical dilemmas and aspects of the business of development and development aid. At a time when ethics and political philosophy within Anglo-American academia were dominated by John Rawls and his conception of justice and fairness,[2] David Crocker (1991) was already arguing for the importance of values and ethical analysis in development policy and practice, and he has for over two decades highlighted the importance of Sen and later Nussbaum's ideas for a more fair understanding of development. Crocker (1991, 2008) identifies as other sources of development ethics the debate on food aid to famine-hit countries in the mid-1970s, particularly the debate involving Peter Singer (1972) and Garret Hardin (1974).[3] During the 1980s, the topic continued to develop with a transition from an 'ethic of aid' to an 'ethic of development', which included basic needs approaches and early versions of the human rights-based approaches (Aiken and LaFollete 1995; Crocker 1991; Dower 1988; Nickel 1987; O'Neill 1986; Shue 1980; Streeten *et al.* 1981). Many of these authors have argued for the ethical investigation of meanings and practices in development, often appealing to some sort of fundamental normative concept relating to the notion of need, right or duty. It is also among these Anglo-American philosophers that early work on the right to development appears directly related to contemporary debates about international development practices (Aman 1991; Penz 1991; Nickel 1987). And it is within this cluster of writers that the first debates began concerning what ought to be the fundamental concerns in development ('needs,' 'rights' or 'capabilities'); a debate that has been taken up by most UN agencies and development practitioners.

Although the issue of poverty and marginalisation has been a main focus of development ethicists, other important topics include the following: reflections on the role of human rights more broadly as key to stable and peaceful societies and fair global relations; investigations of the ways in which bottom-up development may be achieved through deepening democratic processes; specific issues such as the ethical dilemmas entailed by development-induced displacement, globalisation, global citizenship and cosmopolitanism; synergies with other global normative discourses such as human rights and human security, leadership and democratic deliberation, virtue ethics and more instrumental approaches such as global public goods, corruption and accountability (Crocker 2006a; Crocker and Schwenke 2005; Dower 1998, 2003; Chatterjee and McLean 2004; Drydyk 2005; Drydyk *et al.* 2008; Gasper 2004; St. Clair 2006c; Wamala 2008; Young 2004). The authors referred to here, who are primarily Anglo-American, have been reflecting upon issues that have repeatedly arisen during the now many decades long development debate. It would be misleading to suggest that the fundamental questions have been taken up only recently and among Western academics, but our primary interest in this book is in the 'development' era; and it is in this context useful to single out two key questions that have continually arisen. One is 'why development?' – questioning the project of economic growth and modernisation (and later globalisation). The other is 'what causes underdevelopment?' – locating poor people in an international context of structural inequality. Each raises fundamental ethical issues; and both relate to economics and the market system: whether criticising a narrow interpretation of the aim of development as merely economic growth, or the inequities of the global capitalist system.

In his authoritative history of economic development, Arndt asserts that 'economic development in the Third World as a major interest of Western governments, of economists, and of public opinion generally, was born during World War II' (Arndt 1987: 43, quoted in Helleiner 2007: 29).Often quoted in accounts of development aid is Truman's 'Point Four' programme in his inauguration speech as President in 1949: 'We must embark on a bold new program for making the benefits of our scientific advances and industrial progress available for the improvement and growth of undeveloped areas'. Indeed, this is by many claimed to be the beginning of the development era. But in a recent paper, Eric Helleiner[4] emphasises 'the significance of US-Latin America relations in the early 1940s as the incubator for this innovation' (Helleiner 2007: 29). He convincingly argues that Latin American countries were largely responsible for the initiative to establish major international organisations, including the World Bank. In December 1933, a number of Latin American delegations to the seventh International Conference of American States in Montevideo proposed the establishment of an Inter-American Bank (IAB) (Helleiner 2007: 3). The USA was initially wary, but in 1940 became much more supportive, thanks to 'a broader shift in Roosevelt's "Good Neighbour Policy" towards Latin America' (Helleiner 2007: 4). Helleiner quotes the US official spearheading the initiative, arguing that imperialism was 'dead as the dinosaur', and that 'we are both morally and economically better off as the American nations strengthen their economic position' (Berle 1941, quoted in Helleiner 2007: 7).

The new policy towards Latin America in the 1930s was much influenced by New Deal ideology, and the desire to counter the power of Wall Street (Helleiner 2007: 8). The US Treasury secretary, Henry Morgenthau, and his assistant Harry Dexter White, successfully insisted 'that the IAB be government controlled rather than a creature of central banks'. White is famous as the US representative in the meetings at Bretton Woods in 1944 that established the World Bank and IMF. (The standard account has him opposing some of the more radical innovations in the international monetary system proposed by the British representative, John Maynard Keynes.) Helleiner's well documented account not only shows that White had by 1944 already been substantially involved in proposals for establishing international development institutions, but that countries from the South, and especially from Latin America,[5] played a very active role in establishing the World Bank as an organisation for development rather than reconstruction (Helleiner 2007: 21).

From Latin America came not only pressure to establish international development institutions, but also the first clearly articulated criticisms of the international economic system (although one should not ignore traditions of criticism and political activism in other parts of the world[6]). The so called dependency school produced a body of scholarly and policy work focused on the divisions of wealth and power between the North and the South and arguing that such inequalities reflected a system of exploitation and the perpetuation of marginality. These authors defended the need for substantial transformations of social and economic structures on an international scale, not only in countries of the 'Third World'. Thus, poverty and development were seen as 'structural' problems with structural solutions. The more radical authors of the dependency school reinterpreted Marxist criticisms of capitalism and highlighted how poor countries were 'dependent' on the rich. They presented a theory regarding what are today seen as the relational forces that characterise globalisation: advanced economies need the perpetuation of the problems facing poor countries in order to maintain existing privileges and the sources of their wealth; similarly, global elites are dependent on the existence and perpetuation of marginal groups. Accordingly, the world is divided between the core (rich countries) and the periphery (developing and less developed countries) and the advantages of the former are drawn from exploitation of the latter. There was at this time an underlying, and at times very explicit, demand for righting the structural socio-economic and political injustice. The main tenets of the dependency school have been adopted by contemporary world systems theory, and have spread to contemporary works on critical globalisation and critical development studies. These ideas were found also, though in less radical form,[7] in the Economic Commission for Latin America (ECLA), one of the regional commissions of the United Nations, created in 1948 and closely associated with its first leader, Raul Prebisch.[8]

In the late 1960s, Latin America was also the cradle of liberation theology – a powerful mixture of religion and activism – that places at its centre of analysis the role of values in relationship to the poor, questions of justice on earth and human rights as guarantors of people's dignity. One of the fundamental tenets of liberation theology is the concept of 'preferential option for the poor'. This can be interpreted both as a demand for affirmative action policies for the poor (that is, giving preference to their demands because of their vulnerable position); but also as granting the poor agency and dignity, voice and action in order 'to claim rights'. Liberation theologians were amongst the first to propose that socio-economic rights be used as the instrument for lifting people out or poverty and protecting the marginalised. The notion of 'liberation' as an ethic and as a substitute for 'development' is very alive in Latin America and the Caribbean today, not only among liberation theologians. It survives in the critical work of influential figures representing a hybrid and highly interdisciplinary space of reflection and social critique, and also methodological and empirical research approaches. It has produced and continues to produce very important works linking Marxian critiques of modernity, early critics of development, theology and political and ethical and political philosophy with contemporary critiques of neo-liberal economic globalisation. Amongst the most visible and influential liberation thinkers is Enrique Dussel (1978, 2007) who characterises the present era as 'the age of globalization and exclusion'.

In Latin America the debate was strongly influenced by Catholic theology and Christian ethics.[9] As a reaction to the documents from the Second Vatican Council (1962–65) and their renewed focus on the role of the church in the modern world, the Latin American bishops tried to adapt the church's new orientation to their own reality. (For example, at the second Latin American Bishops' Conference – known as CELAM II by its Spanish acronym – in Medellin in 1968.) The renewed interest of the Catholic church in worldly matters, as well as the belief that the church had a duty to participate in the development debate, was an important element in the integration of ethics, economics, and development.

One of the most influential sources of liberation theology and its key thesis – 'the option for the poor' – was Pope Paul VI's famous *Populorum Progressio*. And a major 'ghostwriter' of this document was Louis Joseph Lebret (1897–1966), the first intellectual who explicitly talks about 'human development' within the context of international development, and one of the key inspirations of Denis Goulet – the pioneer of the field of development ethics (Novak 1984: 134 in Hebblethwaite 1994: 484).[10] Lebret was a French Catholic theologian whose ideas heavily influenced the church's thinking about development, and the founder in 1941 of the Economy and Humanism (Economie et Humanisme) movement;[11] an attempt to create an alternative conception of economics through dialogue with philosophy, theology and the social sciences, but also built from below, with ethnographic work as its basis. After WWII he sought to apply his methodological insights in the South – working in various Latin American countries, in Africa and the Lebanon. In Latin America, his work had enormous consequences.

> Lebret worked extensively on a humanistic approach to national and international development. He 'never tired of quoting with approval the phrase coined by Francois Perroux', his colleague, that development is for 'every person and the whole person' ('tous les hommes et tout l'homme').
>
> (Goulet 2006a: 58; 2000: 34, in Gasper 2008b: 5)

Lebret is apparently the first thinker to speak explicitly about 'human development' and to relate this to a particular conception of 'economics', closely linked to ethics and values, pioneering the movement that was much later initiated by Mahbub ul Haq and institutionalized in the Human Development Report Office of UNDP (see Chapter 4).[12]

Building on the legacy and inspiration of Lebret, Denis Goulet emerges as the founder of development ethics as a coherent field of study and brings to the Anglo world some of the ideas both from liberation theology and in the tradition of economics and humanism. Goulet is also the first to engage directly with the knowledge production of the then emerging UN institutions – analysing UN reports, and explicitly assessing development policy. As Gasper puts it, for Goulet, development ethics (DE) considers the 'ethical and value questions posed by development theory, planning and practice' (1977: 5); its mission, he proposed, is 'to diagnose value conflicts, to assess policies (actual and possible), and to validate or refute valuations placed on development performance' (1997b: 1168).

(Gasper 2006: 4)

Thus, Goulet offers us a definition of development ethics that directly refers to the professional work of global institutions and aid practitioners. David Crocker, who introduced the work of Goulet to Anglo-American philosophy, characterises the contributions of Goulet 'to get to the roots of the development enterprise, put ethics on the development agenda, criticise morally problematic aspects of theory and practice, and advocate more just and participatory development policies and institutions' (Crocker 2006b, in Goulet 2006a: XIV).

In what is perhaps his most influential work, *The Cruel Choice: A New Concept in the Theory of Development* (1971a), Goulet argued that development as practised by the major donors and multilateral agencies was primarily 'maldevelopment' – bad development; that is, rather than leading to improved well-being and better societies, development was generating pain and disorder in local communities. Instead of seriously engaging with the challenge of how world misery could be eradicated, development aid – Goulet warned – provided a rationalisation for the rich world's desire to domesticate the development of the Third World (1971a: 14). Development experts were 'one eyed giants, blind in their analysis of the goals of development and ignorant of the role of power, and treating instrumentally, the values and knowledge systems of indigenous peoples and the large majority of the population in developing countries' (Goulet 1980).

It is particularly important to note how Goulet has consistently emphasised the central role of moral awareness of the suffering of others, and the behaviour of the non-poor, in the search for fair and equitable development; this includes reflection on the negative consequences of unlimited consumption, which jeopardises environmental sustainability and justifies the lack of solidarity with the poor at home and abroad.[13] Goulet argued for an ethic grounded on people's living experiences, and for embedding ethics in the research methodologies used for development research, planning and project work. We here quote at some length extracts from Des Gasper's recent analysis of the significance and lessons of Goulet for contemporary debates:

This descriptive and explanatory ethics, essential for serious ethically based strategy, requires a particular sort of research methodology, argued Goulet (1971a). He developed an approach from the French researcher Georges Allo for 'integrating the living experience of ordinary people with philosophical investigation and empirical social science research' (Goulet 1992b: 19). For 'in the case of values, the "object" studied has no intelligibility apart from its "subjective" resonances. ...[Further,] values belong to realms of synthesis, not analysis: their proper domains are philosophy, poetry, meta-analytical symbolism. Only under stringent conditions ... is the study of values appropriate to social science. To reduce this synthesis of totality to that mere portion of reality which is measurable is to deprive life of its specificity and to falsify reality itself'.

(Goulet 1971b: 208 in Gasper 2008b: 9)

According to Goulet (1995: 27), the essential task of development ethics is

to render development actions humane to assure that the painful changes launched under the banners of development not produce anti-development, which destroys cultures and exacts undue sacrifices in individual suffering and societal well-being, all in the name of profit, an absolutized ideology, or some alleged efficiency imperative.

The mission of development ethics, Goulet added, is to keep hope alive. The main danger faced by development ethicists, however, is to 'fall into the role played by plantation preachers during the times of slavery – namely, assuring good conscience to the rich while providing spiritual, "other worldly" solace to the victims of unjust structures' (Goulet 1995: 26).

Most of his work predates that of the more recent (yet much more influential) development ethics of Amartya Sen and Martha Nussbaum:

Well before Sen, Haq and Nussbaum, he advocated that 'authentic development aims toward the realization of human capabilities in all spheres' (Goulet 1971b: 205), and that economic growth and technological modernity must be treated as, at best, potential means towards considered human values, not vice versa. At the same time he insisted that principles of ethics and/or religion had to be confronted by and relate to the full realities and complexities of modern economies.

(Goulet 1960: 23 in Gasper 2006: 2)[14]

In his capacity as both an academic and an activist, Goulet continued to be engaged with these questions. In recent years, he has written extensively on ethics and globalisation, drawing on his earlier work and relating to current globalisation processes and the dominance of neo-liberal economic thinking (Goulet 2000, 2005, 2006a).

Des Gasper (2004, 2006, 2008a, 2008b), social economist and policy analyst, has argued convincingly for opening the debate on ethics and development as an interdisciplinary space for broad dialogue with other disciplines, and emphasised the role of power. He emphasises, as we do, the need for development ethics to make the transition to the world of action – to graduate, so to speak from abstract theorising to practices (see also St. Clair 2007). In his work he also stresses the need for dialogue among diverse ethical understandings and the contextual nature of ethics and values. Increasingly following the route marked by Goulet's activist and empirically based value analysis of development, Gasper notes how development ethics, as a body of work, 'arose in the historical context of the gradual emergence of capacities to ensure, for example, clean water and essential drugs for everyone but the absence as yet of a working system of rights and responsibilities that will fulfil those possibilities' (Gasper 2008b: 7). Gasper is one of the most engaged critics of Sen's work – from his earlier work on the role of 'needs' to his later focus on well-being, and his engagement with the human development and the capabilities approach. Following his more recent interests in global normative discourses and their interlinkages (in particular human development, human rights, and human security), Gasper is expanding the scope of development ethics and in an important sense reorienting the field in directions more in tune with Goulet's work, and away from mere philosophical reflection, while acknowledging the importance of detailed and rigorous philosophical analysis (see Gasper 1997, 2002, 2006, 2007a, 2007b, 2008b). Gasper presents Goulet not only as the precursor of Sen, but as also in many respects more radical:

> Goulet employed the same language of freedom as Sen, and likewise posited freedom as a universally held value, but he had more substantive theories of desire and of freedom. He distinguished 'freedom from wants', obtained via the fulfilment of fundamental needs, and 'freedom for wants', where one is autonomous, in charge of and not slave to the determinants of want generation (1971a: ch. 6). In Sen's system the danger of consumerism is a formal possibility not a central concern; in Goulet's system it is central. Often freedom from some constraints is achieved in ways that reduce human autonomy (1971a: 126). Restraint of material desires is an essential requirement for freedom (pp. 121–122), he argued, not only a prudent measure along a path of accumulation. 'Genuine wealth, the [early Fathers of the Christian Church] contend, resides in the internal freedom which makes one use material goods instrumentally to meet needs, and as a springboard for cultivating those higher spiritual goods which alone bring deeper satisfactions: virtue, friendship, truth, and beauty' (Goulet 2006a: 146). There is nothing specifically Christian in such claims, which are found in many traditions, and for example in the work of the 19th century British economist Alfred Marshall, as well as in the accumulated results of modern research on well-being. Voicing such claims, in advance of and even now after these research findings, does not ensure popularity or attention; many writers prefer to pass by on the other side.
>
> (Gasper 2008b: 11)

Many philosophers also remain silent with regard to the economics of the market and neo-liberal-driven globalisation. The result may be a growing rhetoric in terms of freedoms and capabilities coexisting with a grossly unjust global system. This is of particular importance as the character and particularities of development and the role of development aid are being substantially affected by the rapid changes caused by neo-liberal economic globalisation. This is a criticism widely encountered in critical globalisation studies (Gills 2006; Patomaki 2006; Robinson 2002). A variety of other criticisms have been made of the school of thought built around Sen's work. One is that it is too narrow and insufficiently political; too philosophical, and ill-equipped to relate to questions of power. Another, that the approach is simply too dominated by economics, albeit a more normatively based conception of economics than the mainstream. Philosophical analysis is not ideal for policy dialogue, and if the overarching goal is the actual influence of policy, views such as Nussbaum's are too easily relegated. From our standpoint in this book, the main weakness of this body of work is that it does not, at least so far, address the responsibilities of global institutions. As some of our examples show, the language of capabilities can be used by multilateral organisations without necessarily changing the way they approach development and poverty issues; without leading them to question neo-liberal economic globalisation or debate their own institutions' responsibilities.

But the capabilities approach has achieved what can be called a transition from economism to human development; a very significant step towards a more ethically grounded conception and practice of development with consequences for the poor (Alkire 2002).[15] This contrasts with the ethics of development as articulated by Goulet (or earlier by Lebret and liberation theologians), which were unpopular – at a time when the mainly technocratic and bureaucratic business of development was taking off – and did not exert significant influence in policy circles. Sen enjoys legitimacy and influence thanks to his status within economics; which would not be accorded to other social sciences or philosophy. Furthermore, the capabilities approach has been able to strengthen UNDP in terms of 'ideas' vis-à-vis the Bank (Gasper 2004; McNeill 2007a; St. Clair 2003, 2007). The impact of the capabilities approach and human development as 'alternative economics in action' is very important, as it has filtered ethics into the multilateral system through influencing the notion of 'economics' and economic analysis and thus the key expert knowledge that drives these institutions. Current work on the capabilities approach is largely focused on developing methodologies to measure and operationalise capabilities, and to find strategic avenues to make this alternative view of development and poverty influential in the arena of policy and politics. Research groups, such as the Oxford Poverty and Human Development Initiative, are building up the capabilities approach in strategic ways and with a clear aim to influence policy-making and global actors (see Alkire and Ritchie 2008; Chiappero-Martinetti forthcoming; Comim *et al.* 2008; Deneulin 2006; Robeyns 2006).[16]

At the same time, capability theorists are also driven by other powerful ideas – primarily human rights. The relation between capabilities and rights, especially since Sen's later formulation of his ideas in terms of 'freedom', is an ongoing debate among capability theorists. The literature on this topic has been expanding, with the growth of the human rights discourse among development organisations and experts.

In response to increasing concern with globalisation, there has recently been a rapid development in the field of global ethics, and amongst non-philosophers the closely related concept of 'cosmopolitanism'. But, as with development ethics, it is important to be aware of the origins of global ethics as a concept and intellectual tradition and to acknowledge its roots in religious movements. Amongst the first to use the term 'global ethic' and to build a fully developed conception (notice the singular of the term ethic), was German Catholic theologian Hans Kung, well known for his confrontation with the authority and infallibility of the Pope.[17] By the use of this term, Kung (1991, 1998) sought to refer to an ethic that relates to all cultures, all religions and for all societies – attempting to draw on the similarities of all religions rather than their differences. He was one of the key authors of the 'Declaration of the Religions for a Global Ethic', endorsed by the Parliament of the World's Religions in 1993, the institution most active in promoting 'interfaith dialogue'; a theme later taken up by the World Bank (see Chapter 5). In the late 1990s, Hans Kung further developed his notion of a global ethic to directly address questions of economics and global politics. He took as a point of departure what is an old idea in moral and political philosophy:

> Just as within the state every government, though it needs power as a basis of its authority, also needs the moral basis of the consent of the governed, so an international order cannot be based on power alone, for the simple reason that mankind will in the long run always revolt against naked power. Any international order presupposes a substantial measure of general consent.
>
> (Kung 1998: 48)

Mention should also be made of the 1995 report of the World Commission on Culture and Development, organised by UNESCO under the leadership of former UN secretary-general Perez de Cuellar, which begins with a chapter entitled 'A New Global Ethics'. In addition to seeking some common ground between varied cultures, the report also asserts that

> There is evolving in our time a global civic culture, a culture which contains further elements to be incorporated in a new global ethics. The *idea of human rights*, the *principle of democratic legitimacy, public accountability* and the emerging *ethos of evidence and proof* are the prime candidates for consideration.
>
> (UNESCO 1995: 36, emphasis in the original)

A conception of global ethics – usually expressed in the plural – has recently been adopted by a number of researchers, which is rather different from that of Hans Kung, drawing also on secular ethical traditions (although most global ethics theorists do credit the use of the term to theology and Hans Kung). The term 'global' here refers not necessarily to a set of shared values and shared responsibilities, as Kung had argued, but to a set of global problems that demand the attention of ethicists. Global ethics has undeniably 'taken off' – with debates about globalisation, and rapidly growing attempts to conceptualise critical globalisation perspectives. The growth of this emergent field is evident from new journals (such as the *Journal of Global Ethics*), or special issues, publications (such as Commers *et al.* 2008), and new research centres on global ethics. One such centre offers the following definition of global ethics, which is quite representative of the view from Anglo academia:

> Global ethics deals with the moral questions that arise from globalization. Some of the most pressing of these arise from the great systematic disparities of wealth, health, longevity, security, and freedom between the North and South. What obligations have individuals and governments in the North to improve the lives of people in the South? How might international trading arrangements be made fairer? How might military intervention be better regulated? How might the local tyrannies of warlords or criminal gangs be undone? How far should international institutions have power to make decisions that go against the interests of governments and individuals in the North? What role does corruption play in maintaining an unjust world? How far are local elites in the South culpable for the extremes of the North/South divide? How far must the ways of life of individuals change for the sake of the worst off elsewhere, or for the sake of reversing climate change? Other questions arise from the way in which it is becoming easier for people to become exposed to the cultural differences that aren't being wiped out by globalization. Can people learn from one another about how to live? ... Serious religious observance is an important part of life in very large numbers of countries. Are non-religious people in the West somehow blind to an important source of value?[18]

Another of the new centres of global ethics, in Italy, defines the field 'as normative dilemmas raised by public choices regarding globalization'.[19] And a third asserts that global ethics is both about 'the ethics of globalisation' and 'ethics under globalisation'.[20] Included in this field are attempts to relate to non-Western cultures and values and to offer perspectives that can accommodate diversity. Important in this regard is literature concerning identity and culture and their significance in development work (Appadurai 2002; Appiah 2006; Sen 2005). There is also, as mentioned earlier, a parallel set of writings on global ethics under the label *cosmopolitanism*. The concept of global ethics also finds a place among activists, but more often under the label of global justice and global responsibilities.

Against this perhaps bewildering variety of perspectives and discourses, there is one that has emerged as most widely accepted – based on the concept of human rights, which may be characterised as the 'global ethic of our secular age', an idea we take from Canadian philosopher Charles Taylor's *A Secular Age* (2007), a history of embedding and disembedding of religious values from modernity and contemporary understandings of ourselves as human beings and our globalised age. In the next section, we trace the progress of this concept in the development field, culminating in the convergence of human rights and poverty.

Human rights: the global ethic of a secular age

It is not coincidental that most of the development aid organisations emerge at the same time as the UN Declaration of Human Rights. Both can be seen as reactions to World War II; though both also have roots in earlier initiatives. After WWII, debates about human rights and development are largely separate, following parallel tracks; they converge at the beginning of the new millennium when preoccupation with a global moral order arises again, in the context of globalisation. Clearly, the Holocaust was 'a moral shock', and the colonial system perceived as illegitimate, but the notion of freedom expressed by Franklin Delano Roosevelt in his address to the US Congress on 6 January 1941 was an optimistic statement about the possibilities of the times to change the course of history and the need for 'development', underlined by what he called a new moral order – across the whole world:

> We look forward to a world founded upon four essential human freedoms.
>   The first is freedom of speech and expression – everywhere in the world.
>   The second is freedom of every person to worship God in his own way – everywhere in the world.
>   The third is freedom from want ... everywhere in the world.
>   The fourth is freedom from fear ... anywhere in the world.
>   ... This nation has placed its destiny in the hands and heads and hearts of its millions of free men and women; and its faith in freedom under the guidance of God. *Freedom means the supremacy of human rights everywhere.* ...
>
> (Roosevelt 1941, emphasis added)

Roosevelt's speech was the 'justification' for the US entering WWII. But the way in which it unpacks the notion of 'freedom' points the way to how the concept of universal human rights takes off as a coherent body of global norms aiming to speak to all cultures and all religions. The President's wife, Eleanor Roosevelt, the first chairperson of the UN Human Rights Commission, was also inspired by these four freedoms in drafting the Universal Declaration of Human Rights which was adopted by the General Assembly on 10 December 1948. But in the early years after WWII, as new multilateral organisations emerge, 'development' becomes a political project directly related to the Cold War, and development and human rights take divergent paths; (one might also argue that the global moral order envisioned by Roosevelt was abandoned with the atomic bombs that put an end to WWII). Even though The International Covenant on Economic, Social and Cultural Rights was signed in 1966, the walls separating the West from the East served to intensify the separation between types of freedoms and corresponding rights that has been so pervasive in the philosophical and legal literature of Western societies; namely, the distinction between liberal rights (associated with personal freedom, property, and bodily harm protection) and socio-economic rights (focused on the minimum necessary for the respect and protection of people's dignity). These dichotomies entail two very different conceptions of freedom (positive and negative freedom) entrenched also by the liberal intellectual tradition in the West and reinforced by the role of market-based relations and capitalism. It is highly relevant for current attempts to draw relations between human rights, and development, that the United States has never recognised socio-economic rights and that the term 'freedom' may have become somehow 'perverted' in the hands of powerful actors; resulting in a language that may not necessarily lead to 'good and fair development', with often little resemblance to the meaning of human rights as tools to protect people's dignity, that one sees in histories of activism and resistance.

Universal human rights can be traced much earlier in time, outside the political project of the UN system, as an emerging case of an international political morality as well as a key global ethic. First, there is a very strong tradition among human rights experts that the origins of a universal conception of human rights as related to the protection of the dignity of all people are to be found in the Spanish conquest of the American continent, and not only in the European enlightenment intellectual tradition, the French Revolution and related social movements of critique, contestation and social transformation during the eighteenth century such as Mary Wollstonecraft's declaration of the rights of women (1792).[21] Seeking the genesis of universal human rights leads to the work of former coloniser and later Dominican priest and first bishop of Chiapas, Bartolome de las Casas (1484–1566). De las Casas is recognised as the first historical figure to claim that all human beings (referring to indigenous peoples of the Americas) had entitlements, and dedicated his life and works to denounce the brutality and maldevelopment (to use the term invented by Goulet) entailed by the Spanish conquest. The spirit of De las Casas has survived along the centuries in the region and inspired many social movements for freedom and transformation, and, as we have stated above, human rights were clear guidelines of the Catholic theology of Paul VI, and the liberation theology and liberation theorists in the Latin American continent. In the same way Latin America had especial influence in the creation of the UN system as we argued earlier, Latin American thinkers also participated actively in the drafting of the

Universal Declaration, arguably because of a particularly strong human rights tradition in the region (Carozza 2003). But as it emerges within the UN system, and with the dominance of powerful advanced countries, the perversion of freedom we mention above has led to human rights discourse being identified as a tool of advanced economies, and their intellectual traditions of political liberalism, to domesticate the South. The first attempts to overcome the dominance of liberty rights at the expense of socio-economic and cultural rights were not very successful, and the sense of activism and resistance against perceived injustices that human rights has historically had, the political and moral power of human rights, is downplayed by an excessive legalism and a strong focus on nation-states as duty bearers.

In 1986, at the same time that structural adjustment policies, with their detrimental effects on the poor, were so powerfully influencing development policies, there was a first attempt to formalise the relations between development and human rights and to unify this 'dichotomy of freedoms' with the Right to Development and the Vienna Declaration. Articles one and two of the Right to Development express clearly its scope:

> 1. The right to development is an inalienable human right by virtue of which every human person and all peoples are entitled to participate in, contribute to, and enjoy economic, social, cultural and political development, in which all human rights and fundamental freedoms can be fully realized.
> 2. The human right to development also implies the full realization of the right of peoples to self-determination, which includes, subject to the relevant provisions of both International Covenants on Human Rights, the exercise of their inalienable right to full sovereignty over all their natural wealth and resources.

Note here how the language of point 2 recalls what had been a compromise in the covenant on socio-economic rights, that their implementation was to be progressive, dependent on available resources, and the focus on the states themselves as the main bearers of responsibilities, avoiding direct reference to global responsibilities.

The Vienna Declaration, also formally signed in 1986, may be seen as another attempt at reinforcing the interrelations between liberty rights and socio-economic rights.

The Vienna Declaration states that 'The international community should support the strengthening and promoting of democracy, development and respect for human rights and fundamental freedoms in the entire world' (Vienna Declaration, P1, and 8).

And, regarding poverty: "The existence of widespread extreme poverty inhibits the full and effective enjoyment of human rights; its immediate alleviation and eventual elimination must remain a high priority for the international community' (Vienna Declaration, part I, and 14).

Another important milestone was the creation of the Office of the High Commissioner for Human Rights (OHCHR) in 1993. OHCHR has been very important in raising moral awareness about how human rights crosses paths with poverty, by producing and commissioning work on the relationship between poverty and human rights. It appointed a series of special rapporteurs not only on poverty but also on many specific rights with direct relevance for the poor (for example, a Special Rapporteur for the right to food, to health, to water). The work of Arjun Sengupta, special rapporteur for extreme poverty and human rights, deserves special attention. Not only did he provide intellectual foundations for the linkages between poverty and human rights, but he also made connections with the Right to Development. As former UN independent expert on the Right to Development for the Human Rights Commission, Sengupta has contributed to the materialisation of the Vienna Declaration by focusing attention on the implementation of the right to development via the role of the international community in supporting states to meet their duties (Sengupta 2000). If the right to development is to be considered a full right, then the fundamentals of equity and justice must guide all processes of development, from questions of production to the trade-offs between equity and growth, Sengupta argues; and he adds that respect for the agency of the poor and their participation in policies and projects that will affect their lives is one of the key aspects of a coherent implementation of human rights principles (Sengupta 2000). He developed a step-by-step implementation process that could guide the actions of the multilaterals we study here, and provide a point of departure for global debate on the feasible and pragmatic integration of human rights with the fight against poverty (see also Sengupta 2002). Sengupta has later developed concrete arguments about how and why poverty is best seen as a violation of human rights (to which we turn later).

But neither the Right to Development nor the principle of the Vienna Declaration had direct impact on development policy and practices. It was with the leadership of former UN Secretary-General Kofi Annan, and the Millennium Declaration, that human rights, poverty and development finally converged through Annan's advocacy and mainstreaming mandate through the whole UN system. Mary Robinson, appointed by Annan, has brought charisma and leadership as High Commissioner for Human Rights (from 1997 to 2002), and has engaged personally in dialogue with most UN agencies and the Bretton Woods institutions even after the end of her term. Unlike earlier attempts, the Millennium Declaration clearly argues for a united global society, and speaks the language of global responsibilities, as well as reaffirming both the UN Charter and the Universal Declaration:

> We recognize that, in addition to our separate responsibilities to our individual societies, we have a collective responsibility to uphold the principles of human dignity, equality and equity at the global level. As leaders we have a duty therefore to all the world's people, especially the

most vulnerable and, in particular, the children of the world, to whom the future belongs.[22]

But note also that the Millennium Declaration reaffirms the sovereignty of states:

> We rededicate ourselves to support all efforts to uphold the sovereign equality of all States, respect for their territorial integrity and political independence ... non-interference in the internal affairs of States, respect for human rights and fundamental freedoms, respect for the equal rights of all without distinction as to race, sex, language or religion and international cooperation in solving international problems of an economic, social, cultural or humanitarian character.

The declaration clearly states that certain fundamental values are essential to international relations in the twenty-first century. These include:

- Freedom: Men and women have the right to live their lives and raise their children in dignity, free from hunger and from the fear of violence, oppression or injustice. Democratic and participatory governance based on the will of the people best assures these rights.
- Equality
- Solidarity
- Tolerance
- Respect for nature
- Shared responsibility: Responsibility for managing worldwide economic and social development, as well as threats to international peace and security, must be shared among the nations of the world and should be exercised multilaterally. As the most universal and most representative organisation in the world, the United Nations must play the central role.

Regarding poverty and development the declaration says:

> We will spare no effort to free our fellow men, women and children from the abject and dehumanizing conditions of extreme poverty, to which more than a billion of them are currently subjected. We are committed to making the right to development a reality for everyone and to freeing the entire human race from want.

And it further clearly states the need for both national and global conditions to eradicate poverty, including specific references to good governance at the global level in relation to finance and trade: 'We are committed to an open, equitable, rule-based, predictable and non-discriminatory multilateral trading and financial system.' Last, the Millennium Declaration calls for resources to finance the eradication of poverty through duty- and quota-free access for essentially all exports from the least developed countries, debt relief, and increased development assistance.

The Millennium Declaration crystallises with a series of goals and measurable targets for 2015, the Millennium Development Goals (MDGs), that are today the cornerstone of most development assistance policies of donor countries and the guidelines for most multilateral organisations. (At the time of writing, there is wide agreement that the MDGs will not be achieved.)

Even though the declaration represents a merging between the principles in the UN Charter and the UN human rights declaration together with the later covenants, the MDGs are thin versions of the principles stated in the declaration, leading to less of a burden of responsibility on both states and the global community than the implementation of all human rights (including socio-economic and cultural rights and the right to development) would require.

But human rights have indeed permeated the UN system's language and agenda, and thus even if positive freedom and liberty rights prevail, it is a language difficult to dismiss (despite being over-legalistic and nation-state focused). By 2005, Kofi Annan's last action as secretary-general was to make public a strategy for the reform of the UN presenting its role in a globalised world. Annan's report, *In Larger Freedom: Towards Development, Security and Human Rights for All*, is a holistic interpretation of the convergence among the different key roles of the UN (security, development and human rights). The report is built around three notions of freedom (freedom from want, freedom from fear, and freedom to live a life with dignity). The Millennium Declaration and the related MDGs, and earlier discourses such as basic needs, are now converging with parallel global normative discourses, such as human development (with the capabilities approach as its intellectual foundation), human security (merging the narrow security concerns legacy of the Cold War), and universal human rights (as the undeniable global ethic of globalisation) (Gasper 2007a). There seems to be agreement that there must be a set of principles that underpin the forging of a global community; and of all the global normative discourses, there is no doubt that universal human rights is the most widely accepted. Annan's push for universal human rights in their relation to development has indeed had a major influence in the UN system, including influencing the Bretton Woods institutions.

UNDP produced a forceful argument for a human rights approach to development and poverty in the *Human Development Report 2000* (HDR 2000). We analyse UNDP's promotion of human rights in Chapter 4, but may simply note here that HDR 2000 offers two main arguments to justify the shift in approach:

1 Human rights are double-edged tools that look to the law as well as to morality, and they represent already accepted international standards in both areas;
2 Human rights approaches add analytical force to the implementation of human development, since rights place claims on others (individuals or

institutions) to fulfil their requirements. Rights entail duties, and duties bring with them responsibility, accountability, and even culpability.

Of all the emergent literature on the cross paths between human rights and development, Philip Alston and Mary Robinson's *Human Rights and Development: Towards Mutual Reinforcement*, published in 2005, is perhaps of most importance for our analysis. The book is the result of a conference held in New York in 2004, under the auspices of Mary Robinson's Ethical Globalization Initiative (EGI); the institution she founded after her leaving the post of high commissioner for human rights. The preface of this collection of essays clearly states how Robinson had consulted with James Wolfensohn, then President of the World Bank, and how supportive Wolfensohn was of establishing a dialogue both with academics and with other UN agencies regarding the role of human rights within an institution like the World Bank. As we shall relate in Chapter 5, Wolfensohn also asked the Nordic countries on the board of the WB to help him push for a human rights agenda.

But a more radical use of human rights in relation to poverty also emerges inside and outside of the UN system. In a key document providing both analytical and practical recommendations to link human rights and poverty, the OHCHR's draft guidelines *Human Rights and Poverty Reduction: A Conceptual Framework* (OHCHR 2002), there is explicit mention that poverty is not only a denial but also that it may be seen as a 'violation of human rights'.

> The recognition that the way poor people are forced to live often violates their human rights – or that promoting human rights could alleviate poverty – was a long time in coming. Now a human rights approach to poverty reduction is increasingly being recognized internationally and is gradually being implemented.
>
> (foreword)

The draft guidelines were an attempt to provide input to poverty reduction strategy papers (PRSPs), linking human rights to well established notions such as 'empowerment', 'social capital' and 'accountability', but basing all the analytical relations between rights and poverty on an already normatively-grounded view of poverty – capability poverty – permitting a direct link with freedoms and unfreedoms.

> The reason why the conception of poverty is concerned with basic freedoms is that these are recognized as being fundamentally valuable for minimal human dignity. But the concern for human dignity also motivates the human rights approach, which postulates that people have inalienable rights to these freedoms. If someone has failed to acquire these freedoms, then obviously her rights to these freedoms have not been realized. Therefore, poverty can be defined equivalently as either

the failure of basic freedoms – from the perspective of capabilities, or the non-fulfilment of rights to those freedoms – from the perspective of human rights.

(OHCHR 2002: 10)

The document thus provides a strong argument for the incorporation of human rights in the work of multilaterals working with poverty, such that it may be compatible with their expert work while at the same time keeping the political power of universal human rights in its relation to poverty and explicitly defining the concept of 'poverty as a violation of human rights'.

The three main authors of this OHCHR report have further developed the ideas expressed there. Paul Hunt, at the time of writing, is the special rapporteur on the right to health, and has further developed how a focus on human rights based sectoral policies (on health in this case), can lead to a coherent convergence between rights and poverty. Osmani has been active in deepening the relations between capabilities, freedom and human rights thereby emphasising the moral as well as the legal aspects of rights. As mentioned, Sengupta has also written on poverty as a violation of human rights, and he has actively participated in the UNESCO project we critically examine in Chapter 6 (Sengupta 2007a). Sengupta uses the language of violation in many reports in his current capacity as advisor to the United Nations Human Rights Council, including references to the poor in advanced economies (see for example a report on poverty as a violation of human rights in the United States [Sengupta 2007b]. Thus his work has been taken up by social movements working for the rights of the poor in both the global South and advanced economies.

In short, it seems the idea that poverty may be best seen as a violation of human rights takes off at this time (between 2003 and 2004). But it does not develop much further at the global institutional level; rather, a human rights based approach takes over as the debate focuses on implementation and materialisation of rights, and it seems to do so by toning down the political and moral aspects of human rights. The thinned out version of human rights based approaches to development is now spreading both inside and outside the UN; but the more political and ethical notion of 'poverty as a violation of human rights' has taken off strongly among activists and radical academics, leading to a debate on global justice and global responsibilities.

Critiques of human rights

In parallel with the debates at the UN level and within academia, human rights and poverty have emerged as a key theme among critics of globalisation, following the earlier tradition of using rights language in support of political struggle and activism (Gills 2006; Kiely 2005; Robinson 2002). Writers from David Harvey (2005) to Boaventura de Sousa Santos (2007, 2008) – one of the key theorists of the alter-globalisation movement – are also using the language of rights, albeit in very different formulations. As activist and scholar Paul Farmer claims, promoting social and economic rights is the most important struggle of our time, but we can no longer speak of rights in a depoliticised way. If we forget that human rights are a struggle for shifting power relations and that human rights violations are fundamentally a question of structural violence, all the new rhetoric of rights will lead our generation to simply 'manage social inequality' (Farmer 2003). Paraphrasing the fundamental task of Amnesty International, Farmer eloquently argues in his *Pathologies of Power: Health, Human Rights and the New War on the Poor* that we must 'bear witness' about the plight of the poor, but writing is not necessarily respectful to them, as it may mean no change in their lives. Moving beyond bearing witness requires compassion, solidarity, and amongst all, activism. But Farmer's work can, in our view, be characterised as a form of activism, as it painfully recounts the injustices done to the poor and the persistent violation of the right to health of all poor people even in wealthy and powerful countries like the United States. Farmer's insider account reminds everyone that human rights are about politics and struggle.

The legalistic and rather non-ethical promotion of human rights based approaches is leading to further critique of what is, indeed, a European-centric debate, the distinction between first- and second-generation human rights (liberty versus socio-economic and cultural rights); and the related distinction between traditions of legalising the first sets of rights and not the second, is all too consistent with the basic principles of laissez-faire capitalism (St. Clair 2006d). If liberty rights include a defence of freedom of economic action, rights to a minimum amount of economic means are seemingly impossible within our current market structure. Viewed from that perspective, liberty and economic and social rights are incompatible.

> If there are unrestricted economic rights to run life on commercial lines and accumulate private property, there cannot be rights to food or welfare; if there are rights to food or welfare or health care or employment there cannot be unrestricted rights to engage in commercial activity.
>
> (O'Neill 1986: 107)

Also, respect for human rights requires absolute respect for people's autonomy, which is easily undermined by power relations and by social stigmatisation, two common characteristics of the lives of the poor. Yet autonomy, 'like freedom, requires social conditions for its realization that demand significant constraints on the scope of the market and private property rights ... Protection of autonomy may sometimes require prohibiting the commodification of some things' (Anderson 1993: 142). In short, autonomy requires that many rights are non-tradable.

Moreover, the world has little experience in legislating for, say, the right to food, or the right to health or water, least of all on a global perspective; an important point if the key role of universal human rights in relation to poverty and development is their implementation through legal channels. The non-ethical and legalistic interpretation of human rights shifts the weight of duties towards states and away from global institutions. When the weight of implementing human rights is shifted exclusively to very poor states, the prospects for effective implementation are slight, and the tendency is to fall back on misguided development strategies focusing primarily on economic growth.

Research on the challenges that legal systems, courts, and the judiciary pose for poor people across the globe is showing that implementing socio-economic rights in societies where economies are driven by neo-liberal economic policies, high levels of inequality across sectors of the population, and poor structures promoting social cohesion between the poor and the middle classes, tend to lead to elite capture of the benefits of human rights. On the other hand, historical experiences, such as those of Scandinavian countries, show that the successful implantation of universal social policy went hand-in-hand with economic policies regarding income distribution and high taxation of wealth (Moene and Wallerstein 2006). The main strategy for implementing universal access to health and the assurance of a minimum standard of living for the population of Scandinavian countries was primarily to build social cohesion between sectors of the population and to minimise all sorts of inequalities. This has led to a distaste for both poverty and for excessive wealth, a transformation of values that still maintains these welfare systems amidst neo-liberal pressures. But these experiences and their lessons are overlooked in the emerging legal interpretation of the role of human rights in development by multilateral institutions, primarily because these issues are political. The problem thus, we argue, is not necessarily the legal interpretation of human rights, but rather their depoliticisation. Critical legal theory offers important insights that may help in the eventual formulation of universal human rights as guidelines for development and the eradication of poverty. And parts of the UN system have already echoed this more political and ethical view of human rights in relation to poverty. International law theorists such as, for example, Balakrishnan Rajagopal (2003), argue for a decolonisation of human rights and the resistance against their misuse and abuse by global elites and the global bodies of neo-liberal economic globalisation.

> Human rights and the Third World have always had a troubled and uneasy relationship ever since they were invented as epistemological categories at the end of second World War. Human-rights discourse has generally treated the Third World as an object, as a domain of terrain of deployment of its universal imperatives. Indeed, the very term 'human rights violations' evokes images of Third World Violence – dictators, ethnic violence, and female genital mutilations – whereas first world violence is commonly referred to as 'civil rights' violations.
>
> (2003: 171)

He adds, further, that even with this 'troubled and uneasy relationship', universal human rights can be a territory for the poor to reclaim their humanity, and that universal human rights can indeed be the language of progressive politics and resistance. Indeed, the language of human rights can be used as a political tool for resistance and for action, for driving the power struggle of those abused and marginalised, including the poor. Using the term 'violation of human rights' in relation to poverty, leads to constructing the complex social facts of poverty as a new category of political thought.

There is thus a tension between the need for a workable understanding of universal human rights as a discourse for contestation and challenging of unfair power structures and structural violence, which also serves as a global ethic that unites people and their diverse interests. Even critics from the South who claim that intercultural dialogue about human rights is in its infancy, express approval of the positive roles that human rights language may have for bringing in the voices of the global South (Mutua 2002). In order to achieve this task, critics of globalisation and other scholarship on poverty and human rights, seem to be moving towards a complementary language that would be able to keep all the good of human rights as an undeniable global ethics of our secular age and also keeping this as a political and moral discourse; the language of global justice and global responsibilities to which we now turn.

Global justice: responsibility and response-ability

Critics claim that the development business has been a way to perpetuate the separation between the rich and the poor – a gap which has been accentuated by globalisation and the dominance of neo-liberal economic views; and they view with suspicion the new emphasis on human rights. The moral discourse of global institutions is seen as misguided. Thus, anthropologist James Ferguson criticises the 'de-moralizing' discourse of these institutions, with their amoral scienticism which 'diffuses' or 'sheds away' the real moral issue: the responsibilities of the West and global institutions towards the poor. Following David Cohen (1993) he notes,

> Just as contemporary Germans have had to assess their collective responsibility for the Holocaust ... both sides of the Cold War will have to assess their responsibility for the 'militarization and impoverisation of three-quarters of the globe,' as well as for the creation of 'conditions, interests, orientations, institutions, routines, and cultures that define the possibilities of much of the globe.'
>
> (Cohen 1993: 4, in Ferguson 2006: 178)

Ferguson makes reference to traditional African moral systems, disrupted by 'development' and notes that

It is not only Africans who have traditions of moral discourse capable of generating critique, cleansing and renewal ... the West has its own traditions of accounting for moral responsibility that might well be dusted off and put to work as we survey the landscape of the post-Cold War world.

(Ferguson 2006: 179)

One of the key Western philosophers who has been dusting off Western philosophical traditions in order to address the challenge of global poverty is Thomas Pogge. A former student of John Rawls, Pogge has in recent years developed a view of human rights and poverty that extends the fundamental theses of liberal traditions to the world as a whole, proposing global norms, and pointing to global institutions as the most important actors to bring about world change. In his widely discussed *World Poverty and Human Rights: Cosmopolitan Responsibilities and Reform* (Pogge 2002), fully revised in a second edition published in 2008, Pogge argues that rethinking justice as global requires a reframing of its scope and character. He criticises the pervasive methodological territorialism in Western moral and political philosophy and social theory. We must be careful, says Pogge, in simply using moral and political theory to criticise globalisation. Ethical ideas per se may not lead to a satisfactory answer to why, and how, worldwide actions, relations, practices and institutions are fair or unfair.[23] Moral discourse may reflect the same biases and blind spots that are to be found in orthodox development theories proposed by global institutions. Even John Rawls was not concerned with the global forces that may affect the moral scope of human action, but placed the blame for poverty on the political culture of poor countries (Pogge 2004b: 261). Pogge quotes relevant passages from Rawls' later work where such moral methodological territorialism is evident:

'the causes of the wealth of a people and the forms it takes lie in their political culture and in the religious, philosophical, and moral traditions that support the basic structure of their political and social institutions, as well as in the industriousness and cooperative talents of its members, all supported by their political virtues ... the political culture of a burdened society is all-important ... Crucial also is the country's population policy' (Rawls 1999: 108) ... When societies fail to thrive ... 'the problem is commonly the nature of the public political culture and the religious and philosophical traditions that underlie its institutions. The great social evils in poorer societies are likely to be oppressive government and corrupt elites'.

(Rawls 1993: 77, in Pogge 2004b: 87)

Global justice, in Pogge's account, has an important intellectual framework distinguishable from international or from social justice conceptions. A thorough exposition of Pogge's ideas is beyond the scope of this study;

but we do, as he does, stress the importance of institutions, widely defined. Global justice views events, actions and institutions 'as effects of how our social world is structured – of our laws and conventions, practices and social institutions' (Pogge 2005). The moral analysis and diagnosis that follows from such an institutional perspective seeks explanations and counterfactuals very different from those of such well reputed figures as Rawls. Global justice does not mean that all human beings ought to share the same values; one can conceive of many different notions of justice and espouse complementary ethical theories. As Pogge observes,

> distinct conceptions of global justice will differ in the specific criteria of global justice they propose. But such criteria will coincide in their emphasis on the question about how well is the global order doing, compared to its feasible alternatives, in regard to the fundamental human interests that matter from a moral point of view.
>
> (Pogge 2005: 7)

In Pogge's account, the global system is one of the important reasons for the violation of human rights of the severely poor (Pogge 2002, 2005).[24]

Other philosophers are now following the path opened by Pogge and attempting to reframe their own ideas to accommodate the increasingly apparent injustices associated with globalisation. Nancy Frazer (2005), for example, argues that globalisation forces thinkers to reframe their views of justice. To her own account of a dual notion of justice that concerns itself with both redistribution and recognition (Frazer and Honneth 2003), she adds that struggles for socio-economic justice require a rethinking of the notion of political representation.

All these views are predominantly Western, but much of the edited work we cite above has strong participation from scholars from the global South. Moreover, these lines of argumentation have counterparts in most cultures across the globe, perhaps under different labels and traditions. And globalisation has also led to a level of interconnectedness among scholars from the North and the South that permits dialogue and debate in ways not possible before. Pogge's views are fundamentally in line, for example, with the World Social Forum ideology and its exponents (e.g. Boaventura de Sousa Santos 2007), or with many critical globalisation studies authors (see special issue of *Globalizations* 2006; Gills 2006).

In short, what we hope this chapter has shown is that from the UN system, from social movements and activism, and from Western philosophers there is a very rich literature on which to base a shared conception of global responsibilities. Whereas the debate after WWII centred on ethics, values and universal human rights in relation to poverty and development, in a globalised twenty-first century the debate is centred on global ethics, global justice and global responsibilities.

Pogge's view of responsibility appears to be akin to that expressed by Ferguson: the West and rich countries have responsibility for the past wrongs inflicted on the South and the global poor. He likens the harms done by the rich to the poor to those of the Holocaust, or the massacres in Rwanda. We agree that history should not be ignored, but in seeking an appropriate philosophical approach we favour what the philosopher Iris Young calls a forward-looking perspective on responsibility,[25] and a 'commonsense morality'; somewhat less extreme views which, nevertheless, lead to rather similar political implications. In brief, the question 'who is responsible?' may be restated as 'who is response-able?' – in other words, 'who is capable of responding in such a way as to remedy the harm?'; and the answer, we assert, is international organisations.

In her two key articles 'Responsibility and Global Labor Justice' (2004) and 'Responsibility and Global Justice: A Social Connection Model' (2006), Young pinpoints the central dilemma of what she calls 'structural social injustice'.[26] This, as she notes, is distinct from both the direct wrongful action of an individual agent, and the wilfully repressive policies of a state. Young's philosophy is relational and practical in the sense that she seeks to bring about change. For Young,

> obligations of justice arise between persons by virtue of the social processes that connect them; political institutions are the response to these obligations rather than their basis. Claims that obligations of justice extend globally for some issues, then, are grounded in the fact that some structural social processes connect people across the world without regard to political boundaries.
>
> (Young 2006: 102)

The key question therefore becomes: 'how should moral agents, both individual and collective, think about our responsibilities in relation to structural social injustice?' (Young 2006: 102). In place of what she calls the liability model, and a backward-looking view which seeks to attribute blame from wrongdoing, Young proposes a 'social connection model'.

> From the observation that the social connection model differs from the liability model in that it does not isolate those liable (in ways that implicitly absolve others), it follows that all those who contribute by their actions to the structural processes producing injustice share responsibility for such injustice.
>
> (Young 2006: 122)

Moreover, it is an understanding of responsibility that acknowledges that often actions may continue to happen unless particular remedies are found or solutions reached.

> When conceptualizing responsibility in relation to structural injustice. ... we are concerned with an ongoing set of processes that we understand is

likely to continue producing harm unless there are interventions in it. The temporality of assigning and taking responsibility, then, is more forward-looking than backward-looking.

(Young 2006: 122)

It is thus a forward looking conception of responsibility, rather than an understanding of responsibility as only blame for past wrongdoing.

This, we suggest, is a useful concept for understanding our responsibilities in an age of globalisation. The current international economic and political system is indeed one in which the outcomes are unjust; and we, the rich, who benefit from the system, contribute to the structural social processes which sustain it. Within this system, international organisations – created and maintained by ourselves acting collectively – play an important role in making and applying the rules, and (in the case of development organisations) are mandated to ameliorate the outcomes for the poorest of the poor. This gives these organisations a special responsibility; but, we shall argue, this responsibility is unlikely to be realised under present circumstances. A major hindrance at present is their governance: their answerability to states which – both rich and poor, 'donor' and 'recipient' – are conservative and resistant to change.

Standard models of responsibility in moral and legal theory, Young argues, are not adequate for assigning responsibility for global issues, such as poverty. They

> appear to require that we trace a direct relationship between the action of a person or group and a harm. Although structural processes that produce injustice result from the actions of many persons and the policies of many organizations, in most cases it is not possible to trace which specific actions of which specific agents cause which specific parts of the structural processes or their outcomes.
>
> (Young 2006: 115)

Most of us, most of the time, distance ourselves from a sense of personal responsibility in relation to structural injustice, because we rightly think that we have operated within acceptable norms and cannot see a determinate path between our actions and the structurally caused limitations on the lives of others. Consequently, we tend not to think that we ourselves have obligations to take actions to remedy such injustices. But in the highly globalised world of today, this is not an adequate response to the challenge of poverty (and also issues such as climate change). What may be broadly called 'social structures' operate on a global scale; and 'social structures serve as background conditions for individual actions by presenting actors with options; they provide "channels" that both enable action and constrain it' (Young 2006: 112). Under these circumstances, any conception of responsibility needs to be not individual, but collective (French 1991, 1992). We need a conception of responsibility that is able to account for the new situation of a highly globalised world. As Samuel Scheffler has noted, standard accounts of responsibility, moral sensibility and moral theory lag behind the many fast-paced changes in all types of relationships, and thus the structures that provide the grounds of people's lives and people's choices are also changed. The concepts of responsibility with which we operate are simply outdated. They are a reflection of issues that derive from, and are most suited to, situations of smaller scale interaction.

> We continue to rely on a 'phenomenology of agency', what used to be actual experience of people interacting 'personally' with other people that gives primacy to near effects over remote effects, to individual effects over group effects, and to people's positive actions more than what they have failed to do.
>
> (Young 2004: 373)

Such a conception of agency, and the concept of responsibility derived from it, is not appropriate for understanding and taking responsibility for the large-scale social structural processes that are sources of many problems today.[27]

What we need, says Young, is a social connection model of responsibility, that, following Hannah Arendt, she sees as a form of political responsibility. For Young, political implies far more than government; it refers to the ways in which people organise collectively, and the ways in which we evaluate and reform such collective organisations and the institutions that regulate them. Her approach implies a forward looking notion of responsibility that, rather than allocating blame, seeks to bring about change – collectively. 'Political responsibility seeks not to reckon debts, but aims rather to bring about results, and thus depends on the actions of everyone who is in a position to contribute to the results' (Young 2004: 379). But also,

> Political responsibility ... is necessarily a shared responsibility both because the injustices that call for redress are the product of the mediated actions of many, and thus because they can only be rectified through collective action. For most such injustices, the goal is to change structural processes by reforming institutions or creating new ones that will better regulate the process to prevent harmful outcomes.
>
> (Young 2004: 387)

Iris Young contrasts the social connection (political) model of responsibility with other possible responses to the question of how persons ought to think about their moral responsibilities in relation to threats to well-being that are produced by structural social processes. The first, which she calls the charity view, is consistent with an entitlement theory of justice, and, she believes, is widely held both by philosophers and citizens in the structurally complex societies in which we live. People who do something to prevent threats to others' well-being should be praised for doing so, but no one has obligations to do so. The second, the nation-state view, relates obligations of justice to membership in a political community. As members of a political community, each of us has responsibilities to contribute to making the institutions of this community more just; and our fellow citizens have grounds for complaint if our national institutions fail to treat them justly. The basis of their appeal, on this account, is the fact of their membership with us in a common national community. (She notes that since structural processes are arguably denser within nation-state than across national borders, the social connection model of responsibility often comes to the same practical conclusions as the nation-state view. But she argues that 'the nation-state view begs the question of what are the grounds of obligations of justice. It takes the establishment of political institutions as prior to the responsibilities that individuals have to see to it that their institutions operate justly, and considers the implicit contract citizens make with one another in claiming common citizenship as the ground of obligations of justice.')

On a social connection model of responsibility for justice, on the other hand, the social is ontologically and morally prior to the political. People come to dwell together within institutions that interact together to produce structural consequences. They have obligations of justice towards one another '*even in the absence of shared political institutions*' (emphasis added) because they participate in structured social processes that affect many others. As we argued above, self-conscious political organising is the major means of discharging such obligations. On this account, political institutions are grounded in obligations of justice, rather than the reverse, as the nation-state view would have it. On the social connection model of responsibility moreover, there is no difference in principle between transnational responsibilities for justice and responsibilities in relation to persons in the same city or state as oneself. In today's world, the operation of structural processes that affect the life opportunities of people span locales and nations, and some of them are global in the sense that most people in the world are affected by them. Where structural injustice is transnational, then, some of the responsibilities that agents have under the social connection model are transnational as well. Since discharging such responsibility requires engaging in collective action, such transnational responsibilities give moral weight to projects to establish stronger transnational political institutions.

There are thus two arguments for global justice flowing for the rich elaboration offered by Iris Young, one of which applies even without IOs. The third theory which she considers is the cosmopolitan-utilitarian theory of responsibility. On that view, as Young construes it, moral agents have responsibilities to do something to alleviate suffering or threats to well-being, just because there are sufferers. It does not matter what is the cause of the suffering, nor does the obligation to do something depend on some institutional connection between an agent and those who suffer. All that matters is that an agent be able to do something to help alleviate the suffering or remove the threats to well-being. Each moral agent has the responsibility to do as much as he or she can to contribute to removal of the conditions that cause suffering, right up to the point where his or her own basic well-being is threatened.

On the social connection model, one has obligations of justice to others not in general because morality requires alleviating suffering, but on the more restricted grounds that one participates in social structures that make others vulnerable to harm. In today's world of globalised social structures, this can – with regard to some issues – include everyone in the world. This follows not from the theoretical presuppositions or the principles of the social connection model or a view of responsibility as political, but from the actual facts of particular social processes. The social connection model, according to Young, is located between the two more extreme positions represented by the nation-state view and cosmopolitan utilitarianism.

What is clear is that in order to understand both the sources of injustice and the possibilities for rectifying injustice, normative theory needs to draw more on social theory than is typically the case among contemporary philosophers. Most of the philosophers referred to above, moreover – including Singer, Scheffler and Murphy – write as though each moral agent might discharge their responsibilities by means of their own deliberate action without necessary relation to others. Responsibilities grounded in social connection, Young insists, can normally be discharged only by organised collective action. Thus political responsibility with respect to structural injustice often requires the transforming of institutions and the tasks they assign. This is everyone's task and no one's in particular, and, furthermore, it is a shared task; it implies that individuals reconsider their own responsibilities (Young 2004, 2006).

Another philosopher, Green (2007) argues along similar lines to Young, and spells out quite clearly the differences between the responsibilities of individuals and institutions:

> Both individuals and institutional agents bear responsibilities: They are responsible for avoiding causing certain harms and sometimes for preventing or ameliorating harms even if they did not cause them. There is a rationale for restricting individual responsibility roughly along some familiar lines from commonsense morality. This rationale does not apply to the institutional agents.
>
> (Green 2007: 128)

Commonsense morality is, he says, 'the rough moral code that most of us follow, (which) embodies what Samuel Scheffler calls a *restrictive* conception of responsibility' (our stress). This is more limited than that implied by consequentialist moral theories which, according to Scheffler, differ in that they have no fundamental place for the distinction between action and omission, or for special duties. But he recognises that 'While the restrictive commonsense conception has considerable intuitive appeal, it faces important limitations.' There are global problems such as climate change and global justice that should be regulated by morality, but 'our restrictive conception of responsibility impedes this regulation'. Green proposes institutional responsibility as an alternative. 'Since institutions have different capacities as agents than individuals, there is less reason to apply the restrictive conception of responsibility to them.' Scheffler had argued that part of the explanation for people's failure to do more to aid those who are in need is that the predominant values and norms of our culture do not in fact require them to do so. But Green identifies several of the relevant capacities of IOs, in order to support an expanded and adapted view of responsibility for global problems that are crucial for the analysis we carry out in our work.

By virtue of their hugely greater ability to obtain and make use of information, they 'are more capable of taking the remote effects of their actions into account than individuals are'. Institutions have the power to alter mass behaviour. And they can spread the costs of regulating a problem. And 'In addition, institutions are not hampered by our phenomenal distinction between action and omission.' In brief, institutions have the capacities necessary, are 'able', to bridge the responsibility gap – both moral and practical – which is apparent to those who see extreme poverty as grossly unjust, but are unconvinced by the claim that they, as individuals, are responsible for the situation.

The existence of international institutions, then, renders it possible for individuals to respond to the intuitive demands of global justice; something which, in the absence of such institutions, would for practical reasons be impossible. And because this is possible, it is also, we suggest, a moral duty. What does this imply for the moral responsibility of international organisations, and for the nations that create and, in formal terms, compose them? Those organisations whose explicit purpose is to ameliorate poverty clearly, we suggest, have not merely a formal but also a *moral* responsibility to do so. They are the agents of individuals whose moral duty is to discharge this responsibility. (Those international institutions which have other purposes also, we suggest, have a moral responsibility not to exacerbate poverty.)

International organisations are 'response-able': they are particularly well placed to act by virtue of the powers that we, the people of the world, have given them: the economic resources and expertise that enable them to change the world; and the political legitimacy they enjoy by virtue of their mandates. But in the rest of the book we show how these same powers have acted as constraints on these organisations to behave as moral agents; how the various organisations we have examined have, for very differing reasons, tended to draw back from the moral arena, and been hesitant to embrace the discourse of ethics and human rights.

4 UNDP

The human development paradigm

Since its creation in 1966, UNDP has been at the centre of the United Nations' operational development system, working both at the grassroots level to help build national capacities for sustainable development, and as a leader in development thinking, as demonstrated by its flagship Human Development Reports and its contributions to critical issues such as global public goods and democratic governance. In many ways, it is this important nexus – connecting countries to knowledge and ideas and working with them to strengthen the capacity needed to tackle development challenges – that is UNDP's hallmark.

(UNDP Annual Report 2006)

Introduction

The UNDP provides an interesting case study. It is not strong in terms of either financial resources or expertise, but it draws strength from its special relationship with developing country governments, and it has, in recent years, derived considerable moral authority from its close association with the human development paradigm. In this chapter we first review UNDP's strengths and weaknesses, and then examine its activities in relation to human development, ethics and human rights – showing that it treads a careful path within the constraining walls of political feasibility.

The UNDP is frequently compared – for better or worse – with the World Bank. In this light, it appears as more bureaucratic, but more responsive to the governments of poor countries; less competent, but – thanks largely to the Human Development Reports – as promoting a more 'humane' development agenda.

In his recent history of the UNDP, Craig Murphy draws a rather positive picture of the organisation. He describes it as 'the development programme *of* the developing countries', the intergovernmental organization most trusted by governments in the developing world because it was the most responsive to them' (Murphy 2006: 8). It has, he says, provided 'the most extensive and most consistent presence of the entire UN system throughout the world' (Murphy 2006: 5). 'Not the richest organization in its field by a long way, but usually the one that is the most connected to all the rest' (Murphy 2006: 4).

An earlier, but also comprehensive, assessment is more negative. UNDP is 'the main financing, coordinating and controlling body for the UN's operational development tasks. At no time in its history, however, has UNDP ever succeeded in performing these tasks adequately' (Klingebiel 1999: 2). 'UNDP's history is characterized by crisis-ridden development. The debates on and analyses of UNDP in the 1970s, 1980s and, to a great extent, the 1990s have almost all detected symptoms of crisis' (Klingebiel 1999: 102).

These two accounts are not as inconsistent as may appear. The UNDP is indeed more responsive to developing country governments, but this can also constrain its ability to promote the welfare of their people. And the task of coordinating and controlling the UN's operational tasks around the world is extremely difficult to achieve without substantial reforms to the UN system, which have been effectively resisted over many years.

And the organisation has, of course, changed over time. The 1970s and 1980s was a particularly bad period for UNDP. In the heyday of structural adjustment it played a very modest role. But as criticism of the Bretton Woods institutions increased, the UNDP emerged in a better light – especially thanks to the human development paradigm. (Although it must be noted that the Human Development Reports are not formally endorsed by the UNDP, which was in fact slow to associate itself with what it now presents as its 'flagship' document – see below.) Today, many would argue that the gap between the World Bank and UNDP, in terms of their perspectives and policies, and perhaps also their effectiveness, is less than it was 10–15 years ago, although opinions differ as to which organisation has changed more.[1]

Klingebiel asserts that rather little has been written about the UNDP, at least by researchers, although he does cite a number of evaluations by donors.[2] In addition to his book, and that of Murphy, we draw in the following account primarily on interviews which we carried out with a selection of senior UNDP staff, supplemented by some well informed commentators.

A very brief history

In November 1965, the Expanded Programme on Technical Assistance and the United Nations Special Fund were merged, by Resolution 2029 (XX) in the UN General Assembly, to establish the UNDP. In 1970, against the background of the Jackson Report,[3] the General Assembly enlarged and clarified UNDP's foundations with a 'consensus resolution' which designated UNDP as the central element of the UN system's technical cooperation (Klingebiel 1999: 70). Thus, UNDP, unlike the World Bank or the Inter-American Development Bank, is not a source of investment finance but of technical assistance – in relation to projects, programmes and policies.

The early idealistic period of UNDP is referred to by, among others, Margaret Anstee – the first woman Resident Representative – who contrasts this with its subsequent decline (UNIHP Anstee 2000). She acted as secretary to the Jackson Report mentioned above. This was a comprehensive, and rather damning, assessment of the UN system by a highly respected former under-secretary-general of the United Nations. 'In other words, the machine as a whole has become unmanageable in the strictest use of the word. As a result, it is becoming slower and more unwieldy, like some prehistoric monster' (UN 1969: iii).

Another senior UNDP figure, I. G. Patel, is quoted by Murphy; he

> found much of the culture of the UN development network to be dis- tasteful: wastefully long Governing Council meetings, extraordinarily complex bureaucratic mechanisms 'created for dealing with what was not that much to deal with' and 'a reactionary and conservative staff that constantly criticized the Bretton Woods agencies, even though they were, in many ways, much more progressive than UNDP'.
>
> (Murphy 2006: 152)

In 1995, the Overseas Development Council (ODC) published *A Comparative Assessment*, comparing the UNDP, the International Monetary Fund, the World Bank and UNICEF. With regard to UNDP, its conclusions were generally negative. Its main strengths were found to be

> (1) its close relations with the programme countries' institutions (national ownership, etc.) (2) its good external structure and (3) the conditionality and form of its technical cooperation (grant basis, South– South cooperation, etc.). UNDP's weaknesses, on the other hand are (1) its limited and weak revenue base, (2) its lack of focus, (3) the separation of funding and execution and (4) its underqualified staff.
>
> (Klingebiel 1999: 167)

In the 1990s, with increasingly widespread criticism of the Bretton Woods Institutions, and the success of the Human Development Reports, UNDP's reputation rose somewhat; but the rich countries on whose funds it depended continued to be rather sceptical. According to Murphy, the situation has, however, improved in recent years. He gives credit to Mark Malloch Brown, the Administrator in the period 1999 to 2005, who implemented some substantial reforms.

> By the end of Malloch Brown's tenure in 2005, UNDP was, undoubtedly, a more legitimate organization in the eyes of many developing nations and of most major donors than it had been at the beginning. It was also, in many ways, a much more professional organization.
>
> (Murphy 2006: 298)

But it still had far to go. In the six months after the tsunami of 2004, UNDP delivered only US$35 million of the $122 million that it had available to spend. Murphy quotes Malloch Brown, in reference to this experience: 'If there is an "Achilles heel" of UNDP at the moment, … it is the organizational incapacity to deliver on a scale commensurable with its mission' (Murphy 2006: 49).

One of our interviewees expressed the matter more graphically: 'Mark Malloch Brown was a last ditch rescue effort of a sinking organisation. Love him or hate him you could not ignore him. …his reforms [are] seen as broadly correct, and it is now a consolidation period'. He was succeeded in 2005 by Kemal Derviş (see below).

Governance and budget

The UNDP is governed by an Executive Board, which replaced the larger and more unwieldy governing council in 1994. The chief executive of UNDP (the Administrator) reports annually to the Board which holds an additional two 'regular sessions' each year, at which decisions are taken by consensus. On this Board there are eight members from Africa, seven from Asia, four from Eastern Europe, five from Latin America and the Caribbean, and twelve from Western Europe, who serve on a rotating basis. By comparison with the World Bank there is thus considerably more balance between rich and poor countries. But it is also necessary to recognise the power of the purse, and of the USA.

UNDP's annual income in 2006 consisted of 'core' funding of US$0.9 billion, supplemented by earmarked contributions totalling $3.8 billion. Of this 'non-core' funding, roughly one third each was provided by OECD countries, by non-bilateral partners, and by programme country governments themselves (mainly in Latin America).[4] It is notable that although the total amount is far higher than it was in 1991 (US$1.3 billion), the amount of core funding in 2006 was actually less than in 1991. This can be interpreted as a reflection of mixed donor confidence in UNDP, and a desire for more control; and it is a major problem for the organisation since it severely limits its autonomy.

A high proportion of the core funds come from 'like-minded countries'. The Netherlands, Sweden and Norway topped the list in 2006, closely followed by the United States and the United Kingdom. Although the US is not a significantly greater source of funds than several other countries, it does have considerable influence, not least by virtue of UNDP headquarters being located in New York. But according to Murphy: 'The Programme can never simply be an instrument of any donor's foreign policy. The United States, for example, could veto World Bank loans to Allende's government, but could not change UNDP's commitment to serve Chile' (Murphy 2006: 21). Our interviews confirmed, however, that the threat from the US to propose a cut in UNDP's budget is a continuing concern.

Staff and expertise

The UNDP has over 4,000 staff, from 152 nations, of whom only a minority are at headquarters in New York. As noted above, the ODC's independent assessment identified underqualified staff as one of UNDP's main weaknesses. Another donor evaluation – the Nordic UN Project – concluded that there are serious deficiencies in the training and experience of a large proportion of the staff (Nordic UN Project 1991). Higher management posts are filled on the basis of 'unwritten' nationality criteria (Kienbaum and Partners 1991: 58, quoted in Klingebiel 1999). 'Deficient qualifications are a major feature not only of UNDP's headquarters but also of many field offices' (Klingebiel 1999: 141). Malloch Brown put a major emphasis on staff upgrading, but our interviewees did not claim that UNDP staff were particularly highly qualified. As one interviewee put it: 'I wouldn't say the people at UNDP are different [from the World Bank], except maybe they have one degree less.' Another:

> [it is] striking the low levels of technical competence in UNDP ... but [it is] a whole lot more effective than the UN Secretariat. UNDP reformers have dragged it from the 60s to the late 80s. The UN is still in the 50s/60s.

But those interviewed also emphasised the high motivation of UNDP staff, and the strength derived from the fact that the majority of them work in the field.

Murphy suggests that the structure of the organisation may be in part to blame for the relative weakness of its technical competence: 'After the Consensus [people] were asked whether they wished to be a technical specialist or a line officer in one of the new bureaux; to do both would now be impossible. "Brilliant minds, put into this structure, were (thus) marginalized"' (Murphy 2006: 150–151).

It may also be relevant to note the practice of apportioning senior positions on a 'geographical' basis. According to Murphy,

> An unwritten part of that agreement (following 'the Consensus document'), which has been maintained ever since, was that a national of the region would head each Bureau, located at headquarters, while nationals of major donor countries would head the various cross-regional administrative bureaux concerned with finance, personnel and the like.
>
> (Murphy 2006: 149)

Malloch Brown has emphasised UNDP's role as a 'knowledge organisation'. (It is described as 'the UN's global development network' on the official website.) In recent years, it has been been implementing a new 'T' model, implying that staff should combine breadth and depth in expertise. And the organisation has established centres of expertise outside New York (including a large Poverty Centre in Brasilia, and a more modest Governance Centre in Oslo, Norway). But it can be difficult to match the skills of the staff to the changing agenda. As one interviewee put it: 'You could not convert your forestry specialist into an AIDS expert – the classic UNDP response.' According to Murphy, a particularly valuable initiative is the networks, which connect UNDP staff by internet – sharing views and experience on, for example, human rights. This illustrates a central question facing UNDP: how much and what sort of expertise should the organisation have, and where should this be located? UNDP is, by intention, heavily decentralised; and its role is to advise on, and be supportive of, government policies. It is questionable whether it would be appropriate, even if it were possible, for UNDP to aspire to be a world expert organisation on all the different sectors and issues with which its member countries are involved. (Any aspiration that the UNDP might have to occupy the role of the leading agency of international development is constrained by others in the UN system; on the one hand the World Bank has far greater resources in terms of funds and expertise, on the other hand its sister agencies of the UN, and particularly the specialised agencies, jealously guard their territories.) Malloch Brown told his successor that 'In chasing after business of all sorts, UNDP had become a jack-of-all-trades but seemed the master of none' (Murphy 2006: 295). And the dilemma is very evident from the statement by the Associate Administrator, Ad Melkert, to UNDP's Executive Board in 2007 on 'UNDP and focus':

> at the end of the day UNDP more than any other organization is qualified as 'provider of last resort'. ... programme countries should continue to count upon UNDP to advise and support as necessary. UNDP in turn should invest in quality that comes from focusing on its comparative strengths rather than by the mediocrity that comes from trying to be all things to everyone.
>
> (UNDP 2007)

The issue of expertise links closely with the question of whether UNDP should have an 'official policy' on anything – as discussed below. Some of those interviewed felt that UNDP should have only very broad policies, and generalised expertise. To quote one interviewee:

> The 'policy types' is a relatively recent phenomenon. ... The great criticism five to eight years ago (was that) no-one had a clue what people were doing. Res Reps [resident representatives] had no information. The last ten years were all about figuring out how UNDP will deal with policy. ...Responsive to needs in country – but also build up a cadre of expertise to offer career paths, and to offer intellectual leadership in the world. ... [But] in a knowledge-based organisation: what do you do? [There is] no real profile of the UN expert. Is it an expert in rights-based approaches? In process-oriented development?

The Administrator

Leadership is widely acknowledged as crucial in shaping, though not ultimately determining, the identity of a multilateral organisation. The UNDP

Administrator is the third highest ranking official in the United Nations system – appointed by the UN Secretary-General and confirmed by the General Assembly. James Gustave ('Gus') Speth, who served from 1993 to 1999, was a very different character from his predecessor William H. ('Bill') Draper III, who served from 1986. Speth was more of an academic,with particular interest and experience in environmental issues. (He co-founded the Natural Resources Defense Council, and founded the World Resources Institute in 1982, serving as its President for ten years.)

Mark Malloch Brown came to UNDP from the World Bank, where he had been vice-President for external affairs and vice-President for United Nations affairs. Malloch Brown earlier worked for the *Economist* magazine and founded the Economist Development Report, serving as the report's editor from 1983 to 1986. From 1979 to 1983, he worked for the United Nations High Commissioner for Refugees. The importance of his contribution has already been noted.

Kemal Derviş, who started as the new head of the United Nations Development Programme in August 2005, also had a career in the World Bank, including posts as vice-President for the Middle East and North Africa Region, and vice-President for poverty reduction and economic management. He also had experience as minister for economic affairs and the treasury, and later as a member of parliament, in Turkey. He has published widely, including, in cooperation with the Center for Global Development, a book entitled *A Better Globalization: Legitimacy, Governance and Reform* (co-authored with Ceren Ozer, Brookings Institution Press, 2005) which deals with global development issues and international institutional reform and presents some quite radical proposals, notably that the UN should become responsible for the governance of economic and security relations, led by a reformed Security Council and a new Economic and Social Security Council.

While many people praised Speth's commitment, he was sometimes seen as too 'academic'; Malloch Brown is credited for his management skills and his 'professionalisation' of the organisation. It is too early to say how Kemal Derviş will be remembered in the UNDP. His skills and reputation as an economist are seen as an asset, but opinions vary as to whether UNDP should, or even can, try to establish world-class expertise in this field. He has from an early stage been actively involved in the delicate issue of coordination of UN agencies, notably through his position as ex-officio member of the High Level Panel on UN System Wide Coherence, established by Kofi Annan in 2006.

In-country operations

UNDP has offices in 166 countries. 'The country offices and the Res Reps were the essence of UNDP not only to its staff members, but also to most people working on development in the 1960s, and to the developing countries themselves' (Murphy 2006: 143). This is still the case today. The Res

Reps, although they are in continuing contact with headquarters, enjoy a rather high degree of autonomy; a point which was stressed by several of those interviewed. For example: 'I do think New York is in many ways peripheral.'

Formally, UNDP has a special role as the coordinator of all UN agencies in the field; but, despite repeated discussions in the context of UN reform, this is not easy to achieve in practice, especially with regard to the Bretton Woods institutions. It does, however, enjoy a special standing; to quote one of our interviewees: 'The greatest power of UNDP is the convening power – in country'. According to one interviewee, UNDP is

> the most universal, field-based organisation. More than any other and because of its broad mandate. The obvious mechanism in the field to push a normative agenda – to make sure someone in government is drafting the biannual speech on Convention X, Y, Z. It is the catch-all of all kinds of things. For example, DESA (UN Department of Economic and Social Affairs) needs a Copenhagen + 5 report: you send in the UN Resident Coordinator to get it.

A major task for the Res Rep is 'Country programming'. To quote the Associate Administrator, Ad Melkert, again:

> the majority of UNDP resources are implemented at the country level through the harmonized UN programming process. This process – which includes the Common Country Assessment (CCA), the UN Development Assistance Framework (UNDAF), and the Country Pro-gramme Document (CPD) – is undertaken as a direct response to national development strategies and is aligned with national program-ming cycles. While full government participation is sought throughout the programming process, UNDP Country Programmes have been and will always be fully owned by governments. They are implemented jointly by these national partners and UNDP and subject to approval and review by the Executive Board.
>
> (UNDP 2007)

Referring to eight country studies in the Nordic UN Project, Klingebiel (1999: 146) asserts that 'given these advantages, UNDP operations are gen-erally much appreciated by the programme countries'. But this can also create problems. To quote another interviewee:

> One of the criticisms of UNDP – a little less now I think – is that UNDP Res Reps get too close to the government they serve. But at its crudest it becomes a slush fund for an unsavoury government. Can be complicit. UNDP has never been about economic and political conditionality. ... But we can say we won't work directly through government.

According to Murphy (2006: 14),

> In between [the 1950s and 1990s] UNDP had learned to respond to a persistent criticism that its original vision of 'peace through solidarity' really could be achieved only through solidarity with the *people* of other nations, and not through solidarity with non-democratic *governments*.

But this is not an easy path to tread. Should the organisation not be critical of governments that are corrupt? And where a country's policies are manifestly ill-advised should it not advise, or even try and persuade governments to change? One well informed commentator we interviewed was vehement in his criticism of '"the country is always right" horseshit', arguing that if you are a specialist you have a view – as an expert. 'Not just "if you want a road you can get a road". ... Maybe (it would be) arrogance, but the Res Rep of, say, Tanzania should know something about Tanzanian development; should have some independent views'.

Another important consideration is that 'UNDP's closer identification with the South may have come at a cost: the alienation of the country that had been the major sponsor of the UN development network from the beginning – the United States' (Murphy 2006: 154).

Can advocacy be neutral?

This raises the challenging question of whether UNDP should be – or even can be – neutral; and how this may be combined with an 'advocacy' role. Murphy identifies advocacy as former Administrator Draper's 'second track'. This was certainly an important matter also for Malloch Brown and, to quote a very senior staff member: 'Advocacy is very important. A comparative advantage of UNDP is to be a good advocate. (There are) some basic issues on which we can't be neutral; for example, abject poverty. There is political support for that.'

According to one interviewee, it is 'part and parcel of what we are doing; [but] not a crude advocacy'. Another of those interviewed linked this to what many agree is one of UNDP's major assets – its convening power: 'If I had to single out the most powerful tool it is our convening power, based on our perceived neutrality.'

In emphasising UNDP's neutrality, Murphy makes much of the contrast with the World Bank and bilateral agencies. He cites examples of UNDP's dealings with Romania, during the break-up of the Soviet Union (Murphy 2006: 173); how China, in 1978, regarded UNDP as the 'most trustworthy and independent development organisation' (Murphy 2006: 177); and asserts that only UNDP was initially considered neutral enough to link Iran to non-partisan advice (Murphy 2006: 193). And he quotes the Res Rep of Madagascar, Guindo:

> UNDP has to be close to government, but, in all these situations, I think it's also important that you cultivate good relationships with civil

society ... They should trust you, should see you a neutral, as a broker, instead of siding only with government. It's a very difficult equilibrium to obtain.

(Murphy 2006: 316)

One interviewee contrasted UNDP with UNICEF; to be non-neutral '[leads to] tension between what it champions as a policy issue and the ability to be seen as open, the glue that holds the system together'. Another, when asked whether advocacy is difficult to combine with neutrality, argued that UNDP is 'impartial, not neutral. Not involved in the political dimension. The programme countries are our clients. But not neutral in the sense of Switzerland. We stand for Human Development, the MDGs. ... The flagship document is the HDR'. Another characterised UNDP's conception of neutrality: 'Not too much of an agenda. Even our advocacy of human rights and governance (is) couched in terms of Human Development, not Freedom House.' In brief, the consensus appears to be that although UNDP should not be neutral, its advocacy role relates to the promotion of rather broad issues – which may perhaps be captured by the human development paradigm (see below).

Relations with other agencies

For the UNDP, the World Bank is undoubtedly 'the significant other', although the reverse is not the case. Relations between the two – and more generally between the Bretton Woods institutions and the rest of the UN system – have long been as much competitive as cooperative. Going some way back in history, Murphy notes that 'As the World Bank's Eugene Black readily admitted, the IDA was "an idea to offset the urge for SUNFED [Special United Nations Fund for Economic Development]"' (Murphy 2006: 65). But he also asserts that 'the deepest moral convictions of the officers of the two organizations [UNDP and WB] were the same. Paul Hoffmann worked closely with his World Bank counterpart, Robert S. McNamara' (Murphy 2006: 16).

The period of structural adjustment was a rather crucial one for the two organisations. While ECA (the Economic Commission for Africa) and UNICEF were openly critical of the Bretton Woods institutions, UNDP was more cautious. As Murphy notes, some people

fault UNDP for failing to use the bully pulpit of the Programme's central position in the UN development network to lead a concerted, public, global campaign for what Hans Singer calls the United Nations' socially oriented 'New York Dissent' from the Washington consensus.

(Murphy 2006: 223)

The contrasting positions in the debate as to how UNDP should have acted are well represented by two of the central players. Richard Jolly (deputy executive director for programmes in UNICEF, and later director of UNDP's Human Development Report Office) was convinced that Damiba's cautious strategy came at too high a cost: 'the rest of the United Nations wanted UNDP to take on the role of confronting the Bank' (Murphy 2006: 226). But the head of UNDP's Africa Bureau, Damiba, a twenty-eight-year-old economist from Burkina Faso, was unapologetic. 'If we [UNDP] start to fight the World Bank, the African countries will fight us, because they will go by all means with the World Bank' (Murphy 2006: 227).

This perhaps well summarises the triangular relationship between UNDP, the World Bank and the countries of the South. In the 1990s, UNDP was seen to some extent as explicitly distancing itself from the World Bank. But as one of our interviewees put it:

> The last period has been one of rapprochement. … In the late 90s there was a push for us to make an alternative to PRSPs, but we said 'no, we will try to work on the PRSPs'. Two years ago there was a broad memorandum of understanding [between World Bank and UNDP] as to how we would work together … Kemal Derviş probably has more space to work with. He can work on 'how to make partnerships work'. [But] World Bank still tends to dominate.

Agencies other than World Bank are, of course, of significance to UNDP; with UNICEF being perhaps next in line. But it was striking how consistently those interviewed referred to the World Bank alone. There have for many years been repeated attempts at UN reform, bringing about greater coordination between the agencies, with UNDP accorded a central role. But this has been met by resistance – or at best lack of interest – from the programme countries (Klingebiel 1999: 273) and from UN specialised agencies and funds and programmes other than UNDP (Klingebiel 1999: 274). UNDP has, in principle, a special role with regard to other UN agencies; but in practice this is of rather limited significance.

Internal organisation

Introduction

We shall not attempt to describe all the different units that make up the UNDP in New York, but concentrate on those which are most related to policy: the Regional Bureaux, the Bureau of Development Policy, the Office of Development Studies, and the Human Development Report Office.

When we asked which parts of UNDP were offering policy guidance, we were told by one interviewee: 'All over the place. The most exciting (comes) from HDRO [Human Development Report Office] and the Strategic Office (ODS). Neither has managed to create operational traction. I read them and derive pride [from] human development – its breadth'. One of those interviewed was quite dismissive of those involved in policy in New York: 'What's not significant is the whole group of people who do policy analysis – very little relation to what happens in the field; including the Evaluation people.' But another asserted that 'UNDP tries to provide the home for applied policy' (for example, with regard to governance practice).

The regional bureaux

At headquarters in New York there are five regional bureaux: Africa; Arab States; Asia and the Pacific; Europe and the Commonwealth of Independent States (CIS); Latin America and the Caribbean. These play an important role, in linking the centre to the country offices. To quote one interviewee:

> We are hugely decentralised and country driven. Even compared to say UNICEF, with a much stronger centre. They [staff] feel part of a Regional Bureau more than a unitary corporation. Especially when so much of the finances are driven by the country level.

Each regional bureau, we were told, 'has a culture' reflecting that of its client countries; and 'region speaks to region'. The regional bureaux, we were also told, are not so much the generators of policies, but the filter for communications between headquarters and the field.

Human Development Report Office

The Human Development Report Office (HDRO) is responsible for the production of the annual Human Development Report, first published in 1990. This office occupies an important place in the organisation owing to the considerable significance of the report. The term 'human development' is to be found in publications ranging from academic journals and textbooks to the popular press; as well as the huge volume of written material that emerges from conferences, workshops and the like, associated with development assistance. The importance of the concept is affirmed also by UN secretary-general Kofi Annan who, in an interview under the auspices of the United Nations Intellectual History Project,[5] identified

> a number of areas in which he thought the UN shaped discourse ... but pointed to one in particular. In Annan's words: 'we have defined what development means for the individual through our *Human Development Reports*. ... So we have given a functional and meaningful definition to poverty and development, which wasn't there before.
>
> (quoted in Weiss and Caryannis 2005: 255)

The report, and the human development paradigm, are described and analysed at some length below.

Office of Development Studies (Global Public Goods)

The Office of Development Studies (ODS) was established in 1995 by Inge Kaul who had been, from 1989 to 1994, director of the Human Development Report Office. It focussed very specifically on establishing and promoting the concept of global public goods, and remained until recently a separate unit in the organisation.[6] The primary activity of the unit was the production, and dissemination, of three books on global public goods, on each of which Inge Kaul was the lead editor.[7] These included chapters by a number of well respected economists, including Amartya Sen, and the acknowledged experts on public goods Richard and Peggy Musgrave.

The concept of a public good is well established in economics. As noted in Kaul *et al.* (1999) a public good is 'non-excludable', i.e. it produces benefits which are impossible to prevent everyone from enjoying; and it is 'non-rival', i.e. the consumption of the good by one person does not detract from another's consumption. This implies that it will be under-supplied by the market. In other words, even according to standard economic theory based on a perfect market, the welfare of the people concerned (typically assumed to be a nation) is not maximised by depending merely on the market; welfare could be increased by suitable public intervention. What is novel in the work of Kaul *et al.* is the extension of the concept from the nation to the globe. In one of their policy briefs, the GPG unit begins with a quote from Joseph Stiglitz in support of their argument: 'the concept of global goods is a powerful one. It helps us think through the special responsibilities of the international community ... global public goods provide a central rational [sic] for international collective action'.[8]

Thus, the concept of a public good relates to those issues that will not be adequately dealt with by the market. Extending the concept, as Kaul *et al.* do, shifts focus from the national economy to the global economy. And although the concept is not explicitly value-laden, it implicitly acknowledges the limitations of a market-based approach to resolving problems. Hence, simply by classifying something as a global public good one is, automatically, led to the conclusion that some public body should, in the interests of the common good, seek to ensure that it is provided. Thus, almost by sleight of hand, a normative conclusion is implied by an apparently positive claim. For example, if one agrees that biodiversity is a global public good, one is necessarily committed to the conclusion that public (and by implication international) action should be taken to preserve it. One might perhaps regard this as a technocratic way of approaching ethical issues. Certainly it is seen as an economic approach. It is perhaps for this reason that the work on global public goods has received a rather mixed reception in UNDP. But this may equally be attributable to the internal politics of UNDP, and Inge Kaul's position.

One interviewee described the work on global public goods as 'pure economics ... not a moral motivating thrust', and an attempt to make UNDP 'an alternative World Bank'. One of our interviewees suggested that the impact of the ODS has been limited; it was rather modestly staffed, and the ideas 'did not permeate the organisation' (in contrast to human development). It was also suggested that the ideas were politically controversial, and that Inge Kaul was 'warned off'. The books were widely promoted, and the concept of global public goods attracted considerable attention; but it appears that this was an initiative very closely linked to one person, not strongly embedded in the organisation as a whole.

Bureau of Development Policy (BDP)

The name 'Bureau of Development Policy' implies that it is here one might expect to find the brain of the organisation, but it appears that the situation is not in fact so simple – even if the bureau had sufficiently high-powered staff to provide intellectual leadership. First, there exist other sources of intellectual inspiration at headquarters, notably the Human Development Report Office and the Office of Development Studies.[9] Second, it is unclear how far UNDP should have a centralised, unified policy at all.

One interviewee referred to human development as the 'big overall' topic, and described the BDP as occupying an 'intermediate level', providing support to, and furthering programmes at country and regional level. Another interviewee, commenting on UNDP as a knowledge organisation, said 'We're nowhere close', but suggested instead that 'our real organisational role, maybe, is to build platforms for the really big ideas, rather than the ones in between; not rural development, or governance, but the overall (inclusive) ideas'.

Our impression is that to provide 'global' policy is a particularly difficult, and perhaps even inappropriate, task for UNDP. We argue below that it is not the role of the organisation to develop and promote a global agenda, although it can, and perhaps should, serve as a channel for views and analysis that present issues from a 'Southern' perspective. (The BDP's report on trade – described below – provides an interesting example.)

Should UNDP have global policies?

UNDP is in a difficult situation in seeking to define an appropriate role with regard to policy-making. Its expertise is limited, not only by comparison with the World Bank but even with many of the countries in which it has offices. Moreover, it is unclear, we suggest, whether UNDP *should* be promoting specific policies. By comparison with, say, the IMF, the UNDP emphasises the specifics of each country's situation, the need to take full account of varying contexts – something which militates against 'global' policies applicable to all. Furthermore, to actively promote a particular policy in-country might conflict with its neutrality in relation to that government. For all these reasons, UNDP's approach to policy is at best ambivalent.

It is against this background that one can understand the crucial role played by the human development paradigm in UNDP. For many of the staff it is a source of moral and intellectual guidance, a key to the identity and strength of the organisation. UNDP does not have, and cannot have, comprehensive global policies; but it does have the concept of human development, and the numerous Human Development Reports. It is to this that we now turn.

The human development paradigm

In the global arena, the standing of UNDP was rather low in the 1970s and 1980s. But since the 1990s it has benefited very considerably from its association with the human development paradigm. Indeed, it would not be too much to say that this has proved to be its major asset. In this section, we elaborate on this point, exploring why the concept has proved so powerful, but also demonstrating its limitations; suggesting that it invokes the discourse of ethics and global justice, but still treads cautiously in response to the political pressures that UNDP is subject to.[10]

The first Human Development Report (HDR) of the United Nations Development Programme was published in 1990. According to three of those who played most active roles in its promotion:

> After many decades of development, we are rediscovering the obvious – that people are both the means and the end of development.
>
> (Haq 1995: 3)

> The concept of human development draws on the greatness of human potentiality despite our narrowly circumscribed lives.
>
> (Sen 2006: 256)

> Human development puts people back at centre stage.
>
> (Streeten 1995: x)

Amartya Sen (2006) identifies Mahbub ul Haq as 'the pioneering leader of the human development approach'. He traces its roots to a number of earlier and related concepts – basic needs, physical quality of life, disparities in living conditions – and notes the contribution of some international organisations (such as UNICEF) and relief organisations (such as OXFAM) as well as 'humanists voicing the need for social justice'.

Mahbub ul Haq, in his book *Reflections on Human Development,* explains the background, which may be briefly summarised as follows:

> After the Second World War, however, an obsession grew with economic growth models and national income accounts. ... People as the agents of change and beneficiaries of development were often forgotten. ... The

late 1980s were ripe for a counter-offensive. It was becoming obvious in several countries that human lives were shrivelling even as economic production was expanding.

(Haq 1995: 24)

And he proceeds, 'New questions were being raised about the character, distribution and quality of economic growth' (Haq 1995: 25). Ul Haq had a distinguished career, not only as a professional economist (including as director of World Bank Policy Planning Department, 1970–82), but also – for ten years – as a politician in Pakistan, before his appointment as Special Adviser to the UNDP Administrator. Based on this experience, he became increasingly disillusioned with conventional mainstream economic thinking and its power to bring about development. As he put it: 'When rapid economic growth during the 1960s failed to translate into improvements in the lives of Pakistan's masses, I was forced to challenge many of the premises of my initial work' (Haq 1995: xvii). He presented the idea of preparing an annual human development report to the then Administrator of the UNDP, William Draper III, in the spring of 1989. On receiving the go-ahead to work on the HDR, he contacted Amartya Sen and others to assist him in the task. Some, such as Frances Stewart and Gustav Ranis, were already involved through their participation in a series of North–South roundtables organised by ul Haq in the 1980s.[11] Together with Paul Streeten, they and others had – in the 1970s – collaborated with ul Haq (then at the World Bank) in work on basic needs. In brief, then, the concept of human development may be attributed to the 'visionary economist' ul Haq (Sen 2006) centrally placed in the United Nations development policy system, who was in a position to draw on the intellectual resources of a small group of other well respected economists.

There is no doubt that 'human development' as an idea was very successful, in the sense that it gained a high profile. To quote Sen:

The idea of human development and the commanding presence of the *Human Development Reports* have become solid parts of the contemporary landscape of social thinking in the international community.

(Sen 2000: 17)

Why has the idea been so popular? According to Sen, 'The idea of human development won because the world was ready for it' (Sen 2000: 21). In setting the historical scene for HD, ul Haq draws a parallel with the Redistribution with Growth (RwG) debate of the early 1970s:

The breakthrough (RwG) was simple, as most truths are: Yes, increased productivity is necessary. But let us ask the question, increased productivity of whom and for whom? … The productivity of the poor should be increased. With that intellectual breakthrough, national policy-makers focused on recasting their development planning strategies ... And in the late 1980s, it was necessary to generate a similar intellectual ferment around the concerns of adjustment and growth with human development.

(Haq 1995: 8)

Another well placed commentator, Richard Jolly,[12] notes how the Human Development Reports set out a fundamental alternative to Bretton Woods orthodoxy, and traces the history back to the 1970s, to the debate over basic needs and the work of ILO which 'formed the cutting edge of the UN's contributions to development thinking about national policy in the 1970s' (Jolly 2005: 54). But 'In the 1980s, with rising debt and world recession, action on many of these broader perspectives and priorities was brought to a shuddering halt. With strong political and financial support from the industrialized countries, the locus of international economic policy shifted to the Bretton Woods Institutions' (Jolly 2005: 54). And the development agenda was narrowed. 'The UN was left to take on the role of constructive dissent. In 1985, the United Nations Children's Fund (UNICEF) began promoting the need for "adjustment with a human face". And the Economic Commission for Africa was mobilizing for alternatives in Africa' (Jolly 2005: 55).[13]

In summary, there was in the late 1980s increasing dissatisfaction among many in the development field – both with structural adjustment policies, and the dominance of the World Bank and IMF. In this sense, 'the world was ready for it' (human development). And the circumstances were favourable. Academic authority was provided by Amartya Sen and others in the small group of advisers that ul Haq drew upon.

A crucial reason for the idea's success was that it combined the practical, policy-relevant, with the academically respectable. Clearly some, such as Sen, were more concerned with intellectual rigour, while others, and especially ul Haq himself, were very willing to sacrifice this to some extent to political efficacy. To quote Sen:

> Mahbub's innovation was, in an important sense, a philosophical departure. I say this with hesitation, since Mahbub was always very skeptical of philosophy.

(Sen 2000: 18)

And again:

> Mahbub's impatience with theory, which (I have to confess) I sometimes found quite frustrating, was a great help in this [building agreement]. ... *Mahbub transformed the inquiry into an intensely practical one.*

(Sen 2000: 21, emphasis added)

The concept 'human development' is seen as very relevant to development policy while firmly grounded in academic terms. Equally important – in addition to the concept itself – was the associated Human Development Index, developed by Sen and others (Haq 1995: 47). This was included in the first HDR, in 1990. It proved to be a very powerful complement to the concept of human development (Haq 1995: 45).

HDI has certainly proved a major focus of interest. Ul Haq himself anticipated this, being well aware of the importance of media in the battle for ideas. Variants of the HDI have been developed, relating to more specific themes, such as gender, and some modifications have been made to the index; for example in the HDR 1999. Some issues have, however, been too 'hot', as Streeten relates:

> You have to be careful not to say things that are violating some peoples' interests. Take for example, the freedom debate in the Human Development Reports, and whether to include it in the index or have a separate index. On purely intellectual grounds, it was probably the right thing not to incorporate freedom in the HDI. But to have a separate freedom index would have been very interesting. Yet even Mahbub did not get away with it. We had to drop it.
>
> (UNIHP, Streeten 2001: 127)

There have been, and will no doubt continue to be, lively debates as to how the HDI can be improved, or why it should be abandoned. But it has served, and continues to serve, its purpose: to stake out a credible alternative to GNP which nevertheless could survive in 'the rugged world of measurement' (see quote from Sen below).

In this respect, it satisfied the technocratic demands of development organisations; but it was somewhat critical of the then dominant mainstream economic perspective, and its philosophical foundations. In Sen's words, it was a reaction against a narrow utilitarianism.

> In the intellectual victory that utilitarian accounting achieved in mainstream moral philosophy, quite a bit of the work was done, often implicitly, by the trumped-up belief that it would be somehow analytically mistaken, or at least ferociously clumsy, to have many different things as being simultaneously valuable.
>
> (Sen 2000: 17)

In modern times, he says, 'these ideas can be traced from the famous economist A. C. Pigou' (Sen 1999: 73).

According to Sen, utilitarianism, and the mono-concentration on one variable, utility,

> not only suppressed the claims of rival theories, it also corrupted and deformed the intellectual basis of the claims underlying these theories by making their advocates opt for a subsidiary route to influence via their

effects on utilities. The utilitarian emperor offered small native king-doms, under strict viceregal supervision, to advocates of freedom, rights, equal treatment and many other putative claimants to ethical authority.

(Sen 2000: 20)

And deriving strength from this philosophical position was the concept of GNP:

Riding initially as a kind of younger brother of utility, the concept of real income has managed to get a very special status in applied work in development economics. ... In the rugged world of measurement, the concentration shifted from the foundational concern with utilities ... to a practical involvement with income statistics and evaluations based on this. ... The devotees of what is called 'an operational metric' declared victory over all pluralist rivals. ... It was not so easy to defeat the dom-inance of utility and, in practice, of the GNP or other related income-based measures.

(Sen 2000: 20)

But Sen's analysis needs to be complemented by a political perspective. Why has the utilitarian approach been so dominant? Why has it not been more effectively resisted? Here it is necessary to look behind the power of the World Bank and IMF, and examine the power of the economist and the technocrat in development research and policy.[14] To use Sen's words, the economist is the 'viceregal supervisor'; and the technocrat the 'devotee of an operational metric'. To remedy this situation it is necessary to make space for other dis-ciplines in the making of development policy. All the main characters behind HD (human development) are also economists. Although they were indeed challenging the dominant position of the 'Washington consensus', they were nevertheless doing so from within the economics discipline. Similar, if not more radical, criticisms from other disciplines have largely gone unheard, as noted by Apthorpe (1997), and by Gasper (2002) who asks: 'Are the HDRs really "Human" – or still too economistic?'

When once accepted by UNDP, it has acted as a source of institutional identity, and provided technical, political and even moral guidance. To quote ul Haq once again:

There is a missing moral core in our technological advance. In rich nations and poor, the moral foundations of economic growth are often lacking. And we are too embarrassed even to mention morality any more.

(Haq 1995: 202)

According to ul Haq, the strength of the Human Development Report lay in its 'intellectual independence and its professional integrity – its courage more than its analysis' (Haq 1995: 43). But although the HDRs were published by UNDP, the organisation took some time before giving it institutional backing. In the early years it proceeded with caution; and no-one could, at this stage, envisage how successful the exercise would be. It is no coincidence that the Human Development Report is not an official UNDP statement. As stated clearly in the foreword by William Draper III in 1990 (with minor variations since):[15]

> The views expressed in this Report are those of the team and not necessarily shared by UNDP or its Governing Council or the member governments of UNDP. The essence of any such report must be its independence and its intellectual integrity.
>
> (UNDP 1990: iii)

The independence and integrity of its authors has indeed been its strength; but international institutions are necessarily less outspoken. And they are inevitably slow-moving. Although Draper himself was supportive, the views of UNDP staff and member states were not always so positive. Supporters of structural adjustment views were also found in UNDP in the early 1980s, and St. Clair affirms, quoting Richard Jolly, that it took several years until the idea became officially accepted in UNDP (St. Clair 2003: 216). There is no doubt that even now the HDR would be written differently if the authors did not continue to enjoy the independence that William Draper III and subsequent UNDP Administrators have given them. (The editor of the report is nevertheless required to discuss, and if necessary defend, its content with the senior staff of the organisation before publication.)

Each year since 1990 new topics have been introduced: security, gender, consumption, human rights, climate change, etc.; and the global reports have been translated into more and more languages (now seven). Although produced by a small team, the number of people involved in some way in the production of the HDR is large; including consultants that prepare background papers, and numerous commentators. It has been strikingly successful in terms of publicity.[16] But the pursuit of media attention can create a problem: the need to be innovative every single year; to have something new to present at the press conferences around the world. Forced innovation may even begin to detract from, rather than add to, the merit of the concept. One might counter this by arguing that the novelty lies mainly in applying the idea to different issues (such as technology, or water). The question then arises what theme is chosen. Topics come and go in the development field, and in the attempt to latch on to a passing bandwagon, a concept may suffer painful damage. According to Fukuda-Parr, a longer-term trend in the development of HD in the global reports can be detected. The HD approach, she says, has 'evolved in directions that pay more attention to the agency aspects of human development – to political freedoms and institutions as well as political processes' (Fukuda-Parr 2003: 315).

The danger exists that the idea of HD can lose its cutting edge, and be drained of its political and moral power, like other ideas before it (Bøås and

McNeill 2004). It is widely claimed in UNDP that the World Bank distorted the idea, whether intentionally or otherwise, by interpreting it as almost synonymous with education and health – thus reducing both its political and analytical 'edge'. As Sen notes:

> One can detect some accommodating gestures coming out of the citadels of economic growth – the World Bank and the IMF – though how far this conversion to human development is real rather than rhetorical has yet to be seen.
>
> (Sen 1989: 44)[17]

But human development has, by comparison with other comparable 'ideas' been relatively successful in resisting distortion, partly because it has maintained control over the related concept of the Human Development Index (HDI). But how far has the idea been successful in changing actual policies?

UNDP, ethics and human rights

Does the human development paradigm introduce ethics into the development discourse, and into the policies and practice of the UNDP? It appears from the earlier quote from ul Haq, that he hopes to make good the lack of 'moral foundations of economic growth' (1995: 202). On this view, the paradigm brings in a more 'humane' perspective on development: a concern with equity as much as with growth; a challenge to the dominance of economic, and especially neo-liberal, thinking. It creates a platform for Sen and others outside the organisation who use the language of ethics. But one may ask how far this influences the activities of the UNDP itself. In the following pages we assess this, especially in relation to the issue of human rights.

Starting with Murphy and Klingebiel, we again find a contrast. Murphy is very positive; he claims that the annual Human Development Reports

> clarify the meaning of the otherwise ambiguous concept and have served as cover for successive Administrators, Regional Directors, and ResReps who have used such clarifications as action guides and welcome prods to NGOs and political parties who embrace the goals that UNDP advocates more than do its government partners.
>
> (Murphy 2006: 260–261)

By contrast, Klingebiel argues that 'The political disputes in UNDP's Governing Council in the early 1990s in fact clearly reflected the absence of a political majority in favour of a UNDP that endorses the *Human Development Report* in conceptual and practical terms' (Klingebiel 1999: 3). Elsewhere, Klingebiel does list as the first of UNDP's strengths that 'With the concept of sustainable human development UNDP has succeeded in developing a generally accepted development paradigm at a high level of abstraction' (Klingebiel 1999: 237). But at the same time he lists as its first weakness that 'the development paradigm (SHD) has so far been unable to contribute to effective substantive focusing' (Klingebiel 1999: 237–238).

Again, the difference in opinion may be partly attributed to the fact that much has happened in the period between these two assessments. But Murphy's view appears to be overly positive. Several of those interviewed gave great credit to the concept, but saw it more as a motivating force than a source for policy prescription. For example:

> Operationally worthless. Incredibly exciting, even motivating, but ... The onus is on the producer of the idea to make it connect.

Another critical voice:

> But what does that mean concentrating on if you're trying to use money at the margins? It's almost an extension of trying to be popular. ... Development is not just about GDP per capita. But the next step is what? You could measure development in a variety of ways, yes. Girls' education is important, terrific.

This contrasts starkly with Murphy:

> In fact, the annual Human Development Report has helped to make it [poverty] a priority. It has had an almost immediate impact on the allocation of development funds, especially donor funds, shifting them towards the priority concerns of poverty reduction and social welfare. ... It was also because the persuasiveness of the report's analysis convinced a self-reinforcing cascade of development agencies to change their priorities.
>
> (Murphy 2006: 245)

The concept of human development not only serves as the embodiment of an ethical position, but can also provide a political shield for the protection of critical views – in national or regional Human Development Reports, or other reports that are controversial. Probably the best example of the former is the Human Development Reports on the Arab states. Written by well respected, independent individuals, mainly from the region, the reports have stimulated considerable interest and controversy. They have addressed 'hot' issues (in 2004, the title was *Towards Freedom in the Arab World*; and in 2005, *Towards the Rise of Women in the Arab World*).[18] But even those who object to their content find it hard to reject the data and analysis in the reports. They have thus achieved considerable influence, drawing, in part, on the authority of the concept of human development. The UNDP's own website cites these reports as the example of 'a new advocacy dimension' promoted by Malloch Brown. From the start the report was controversial. There were huge debates – internal and external; it was feared it would upset

Washington, and that every country in the region would attack it. But the Arab Human Development Report provided a very suitable vehicle for addressing controversial issues. The question was posed 'what is holding back development in the region?' And the answer, based on objective analysis, came back: 'gender, education, political rights'. Each year the report met strong criticism, but also strong support; and it has been extremely influential.

A good example of the strategic use of the human development paradigm in a controversial report is *Making Global Trade Work for People* (UNDP 2003), written by a team led by Kamal Malhotra, an economist in the BDP. The product of a lengthy process involving a large number of experts from all over the world, its aim was 'to provide policy-makers, practitioners, civil society groups and others engaged in trade issues with some concrete ideas on how to move forward' (UNDP 2003: xii). Much of the funding for the report came from external sources, notably the Ford and Rockefeller foundations and the Rockefeller Brothers Fund. Its origins can be traced back to the breakdown of the WTO ministerial meeting in Seattle in 1999, which clearly demonstrated the importance of the multilateral trading system for developing countries, but also the highly political nature of trade negotiations. The UNDP could play a role here, but this was obviously going to be a dangerous path to tread. The lead author, Malhotra, recruited a small team of consultant experts to prepare background papers and do additional policy research, including the well respected, heterodox economist Dani Rodrik, to analyse the broader empirical relationship between trade liberalisation, economic growth and poverty reduction. Consultations were held mainly with two sets of actors, developing country governments (including the G77/China) and civil society groups, in a lengthy process which was as important as the final product. The 'Acknowledgements' in the report thus refer to the eminent persons group, the peer review group, the UNDP advisory group, expert reviewers, specific contributions, the brainstorming meeting, and consultations. Nevertheless, controversy surrounded the publication of the report, with the WTO, in particular, unhappy with some of its content; but it finally came out under the imprint of Earthscan with UNDP as a co-sponsor.

To quote the Rockefeller Brothers Fund website:[19]

> Making Global Trade Work for People presents a far-reaching reassessment of the current multilateral trade regime and examines how it can be improved in order to contribute genuinely to human development. Such a 'reassessment' can be threatening to powerful interests, but who can object to anything that 'contributes genuinely to human development'?

In summary, the 'human development' paradigm despite all its faults, is perhaps UNDP's greatest asset. Even if it gives only limited analytical or policy guidance, it can be an instrument of advocacy, or provide moral authority, political 'cover', or a source of identity for the organisation. Its continued significance is indicated by Kemal Derviş in his statement at the annual meeting of the Executive Board in 2006 where he asserts that 'human development is the unifying framework for our activities'.[20] But in practice the Administrator is heavily constrained in putting it into effect, at least insofar as it has implications for the question of human rights – as his other comments at the same meeting, quoted below, indicate.

As noted in Chapter 3 the UN has, for decades, been very active in promoting human rights issues; not only in terms of ideas, but also concrete conventions such as CEDAW (the Convention on the Elimination of All Forms of Discrimination against Women adopted in 1979 by the UN General Assembly) which defined discrimination, and attributed responsibility to the state. In the 1990s, UNDP was one of a number of agencies that linked human rights more specifically to development. In one of his last speeches as Administrator, Gustave Speth claimed that 'For the 1.3 billion people – one third of the population of the developing world – who live on less than a dollar a day, there can be no doubt that poverty is a brutal denial of human rights' (UNDP 1998: 27).

The issue was taken up at length in the *Human Development Report 2000*, entitled 'Human Rights and Human Development'. This presented a coherent view of human rights in both their legal and moral sense, and linked this to the notion of human development. The report saw rights-based approaches as providing possible tools to locate accountability for failures in the social system and responsibilities for present and future action. These insights were further developed in HDR 2002, entitled 'Deepening Democracy in a Fragmented World', which investigated the role of politics in the implementation of human development goals. HDR 2002 touched upon questions related to access to justice, but contained little discussion about moral responsibility. The HDRs 2000 and 2002 do not offer compelling analyses of international and global factors; and the language of choice and freedom may be misleading without clarification of choices *for whom* and *how*, and freedom *for whom* and *about what* (Gasper 2004). Even though UNDP may sometimes come close to viewing poverty as a human rights violation, official expressions of UNDP policy are often quite vague, expressed in statements such as: 'respect for human rights matter for poverty reduction' (UNDP website).

Referring to UNDP's activities in the human rights field, one well informed interviewee summarised it by saying that the organisation might 'for example, set up a human rights commission, or an ombudsman', but added that 'some will be fig leaves' and indicated the risk of co-optation. 'UNDP is not Amnesty International and never will be.' But through 'stealth and advocacy' achievements could be made. One interviewee noted that at the end of the 1990s, UNDP was 'maybe working in six countries on practical human rights programmes; now about fifty plus'.

Another argued that 'It's been helpful to force countries that don't take human rights seriously; given UN a wedge'. But another: 'Now we're not really rights-based. People are not hanging on our every word.' To suggest that

UNDP adopts a human rights approach is 'implying a degree of coherence that does not exist. Compare with UNICEF. They take a rights-based approach. They didn't ask anyone, they just did it. They have a strong advocacy.'
And finally:

> Human rights, for example is a classic case of an idea vying for supremacy that's been botched by its owners, whoever they are. In terms of including a wider set of stakeholders. I don't think it has even taken off as the big idea in the way some say it should. I have received millions of emails on the rights-based approach, but I wouldn't know what to do on the ground, beyond some normative statements about rights.

What UNDP has done is to support 'HURITALK' (human rights talk), an email-based network which offers staff all over the world the opportunity to exchange knowledge and experience, and seek advice on specific questions.[21] And it has funded a number of in-country initiatives.

It is fair to note that UNDP's involvement is limited by the existence of other UN agencies dealing with the same issue.[22] But the most important constraint is certainly political. Faced with as controversial an issue as human rights, UNDP is very cautious about adopting a global, 'top-down' approach; and extremely wary of any hint of conditionality. Just how sensitive is the issue is illustrated by the statement of the Administrator at the annual meeting of the Executive Board in 2007 which gives prominence to a section on 'human development, human rights and national ownership' and begins: 'Within this context, I would like to address the issue of our human rights based approach to development.'[23] This merits quotation at some length.

Derviş begins by citing the statement issued by global leaders at the 2005 World Summit: 'peace and security, development and human rights are the pillars of the United Nations system and the foundations for collective security and well-being'. And he notes their resolution, to 'integrate the promotion and protection of human rights into national policies and to support the further mainstreaming of human rights throughout the United Nations system'.

'These', he says, 'are not just nice words but represent robust ideals that are at the heart of everything we do. As I said to you in an earlier session, I really could not imagine working for the United Nations if I was not totally committed to the cause of human rights.'

'But', he continues,

> 'it is important is to be clear about what we mean when we are talking about a human rights-based approach to programming. UNDP's stance on human rights is not one of political conditionality, but rather one of collaboration and cooperation. ... As consistently highlighted by my two predecessors, UNDP's policy is that equality of rights for all is the indispensable foundation on which Human Development must be built.

The policy, promulgated in 1998, specifies that UNDP should work to promote human rights, primarily through support for the development of national capacities.'

(UNDP 2007)

This cautious, even ambivalent position, may be interpreted as a response to critical views from some member states, as is evident from the earlier presentation of the Draft Strategic Plan 2008 – 2011 to the Board of Governors, in June 2007. Here, we quote from the statement by the Associate Administrator, Ad Melkert:[24]

Mr. President, if you allow me I will refrain from an overall introduction of the Plan given a number of very useful informal meetings over the past few months and the debate following the Administrator's presentation and his response to key issues raised.

Melkert makes three points. The first is:

The draft that we put before you is not sufficiently balanced as it focuses too much on what is new in relation to UN coordination whilst taking more or less for granted the basic presumption of UNDP's 'raison d'être': supporting the achievement of national strategies with full recognition of country ownership as the necessary precondition for development effectiveness. ... the UNDP staff is very committed and indeed directed by the deeply rooted understanding that 'development' as a concept and as a practice will fail if imported or imposed and that building capacity to sustain ownership is the single most decisive contribution that can make a difference. ... While full government participation is sought throughout the programming process, UNDP Country Programmes have been and will always be fully owned by governments. They are implemented jointly by these national partners and UNDP and subject to approval and review by the Executive Board. All of our policies are driven by governments, putting peer pressure on donors to align their support and thus to reduce the transaction costs that are particularly burdensome for least developed countries.

The second point:

The section on 'operational principles' should be rewritten entirely. As the Administrator put it: the explicit recognition that UNDP's contribution to gender equality, human rights and civic engagement is all about capacity development support and *not, I repeat not, about political conditionality.* [Emphasis added]. ... In our work we want to embody the letter and spirit of the UN charter and to bring to the attention of our partners lessons learned during decades of development. ... As to the method, there is no alternative to country ownership in order to have the application of these principles internalized. Leadership at the country level, supportive donor coordination and the great potential of south-south cooperation provide the overarching ways and means to achieve progress. In the long run there is no viable alternative to that and it should be recognized in the new draft.

These two quotes, from the Administrator and Associate Administrator, rather starkly illustrate the dilemma that UNDP faces in seeking to promote human rights. It is clear that the member governments will not countenance anything remotely resembling pressure on them to adopt this agenda.

Conclusion

The Annual Report 2006, quoted at the beginning of this chapter, at the same time as it sets out the organisation's ambitions, effectively recognises its constraints. The UNDP's hallmark, says the Administrator, is 'connecting countries to knowledge and ideas and working with them to strengthen the capacity needed to tackle development challenges'. With regard to 'knowledge' the report claims UNDP to be 'a leader in development thinking, as demonstrated by its flagship Human Development Reports' and adds reference to 'its contributions to critical issues such as global public goods and democratic governance'. The activities listed are indeed where UNDP has most clearly concentrated and made its mark; but it may equally be argued that its potential for achievement here is fairly modest. The combination of limited technical expertise, and inability to exert political pressure on national governments, places UNDP in a weak position – certainly by comparison with the World Bank. What the organisation does have, we suggest, is a degree of moral authority – closely associated with the human development paradigm. And it is primarily this which gives the organisation some opportunity to raise ethical issues and promote human rights.

The organisation has an ambitious global mandate, and, thanks to its decentralised organisation, an extensive global reach. The fact that it has relatively little clout restricts its capacity to bring about major change, but also, ironically, makes its easier for the organisation to avoid the sort of criticism aimed at the Bretton Woods institutions. On the other hand, its major asset – its close association with its member states – acts as a constraint in this regard. It is rather difficult for the UNDP to promote a global agenda on any issue; and it is particularly difficult where the issue is controversial – notably on human rights. Here UNDP's scope for action has proved limited. It is not listed by the Administrator among UNDP's most prominent themes, and the organisation's activities appear to have been mainly concerned with 'connecting countries to knowledge and ideas'.

The human development paradigm has undoubtedly been important for UNDP. It increased its status vis-à-vis other multilateral organisations, and most notably the World Bank, at a time when the organisation was quite weak. The concept has not been particularly useful in providing specific guidance on policy choices, but has provided 'cover' for UNDP staff, at both headquarters and in-country, to push agendas and promote views which may be unwelcome by some. It has given the UNDP a degree of moral authority, which has been valuable for the organisation in its unequal struggle with the World Bank, and others, for influence on the world stage. But although the language of the Human Development Reports is sometimes more outspoken about injustice than that of the WDRs, and the motivating power of the concept is no doubt associated with the moral purpose of poverty reduction, there is little evidence that the paradigm has created much 'ethical space' within UNDP – that it has encouraged and supported discussion of ethical issues within the organisation.

One interviewee, a well informed critic of the organisation, argued that

> some of UN's moral standing should come from the risks they take also intellectually, not just a Greek chorus; not predictable; going against governments occasionally. That's why I see the Joint Inspection Unit, the Human Development Office as critical to legitimacy; alternative voices. ... It should be possible for UN staff to write what they like; obviously within limits.

The UNDP has limited financial resources and expertise – certainly by comparison with the World Bank. It is trying to increase both. (It is almost unthinkable that a multilateral organisation would not seek to increase its budget. And the same applies to expertise; although it is in theory an option to seek to build on expertise other than – and possibly even critical of – mainstream economics.) But there is little prospect of substantial change in either of these respects in the near future. It is not far-fetched to claim that precisely because it has limited financial resources and expertise it is easier for the UNDP to claim moral authority and to maintain the trust of governments in poor countries. For the UNDP, therefore, in contrast to the World Bank, the challenge is how to enjoy the moral authority derived from its close association with the human development paradigm, and seek to promote the ideas associated with it, while at the same time being closely linked with many governments which do not, in practice, adhere to these ideals.

5 The World Bank

The internal dynamics of a complex organisation

Introduction

In this chapter we examine the challenges faced by the World Bank in addressing issues concerning ethics and human rights. We show how, even though the staff have some awareness of the ethical aspects of their work, institutional forces in the organisation constrain how the World Bank thinks and speaks about such matters. We focus our attention particularly on two recent experiences: the production of the *World Development Report* (WDR) 2006 on Equity and Development, and discussions surrounding the World Bank's activities in the human rights field. In this chapter we emphasise the significant role of expert knowledge, and in this case especially economic expertise, and how this shapes or 'frames' ideas (Bøås and McNeill 2004) and thereby also action. In order to understand the significance of expertise in the Bank, it is necessary to study how processes of knowledge formulation are themselves embedded within sets of social relations among professionals in the Bank, as well as relations between the Bank and others outside. Expert knowledge must be seen in the context of social relations among communities of professional advisers, consultants, policy-makers, aid administrators and managers inside and outside the Bank, relating also to its organisational culture (Mosse forthcoming). Bank experts need audiences that legitimise their knowledge. In many cases, these audiences are other bureaucrats or actors that are dependent on funds provided by the Bank to carry out activities that have been defined and promoted by the Bank's experts, thereby generating a circular dynamic between the expertise, the audience, and the legitimacy of that expertise (St. Clair 2006a). Moreover, because of the need to maintain a sense of coherence in an organisation that is highly heterogeneous and complex, new ideas and themes tend to be built upon older and well established WB ideas and discourse; and critical views are excluded, in a process of what Wade (1996) calls 'paradigm maintenance'. Where disagreement arises, consensus is reached through internal negotiation and contestation processes that take place behind closed doors. And ideas that are not suited to the tools of analysis and instruments of policy of the Bank (for example the role of human rights in bringing about fair development processes) tend to be excluded.

The World Bank: a brief overview

There are innumerable books and articles on the World Bank, by both insiders and outsiders – both critical and supportive.[1] Indeed, an active network has been formed of researchers working specifically on the World Bank (Research Alliance for Development – RAD).[2] Even the more specific topic of the World Bank's expertise has been subject to considerable critical study (Broad 2006; Bøas and McNeill 2004; Goldman 2005; McNeill, 2005; Sridhar 2007; St. Clair 2006a, 2006b; Stone and Wright 2006; Wade 2002, 2004; Woods 2006). This is not surprising; besides its financial power through lending and grants, the World Bank is more influential than any other agency in terms of exercising power over the development 'discourse', policy ideas and development policy agenda. And the Bank itself takes pride in its expertise, which it regards as one of the most important sources of its legitimacy as a global development institution. The Bank's expertise is located primarily within economics, and the alleged scientific character of this discipline is used to support claims about the neutrality and importance of the Bank's ideas. Since its creation, the organisation has built up an impressive stock of data and research about developing countries. By defining development-related issues as predominantly economic, it has established and perpetuated its own legitimacy and credibility, and generated demand for the sort of knowledge in which it specialises.

We do not find it necessary to include in this chapter a lengthy description of the Bank's mandate, governance, internal organisation, etc. It is sufficient, we hope, to provide merely enough information to allow comparison with the development agencies that are the subject of other chapters; and some information about those aspects of the organisation's work which concern ethics and human rights – and related topics such as responsibility and accountability.

Established in 1944, the World Bank is the world's largest provider of development assistance, involved in more than 100 countries. In 2007, the total value of loans to its client countries amounted to US$12.8 billion, and its cumulative lending was US$433 billion. Formally, the World Bank is owned by its 185 member countries whose views and interests are represented by a Board of Governors and a Washington-based board of directors. The latter operate in continuous session, and some critics claim that they tend to micro-manage (Woods 2006). Votes on the Board are determined by shareholdings: the USA has just over 16 per cent, followed by Japan (almost 8 per cent), and Germany, France and the UK (each with over 4 per cent). Board decisions are formally determined by majority vote, but in practice consensus is the norm, and the President plays a key role. It is at the annual meetings of the full Board of Governors, and the spring meetings of the Development Committee, that more visible political controversies may arise.

The Bank has about 10,000 staff (including 3,000 in country offices) of whom a high proportion are economists. The staff are, in general, better qualified than their counterparts in other UN agencies; and they know it. (To judge from our interviews in UNDP, and even IDB, this is also acknowledged by other agencies – though not, we are told, by the IMF.) And the Bank can, and does, justifiably claim that it has more staff resources in most fields than the relevant specialised agencies and programmes: 'more agriculturalists than FAO', 'more environmentalists than UNEP', etc. As a result, although Bank staff do attempt to collaborate with others, they tend often to be found arrogant in their dealings with agencies of the UN system. As one interviewee told us, regional banks like the Asian Development Bank (ADB) or the Inter-American Development Bank (IDB) primarily lend money for projects to countries: 'we do the difficult part, to provide them with the best possible knowledge for reducing poverty'.

The president of the World Bank enjoys considerable power. It is widely agreed that Wolfensohn (1995–2005) was the most influential and charismatic leader since Robert McNamara (1968–1981) (Mallaby 2004). And he was very active, some said too active, in setting up new initiatives. Wolfensohn was replaced by Paul Wolfowitz, former US Deputy Secretary of Defense, which proved to be a serious error. Wolfowitz was a most unpopular figure within and outside the Bank, being seen by many as a war criminal on account of his part in the American invasion of Iraq. Following efforts to oust him, he resigned in mid-2007 to be replaced by Robert Zoellick, best known from his work as US trade representative.

Although it does have numerous country offices, these enjoy only a limited degree of autonomy; by contrast with UNDP, the Bank is very much steered from Washington. The Bank's relations with its 'client' countries are now rather more equal than they were in the period of structural adjustment programmes and their associated conditionality, but the relationship is still very different from that of the 'partnership' model of UNDP.

The Bank has gone through numerous reorganisations, and there is no need here to describe its current organisation in any detail. (The combination of departments, 'networks', families and so on is confusing even to insiders.) It engages in an extremely wide range of activities, and faces continuing criticism of 'mission creep' – a tendency to expand activities beyond its range of competence and lose focus on its 'core business'. The latter is defined as lending money; and indeed the Bank measures performance in terms of the amount of money it successfully lends. Thus, operations, and individual staff members, are subject to assessment according to the number of person-months per dollar lent. This, together with the dominance of economists, is crucial for understanding the driving forces in the institution: the imperative of 'operationalising' ideas, and the resulting 'economic-technocratic nexus' (Bøås and McNeill 2004) that allows little space for issues such as ethics and human rights.

The World Bank has for many years sought, and most would say achieved, a dominant position with regard to the 'global development discourse'. This is manifest not only in the dominance of its ideas and policies, but even its terminology (McNeill 2004), and in the realm of statistics, where the attribution of World Bank as a source is often used as a guarantee of reliability. Under Wolfensohn it explicitly took on the role of 'knowledge bank'. (As noted above, UNDP made a similar claim.) Certainly it produces innumerable publications: most notably the annual WDR,[3] but also more academic publications such as the *World Bank Research Observer*, and many influential documents, some of which continue to be referred to years later. In Africa, for example, the Berg Report of 1981, *Accelerated Development in Sub-Saharan Africa: An Agenda for Action* (WB 1981), or *Sub-Saharan Africa: From Crisis to Sustainable Growth* (WB 1989). And the World Bank hosts innumerable conferences, including the ABCDE – Annual Bank Conference on Development Economics. Ten years ago it established the Global Development Network (GDN)[4] based in Washington, which has since been 'spun off' as an independent organisation. Here again we see clear parallels, if not competition, with the UNDP and its Global Knowledge Partnership.[5]

Ethics and human rights on the agenda

In Chapter 3, we have indicated how and why ethics and human rights came to occupy a prominent place in the global development discourse in recent years. Especially in the case of the World Bank, this can be seen as largely a response to external criticism from civil society. The organisation, together with the IMF and WTO, was regarded by many NGOs as the visible embodiment of the forces of globalisation; as such, it came under heavy attack, manifested in the '50 Years is Enough' campaign and pitched battles in the streets of Seattle, and subsequently in other cities where annual meetings were located. One response by the Bank was to increase accountability mechanisms, and participate in collaborative exercises which included civil society. The Joint Inspection Panel is an example of such a mechanism, created to evaluate requests for inspections from private citizens, in areas affected by the projects financed by the World Bank.[6] But this was established earlier, in 1993. More relevant here is the Structural Adjustment Participatory Review Initiative (SAPRI), launched in 1997 as the result of a challenge to President Wolfensohn by a global network of NGOs engaged in the '50 Years is Enough' campaign.[7] Other examples are the *Extractive Industries Review*[8] and the World Commission on Dams.[9]

In addition to engaging in (sometimes unsatisfactory) dialogue and collaboration with NGOs, Wolfensohn also gave his support to the major, and very high-profile, *Voices of the Poor* study, led by sociologist Deepa Narayan,[10] which sought to associate the Bank more directly with its ultimate 'clients'. This helped to give some credibility to the work of 'non-economist social scientists' (as they are known in the Bank) although they remain a marginalised group in terms of power and influence.

More specifically relating to our concerns in this book, two initiatives deserve mention. First, the appointment in 2000 of Katherine Marshall as

Director, Development Dialogue on Ethics and Values. Her department, created after the *World Development Report 2000/1: Attacking Poverty*, was in charge of coordinating the World Faiths Development Dialogue, co-founded by James D. Wolfensohn and Lord George Carey, and later extended to include ethical values more generally. This initiative was not particularly welcomed by the Board, and has had a marginal role in the Bank.[11]

In relation to human rights, another relevant Wolfensohn initiative was the appointment of Alfredo Sfeir-Younis as his Advisor on Human Rights, in 2003.[12] The appointment could be interpreted as a clear sign of the Bank's commitment to engage with human rights issues, and more generally to address concerns for the organisation's moral responsibilities, but the advisor had very little influence over policy. It appears that there was a wide gap between his world-view and that of the Bank, and Sfeir-Younis left his position in summer 2005. More important, in terms of influencing Bank policy in this field, was the Chief General Counsel, Roberto Dañino, as discussed below.

Both Katherine Marshall and Alfredo Sfeir-Younis faced the challenge of introducing into the Bank topics that did not easily fit. It is not simply that questions of ethics and human rights had rarely before been directly addressed; the very language and discourse of the Bank rendered it difficult to do so. Sfeir-Younis made some attempts to confront and criticise the dominance of conventional economic thinking, but this was not well received – if indeed it was well understood.[13] But the time was apparently ripe for the Bank to address the issue of human rights.

Following this brief introduction, we now turn to the first of our two objects of study – the *World Development Report 2006* – which exemplifies our main argument: the power of economic expertise in shaping the thoughts, and thereby the actions, of this huge international institution.

WDR 2006: equity and development

The annual World Development Report of the World Bank is the organisation's flagship publication.[14] It serves the purpose of synthesising and, where possible, advancing what the Bank regards as state-of-the-art development thinking on the topic selected for that year, for example agriculture, poverty or sustainable development. It is perhaps the most important way in which the Bank seeks to display its dominant position in the field of development research and policy.[15] The WDR is very widely distributed, and attracts considerable attention both from the media and from the community of development practitioners, as well as political leaders in the global South. In this section it is the World Bank's *World Development Report 2006: Equity and Development* (hereafter, WDR 2006) that is our focus of attention.

The process of preparing the report began in 2004, and we begin our account with a workshop in Oslo in September 2004 which we co-organised, and which constituted one of the first consultations on the report.[16] The workshop had a dual purpose. It was primarily a response to President Wolfensohn's request to the Nordic countries to help him build a case for the integration of human rights in the Bank's work. In addition, half a day was devoted to discussing the WDR 2006 outline and how the report could better incorporate a human rights perspective. There were presentations from scholars working on the role of rights-based approaches to development, and development ethicists.

Particular issues which participants emphasised were, first, what sort of evidence is relevant for asserting that equity matters, and, second, whether the argument that equity does matter should be based on intrinsic or instrumental grounds. The following points (and a few others) are documented in the World Bank's own record of 'important comments' from the workshop.[17] First, as background, it was noted that 'The climate in the Bank with respect to the HR approach has changed; the current General Counsel thinks HR [human rights] should be part of the Bank's discourse. This is a major change with respect to the past.' Second, on the intrinsic argument:

> We really ought to refer to the human rights approach when talking about why equity matters intrinsically. More than a hundred countries have ratified the various Human Rights covenants that sanctions economic, social, and political rights.

And third, as a comment on arguments presented that inequality matters instrumentally:

> We need to clarify instrumentally to what. Arguably the goal is poverty reduction (not growth per se), with poverty intended broadly. This links to [the] question of addressing WHY reducing inequalities, before addressing the WHAT to do and HOW TO DO IT questions.
>
> (capitals in the original)

Three important issues raised at this workshop form the main basis for our analysis that follows. The first is what empirical evidence is regarded as relevant for demonstrating that equity matters. The second is whether one adopts an intrinsic or an instrumental argument for why equity matters. The third is how the World Bank addresses human rights issues, both in this WDR and in the World Bank more generally. (Clearly, an intrinsic argument for equity is closely linked to a human rights approach.) These issues exemplify the economic-technocratic nature of the Bank; they also give valuable insights into the internal dynamics of regimes of truth in the development field, and what drives institutional knowledge processes and the professional communities involved. The issues we address thus illustrate the context and social processes – both within and outside the Bank – that influence the activities of the organisation.

We may begin by briefly summarising the structure and contents of the final published version of the WDR 2006.[18] *World Development Report 2006: Equity and Development* is divided into three parts. Part I considers the evidence on inequality of opportunity within and across countries. Part II asks why equity matters. Part III addresses how public action can level the political and economic playing fields in both the domestic and international arenas. The report demonstrates, convincingly and with a wealth of empirical data, that huge inequalities of opportunity exist in practice – both within and between countries. It addresses political issues more explicitly than has often been the case in WDRs, and in World Bank reports more generally. The language is sometimes unusually strong for a WDR – referring to 'staggering inequalities' between countries, and using the term 'elite capture' several times. But it also emphasises continuity and consistency with previous reports and with World Bank policy in general. Thus it links the overall argument for equity with the two pillars of Bank policy – 'opportunity' and 'empowerment' – set out in the WDR 2000/1. (There are two basic issues which repeatedly arise in WDRs, and indeed in the work of the World Bank generally: 'equity versus growth', and 'state versus market'. In practice, the Bank's position on both tends to be ambivalent, and formalised in terms of these two 'pillars'.) Indeed, the 2006 publication clearly specifies:

> This is not intended as a new framework. It means integrating and extending existing frameworks: equity is central both to the investment environment and to the agenda of empowerment.
>
> (World Bank 2006: 3–4)

Or, as Wolfowitz puts it in the foreword:

> In my view, the evidence that equity and economic efficiency as well as growth are complementary in the long run helps to integrate the main two components of the World Bank's poverty reduction strategy. ... This report shows that the two pillars are not independent from each other in supporting development, but instead are intricately linked with one another.
>
> (World Bank 2006: xi–xii)

In preparing the report, Bank experts were concerned with providing strong evidence that equity matters. It is common for Bank staff to stress the importance of analytical rigour combined with reliable empirical 'evidence', with a preference for quantitative data. As one of our interviewees put it, in referring to the Bank's identity: 'fundamentally that we make the soft stuff hard. So we make hard [those] economic and social analyses of things'. Even if the Bank is often guilty of 'economic fundamentalism', as one interviewee put it, 'in many of us is the suspicion, rightly or wrongly, that we are able to formulate causal statements rigorously and then test them. ... Other disciplines do also ... but we think they do that less than we do'.[19]

Empirical work, data and surveys in developing countries are strengths of the Bank, key characteristics of the identity of the institution as an 'expert bureaucracy' in development work, and also key elements in the way in which the Bank builds and sustains its legitimacy (St. Clair 2006a). In our interviews with staff this was a recurrent theme. The most fundamental aspects of the self-identity of the institution are its mandate (to reduce poverty) and its technical expertise (economic analysis). Yet, as critics have argued, these hard empirical facts derive from the Bank's often privileged knowledge, and are based on social relations between those seeking to establish statistical data on client countries and the officials and actors providing it (Goldman 2005; Griffiths 2003; Harper 2000). In the following analysis, we begin with the issue of what evidence counts, before turning to the 'intrinsic versus instrumental' question; and finally to human rights. In examining these issues we will pay particular attention to three significant phenomena: changes in the WDR text over time – as the report moves from outline, to draft, to final version; differences between the report's overview and the much longer main text; and incongruities within the text that are indicative of rewriting and compromise (Sindzingre 2004).[20] We shall give examples of each.[21]

First, regarding the relative merits of different types of empirical evidence, what is of particular relevance for our purpose is the debate on the significance attached to research from a relatively new branch of economics, namely 'experimental economics'. In brief, this involves testing human (economic) behaviour under 'laboratory' conditions – often with economics students as its 'guinea pigs'.[22] Its attraction, for economists, is that it is seen as cutting-edge economic research; although even within the discipline there are some who criticise this method, or at least regard it as being as yet under-developed.

There was debate within the team (see below) as to how much weight should be attached to such evidence. And at the public consultation in Dakar, Senegal, in January 2005, Desmond McNeill criticised this type of argument. As recorded on the World Bank website, he maintained that 'on the intrinsic argument, the best literature to draw from may not be the behavioural economics literature. Other disciplines have been saying these things for a long time.' McNeill subsequently made direct contact by email with the team, strongly arguing that experimental economics evidence should not be given a dominant place in the argument as to why equity matters. At one stage it appeared that findings from experimental economics would be given considerable weight, but in the final version of the report this was in fact presented as only one of several forms of evidence, along with reference to 'religions from Islam to Buddhism and secular philosophical traditions from Plato to Sen'. (For more detail, see World Bank 2006: 76.)

The second, even more revealing question is whether the case for equity in development is made on intrinsic or instrumental grounds. As noted, this issue was raised at an early stage in the report process (at the workshop in Oslo), and it was taken up again at later stages. Although the World Bank staff generally appeared to favour an instrumental argument, the matter was still apparently not fully resolved in the final version; the persistence of differing views on this question is evident both in incoherence in the report, and in variation between overview and main text.

Bank experts relate first and foremost to economists, and need to position the notion of equity within the dominant rationality of economics and market relations. This favours an instrumental view (see McNeill 2004, on social capital, and Sridhar 2007, on nutrition). 'This is what we do', a senior staff member told us, 'we do not fund education because it's a good thing to do. We fund education because it's good for economic development.' But the notion of equity is ambivalent, having, as it does, an undeniable intrinsic meaning (as fairness and as a determinant of justice). For those involved in producing this WDR, it was impossible to avoid references to equity as an intrinsic value. But the report, it may be argued, is marked throughout by equivocation between the two meanings of the term equity; the obvious tensions between the scientific rationale of economics and the cognitive premises of ethical, or intrinsic, values and arguments. It illustrates the difficulties that Bank staff have when stepping outside mere economic argumentation, moving into a dangerous territory where the Bank may not have the best expertise. We do not claim that Bank experts consciously refuse to step outside economics because of mere arrogance; it is rather a matter of the perceived legitimacy of the Bank as an institution, and the 'obligation' of the staff to maintain such legitimacy.

Regarding the tensions between intrinsic and instrumental argumentation, it is instructive to look at the overall process of building a WDR, and to distinguish between the main text of the report and the Overview. The draft report is written by its main authors, with the support of their team. But it has to be approved by the Chief Economist and the President, and 'signed off' by the Executive Board. In the process it is likely to be modified and, if controversial, glossed. It is not unusual that, in such processes, more attention is focused on the 'Executive Summary', or Overview, than on the much lengthier main text. Disagreements are therefore revealed both by incoherence in the main text, and by variation in emphasis, or even substance, between the main text and the Overview. Examples of both can be found.

The relevant section of the report is part II: 'Why Equity Matters'. (It is significant to note that the title of this part was changed during the process of consultations from 'Does Inequality Matter?', a title that led to a storm of protests from commentators, largely NGOs.[23]) This contains very few explicit references to the word 'intrinsic'. It does, however, state, 'To the philosophical and legal arguments for equity ... we add a final argument [the instrumental]' (World Bank 2006: 84). This wording seems to imply that the authors primarily emphasise intrinsic arguments. But a very different impression is given in the Overview. Here, it is primarily instrumental arguments for equity that are emphasised. The intrinsic argument is mentioned, but is not predominant. For example:

So a portion of the economic and political inequalities we observe around the world is attributable to unequal opportunities. This inequality is objectionable on both intrinsic and instrumental grounds. It contributes to economic inefficiency, political conflict, and institutional frailty.

(World Bank 2006: 9)

The latter argument ('It contributes to ...') is, of course, purely instrumental. The issue is also addressed in chapter 10 of the report, which provides a good example of how the pursuit of compromise can lead to merely vacuous statements such as: 'Greater global equity is desirable for itself to all those who find equity intrinsically valuable' (World Bank 2006: 206).

In summary, the report argues on both intrinsic and instrumental grounds. In the main text, the former is more emphasised; in the Overview (subject to approval at the highest level) the instrumental argument predominates.[24] This predominance of instrumental argumentation can be seen as a way of avoiding the territory of human rights based analysis, an arena which the Bank has been reluctant to enter, under the presumption that this conflicts with its 'apolitical' mandate, but also because the type of analysis that human rights demands from Bank experts takes them outside their usual area of technical work. It is to this issue that we now turn.

A month after the Oslo workshop, on 15 November 2004, Asunción Lera St. Clair was invited to present a summary of the main points at a consultation at the Bank headquarters. This was organised jointly by the World Bank's Social Development Department, the WDR 2006 team, and the UK Department for International Development (DfID) to discuss several background papers prepared for the WDR 2006 (with DfID and World Bank funding). St. Clair summarised the main recommendations from Oslo, arguing that there was a clear opportunity to bring human rights issues into the WDR 2006. Rather than avoiding the issue, a Bank report on equity could emphasise the need for combining policies for economic efficiency and social equality; an opportunity to use historical and empirical examples where a combination of economic and social policy had led to growth combined with low levels of poverty – such as in Scandinavian countries. St. Clair presented examples discussed in the Oslo workshop where human rights views on education and health, or rights in relation to access to justice, were in fact consistent with other ideas and proposals flowing from the Bank's work and coherent with the notion of equity argued for in the WDR. Her presentation, however, warned of a possible depoliticisation of human rights and the seemingly equivocal meaning of equity in the draft, possibly leading to trade-offs between intrinsic values (the dignity of all human beings) and instrumental values. One of the conclusions of the Oslo workshop was that human rights should not be addressed by the Bank unless this was done well and in a concerted way which was consistent with other UN agencies' rights-based work; that human rights in development should not be treated merely as a value-added issue, or as a way to place the burdens of responsibility on client countries, but as a challenge to Bank experts to question the 'why' and 'how' of development assistance.

In the sometimes heated discussion that followed, some argued very vehemently that it was not the role of the Bank to address questions of human rights. Although this view is often based on an interpretation of the Bank's mandate (see below), the major concern here derived from discomfort with the 'intrinsic' argument for equity, which does not fit well with the dominant economic perspective. One of the key cognitive values of economics is the notion of a trade-off – whether in seeking to understand people's behaviour, or to advise on policies. This leads to serious incompatibilities with ethical argumentation based on intrinsic values. By definition, something that is intrinsic is non-tradable. The conception of human dignity (regardless of whether based on religious or secular foundations) is the key element of human rights norms. What relates most clearly the term 'equity' to 'human rights' is precisely the non-tradable character of human dignity. As both Amartya Sen and Thomas Pogge argue, human rights ought to be seen as moral as well as legal issues; the moral ground of human rights is the equal moral worth of all human beings regardless of age, sex, country of origin, ethnicity, etc. (Pogge 2007; Sen 2005).

This intrinsic argument for equity is very different from the instrumental argument (that increasing equity is an effective approach for the design and implementation of policies to promote development). We often heard from staff interviewed that one of the problems of rights perspectives is that it was not empirically proven to be economically sound to implement, say, the right to education or the right to health for all. As one respondent told us 'vaccinating the last 5 percent of children in a poor country may not be the most effective way to have health for all'. We were also told that implementing socio-economic rights was simply 'expensive' or incompatible with the unstructured, informal labour situation in which most poor people live. It is undoubtedly difficult for economists to include intrinsic values in their analyses. But the remedy is not necessarily a new economics (though some would certainly favour this); it is sufficient, we suggest, to recognise the limitations of economics in this regard, and draw also on the cognitive and analytical tools of other disciplines (for example ethics, but also other social sciences) in seeking to promote development and poverty reduction. The problem lies in the self-identity of the Bank staff, and the Bank's need to maintain a position of expertise-based power derived from economics.

The Outline of the report (July 2004), made clear reference to the linkages between an intrinsic meaning of equity and the role that human rights and rights-based approaches to issues such as health and education can play in actually moving towards equitable societies. In the section 'Towards equity in assets, incomes and agency', the Outline states

> In some of these areas, such as basic education and health, rights-based approaches may be valuable ways of achieving greater equity. The report

would explore empirical evidence on whether such explicit pursuit of economic and social rights is effective in achieving improvements in well-being of poorer groups in these dimensions (see Drèze, 2004, for an argument that such approaches can be useful in mobilizing public action in the cases of education and basic food in India).

(World Bank 2006, Outline of July 2004: 18)

But the final version of the WDR does not argue for such a link. Human rights references are here tangential to the core of the arguments, and are used simply to argue that an intrinsic meaning of equity is consistent with human rights covenants (see World Bank 2006: 7). In general, the WDR is very cautious in referring to moral arguments.[25] For example:

The international human rights regime testifies to the shared belief that all should have equal rights and be spared extreme deprivation. Some *even* argue that there is a powerful moral case for rich countries to take action, because of the huge disparities and *(arguably)* because they partly created and perpetuate global inequities.

(World Bank 2006: 206, emphasis added)

What we found in our conversations and interviews with Bank staff was that their position is unproblematic once new issues and ideas have been widely accepted – for example 'education for all', or even that the primary goal of development ought to be poverty reduction. The problem arises when they face the need to integrate 'new ideas' – as was the case, we were told, of linking human rights and equity in a major report. The importance of equity is not widely accepted among some groups. For the very wealthy, it may simply threaten their privileges; and among certain economists it is seen as running counter to efficiency. Adding human rights, and thus the intrinsic meaning of equity, was too much of a challenge for some of those working on the report.

'I tend to think of myself as reasonably open minded', one of the members of the editorial team told us, but

when a new concept arises the fundamental thinking I go through is: where does this fit? ... and if it does not fit, ... then I temporarily reject it. ... This resistance is exacerbated by the need to have a written document in say effectively six to seven months on a large concept, and in an accessible language and that has to satisfy two constraints: up to scratch vis à vis the status of knowledge of the profession and the need to satisfy a whole group of constituencies.

Even if some of the staff on the WDR editorial team were sympathetic to including references to human rights or ethically grounded arguments, the overall process discourages the taking of risk. Part of the problem is simply the short time allocated to the preparation of the WDR. 'I think we do too many big reports', we heard in one of our interviews, 'we do too many WDRs in particular. We need two years for the WDR ... maybe then people will be more able to be more open minded or at least there will be more time to think through the things that do not fit'. As an institution, the Bank continues to produce innumerable reports and annual WDRs, and it has to satisfy many, often competing, audiences.

That the final version of this WDR 2006 reveals some of the tensions and limitations of a primarily economic analysis is due not only to the topic itself, but to the particular set of circumstances at the Bank at the time of the production of the WDR, and the social relations between experts and bureaucrats and among various sections and departments in the Bank as well as relations with others outside the Bank. It is to these that we now return.

Processes of knowledge production need audiences that legitimise their knowledge outputs. This is a common characteristic of all types of expertise, which depends always on the relations between cognitive authority and audiences (Turner 2004). The knowledge claims of experts cannot be legitimised simply by the fact that their audience recognises that they are indeed expert. There are different types of audiences and legitimising processes, and also different kinds of dynamics that may lead to very different relations between experts and the sources of legitimacy of their expertise. One of the main reasons that World Bank knowledge cannot be said to be 'objective, solid science' is because of the ways in which the Bank's documents build legitimacy and credibility (St. Clair 2006a, 2006b). This process deserves close scrutiny. With WDRs it starts with the choice of topic and of authors. 2006 was the first WDR under the direction of the new Senior Vice-President and Chief Economist, Francois Bourguignon. It began under the presidency of James Wolfensohn, but was written largely under the presidency of Paul Wolfowitz (from June 2005). The report was co-directed by Francisco H. G. Ferreira and Michael Walton, two economists well regarded in the Bank who had already collaborated (along with two others) on a report entitled *Inequality in Latin America and the Caribbean: Breaking with History?* released in 2003, which was by Bank standards rather radical.[26]

The team was, like most WDRs, entirely dominated by economists. In addition to Walton and Ferreira, all but two of the fourteen other core team members were economists. There were five advisors, four of them economists trained and currently employed in the USA or UK.[27] The only non-economist was Arjun Appadurai, a professor of anthropology at the New School, New York; but he excluded himself from the task at an early stage due to other pressing commitments.

Responsibility for the WDR is located in the Development Economics Vice-Presidency (DEC).[28] DEC is now the largest development research body in the world, and entirely dominated by economists. In an insightful article, Broad analyses in detail the mechanisms by which DEC produces research that is biased towards the neo-liberal paradigm, showing how 'research that has "resonance" with the paradigm is elevated and dissonant research is discouraged' (Broad 2006: 412).[29] Various other departments normally have an interest and an input, depending on the topic (see below).

In order to understand the WDRs – indeed, any such document – it is necessary to ask who the authors consider to be their audience, and whose judgement matters. For whom is this report written? We may distinguish several audiences. Colleagues within the Bank are important. Those who prepare the report, even if they are not long-term Bank staff, have often absorbed the Bank 'culture'. They are accustomed to peer review, often quite critical, from colleagues – and especially from economists. They need to show that the report is rigorous, according to the criteria of that discipline. But this audience also serves to ensure coherence with other well established views in the Bank and consistency with general trends in the organisation. If a Bank report does not satisfy key audiences within the Bank or sister organisations, it would not have sufficient legitimacy. To varying extents, the authors also want to impress, or at least protect against criticism from, academic economists outside the Bank. They can do this by ensuring that their arguments are rigorous (even if doubts remain about the accuracy of the data used), and by demonstrating their knowledge of new ideas within the discipline (i.e. being at the research frontier). Here the view of advisors would carry considerable weight – for example Angus Deaton, President of the American Economic Association.

It is often stated that 'ministers of finance in developing countries' are the target audience of the WDR. The implication is that the document is aimed primarily at the governments in poor countries (the 'clients' of the World Bank), and especially at those who have both the power and the technical competence to make use of the report. Such people are, of course, also politicians; but the implication is that they too will be convinced by sound economic arguments.[30] Another audience is constituted by the report's outside commentators and critics: especially, since the late 1990s, NGOs, politicians on both the right and the left, and the media.[31] While most NGOs regard the bank as a haven for neo-liberals, Republicans and even the *Economist* magazine sometimes treat the Bank as alarmingly socialist. It is, however, the NGOs that are usually most detailed and outspoken in their criticism, and the Bank tries not to provoke this quite influential audience more than is necessary.

The report must be approved by the President and 'signed off' by the Executive Board, who, in this sense, form the most important audience and should be placed top of the list. The President is likely to be particularly concerned about the main message of the report, and hence with the wording of the 'Executive Summary'. The views of individual member countries may range from objections to the very fact that an issue (such as equity) is addressed at all, to objections about specific 'boxes' or empirical examples in the report which reflect badly on them. As noted, these pressures can lead to real modifications in the report as a whole, but may also be unresolved, leading to incongruities or inconsistencies in argument or to noticeable differences between the executive summary and the full text. In addition to these various audiences, there are others who may have some influence on the process and product; notable among these are bilateral donors, which we analyse below, and, depending on the topic, other departments of the Bank. In this case, the Social Development Department (SDD) and the Legal Department deserve particular mention. The SDD has a weak position in the Bank.[32] As Mosse argues (Mosse forthcoming b), non-economist social scientists in the Bank are 'a marginal group'. They occupy a threatened professional space, seen as contributing little in practical terms. The number of such social scientists in the Bank has increased (Miller-Adams 1999), starting from the initial appointment of Michael Cernea in 1974 (Cernea 1995) but, as Mosse argues, with this has come a change in their role, from criticising to promoting what might be called a 'technocratic' application of their expertise. They are faced with a twin dilemma: whether to be 'critical' or 'constructive'; and whether to couch their expertise in the language of the dominant discipline of economics. Our experience in witnessing the process of building the WDR 2006 is an illustration of Mosse's claim that non-economist social scientists are preoccupied to protect their own cognitive space, while having little power. To quote Mosse: 'they make the organisation work better without changing what it does, even contributing to the unreliable notion that the organisation is knowledge-led' (Mosse forthcoming b: 000). The topic chosen for WDR 2006 provided the SDD a good opportunity to become involved, but they apparently felt the need to proceed with caution. At the seminar in November 2004, St. Clair experienced resistance both from the SDD and DfID researchers, which she understood to be motivated by concerns that pushing the human rights issues too hard would have negative consequences: for the text (which might actually be weakened) and/or for the department and the staff promoting the issue (who might be criticised for overstepping their boundaries).[33] But discussion on human rights was something that the Legal Department, and in particular the Chief General Counsel Roberto Dañino, was interested to promote, and it is to this – our second object of study – that we now turn.

Human rights

In the past, the Bank's policy regarding the role of human rights in the organisation's work has been rather unclear, if not absent. In recent years, one can find declarative statements about 'the mainstreaming of human rights into everything we do' (World Bank 2002); but to judge from the summary of a meeting addressing human rights in the Bank, staff members were doubtful as to whether 'an economic development institution (should) embrace the fundamental values, elements, and instruments of a human rights approach to sustainable development' (World Bank 2002). There appears to be a reluctance to address rights directly – although human rights has begun to enter into the 'country dialogue' in Country Assistance Strategies, e.g. in Nepal.

Traditionally, the World Bank interpreted its Articles of Agreement in narrow economic terms which effectively excluded the issue. In the early 1990s, when 'good governance' came on the agenda, the then General Counsel, Ibrahim Shihata, reinterpreted this mandate somewhat more widely, opening up for some inclusion of 'political' issues. He retired in 1998, and no significant changes were made under the acting General Counsels who served subsequently until Dañino, former Prime Minister of Peru and ambassador to the USA, was appointed Senior Vice President and General Counsel in late 2003, and adopted a more proactive role. One of the first things he did was to set up a Work Group on Human Rights within the Legal Vice Presidency. 'The group was established not only because of (his) personal conviction that work in this area is a moral imperative, but also because of (his) sense that human rights are progressively becoming an explicit and integral part of the Bank's work' (Dañino 2006: 298). In taking an initiative in this field, he was sticking his neck out politically, but he received the backing of Wolfensohn who, in 2004, asked the Nordic-Baltic Office in the WB to assist in raising the issue of human rights in the Bank.

In brief, after a long period in which human rights was virtually off the agenda in the World Bank, the issue was, early in the new millennium, up for debate. To understand the dynamics of this debate, it is useful to distinguish three main, to some extent interrelated, constraining factors: a reluctance on the part of several Board members, especially but not solely, 'part 2' ('client') countries to discuss human rights; views concerning the correct interpretation of the Bank's mandate; and the dominance of economic thinking among the staff, just described.

In some member countries there is no doubt a desire to keep the Bank out of this area, whether to avoid unwelcome criticism or from a fear that this may make it more difficult to obtain loans.[34] Executive Directors may therefore choose to favour a narrow interpretation of the Bank's mandate. In order to promote the human rights issue, a 'Nordic' paper on human rights was prepared, but it was not presented in the Board, apparently for fear that it would be too controversial. However, a number of activities were set in motion 'under the radar', as described below. (Even among the Nordic countries there was some disagreement as to how far the issue should be pushed. Differences of view here are attributable in part to the fact that some Executive Directors are from the country's Ministry of Finance while others are from the Ministry of Foreign Affairs.)

The Articles of Agreement of the Bank state that 'The Bank and its officers shall not interfere in the political affairs of any member country. ... Only economic considerations shall be relevant to their decisions'. In interpreting this mandate, the Chief Legal Counsel plays a crucial role, and therefore the less restrictive and more proactive approach of Dañino was extremely important; not merely allowing but actively encouraging inclusion of human rights considerations in the bank's work.

But how to counter the resistance of Board members? An attractive solution was to argue the case for human rights on economic grounds. This would make it easier both to claim that the issue fell within the Bank's mandate, and to gain ready acceptance among the staff of the Bank. Such an approach promised to overcome all the three barriers just identified: the issue could be presented as 'economic', thus clearly within the Bank's mandate, unthreatening for Board members, and in line with the dominant discourse of the Bank.

The decision by the Bank to consider addressing human rights issues was, in part, a response to criticism and pressure from NGOs. But there was also, as mentioned in Chapter 2, pressure throughout the whole UN system stemming from the lead given by Secretary-General Kofi Annan, followed up by Mary Robinson, who helped Wolfensohn organise a major conference on human rights and the role of the Bank (Alston and Robinson 2005). The debate coordinated by Alston and Robinson, concerning how to link human rights to development work, often focused on client countries' obligations; but within the community of legal scholars there was also an important debate about the extent to which the Bank is bound to respect and/or promote international law. One of those who have made detailed investigations of the possible legal obligations of the Bank (Skogly 2001: 46) argues that the institution was established according to international law, 'through the adoption, ratification and entry into force of their Articles of Agreement as treaties among states'; and that from the Articles of Agreement it follows that the Bank is a legal person with duties and responsibilities, arguably in the same way as business corporations are treated as legal persons. This means, according to Skogly, that the Bank has a responsibility to carry its mandate 'within the framework of international law' (Skogly 2001: 47). From this, it follows that the Bank is also obliged to respect human rights as articulated by the UN charter, as well as by customary international law and 'general principles' of law (Darrow 2003). This obligation entails that Bank programmes and policies ought not to violate human rights. Skogly adds, furthermore, that such obligation is not only negative, but also positive. According to her, even though the Bank has recognised its positive role in the promotion of economic, cultural and social rights, there is no indication as to how this is ensured or monitored (Skogly 2001: 55). Regarding positive obligations to protect and to fulfil people's rights, it may be argued, from a legal perspective, that although the Bank itself does not hold full (perfect) human rights obligations (as it is not a ratifying party to human rights treaties), it has implicit obligations to the degree that its member states are committed by ratification. According to the principle of extraterritorial obligations, it can be argued that member states are bound by the conventions they have ratified with regard to their behaviour through the Bank's operations.

In short, some scholars consider that the Bank is legally bound to comply with and even to promote human rights. Perhaps the most detailed attempt to provide guiding principles is found in the 'Tilburg Guiding Principles of World Bank, IMF and Human Rights' (Van Genugten *et al.* 2003; see also Van Genugten and Perez-Bustillo 2001). According to Van Genugten (2003), what is important is that new approaches and directions in the Bank – such as governance, social safety nets, or efforts to encourage countries to meet health and education targets – be expanded and evaluated according to both socio-economic and cultural rights, national regulations and international human rights laws. Even though a focus on poverty issues is important, it is *per se* not sufficient to guarantee protection of basic rights nor necessarily consistent, procedurally, with rights broadly understood.

In December 2005, the Legal Department organised its annual Legal Forum around the WDR 2006, under the title 'Law, Equity and Development'. Roberto Dañino used the occasion to present his legal opinion on the role that the Bank has in following human rights norms (Dañino 2006). He argued that there is no reason why the Bank should not demand from its clients respect for human rights; but he fell short of committing the Bank as an institution to be subject to human rights law – because human rights law, he claimed, applies to countries rather than to multilateral institutions. This event, and the counsel's opinion, was an important indication of Dañino's commitment to the issue. But Paul Wolfowitz, who took over as President of the Bank in mid-2005, showed limited enthusiasm for this agenda,[35] and Dañino left the Bank in January 2006. He was replaced by Ana Palacio, former Foreign Minister of Spain and good friend of Wolfowitz. It appeared that she was willing to continue the same line pursued by her predecessor.[36] But when Wolfowitz departed, her position became increasingly difficult and she resigned from the Bank shortly before the time of writing.

In his presentation at the Legal Forum, Dañino presented ongoing work in his department on a 'matrix that charts human rights against the activities of the Bank to help it get a better understanding of the interconnections between the work of the Bank and each member's human rights obligations' (Dañino 2006: 296). This is one example of his more proactive approach. In recent years, the Legal Department has not restricted itself to dealing with contracts and advising on the legal aspects of projects and policies; it has engaged in law as a 'sector', supporting projects such as those concerned to improve the operations of courts, and has addressed issues in connection with human rights and more recently supported research on access to justice. And the Nordic countries wished to provide further support to such activities.

In addition to being represented in the Board, donor countries have some power to influence the processes of building knowledge in the Bank by providing technical and financial assistance through trust funds. For example, Britain (DfID) financed a number of background papers for WDR 2006, prepared in collaboration with the Social Development Department. (DfID had, in 2004, sponsored a study on empowerment, *Power, Rights and Poverty Reduction*, which was also used as background material in the Oslo workshop mentioned above.) Another example is the Norway-Finland Trust Fund for Environmentally and Socially Sustainable Development, which has provided almost 10 million dollars a year for the last five years, much of it to support social development activities.[37] These are only two of many such funds, which now account for a substantial proportion of the funds that World Bank receives. With regard to the proposed Nordic Trust Fund, there are two aspects of particular interest in the context of this book: the discussion as to whether to keep the fund 'under the radar', and whether to argue the case for human rights work in the Bank in purely economic terms.

The former issue is a delicate one. It might, perhaps, be possible to set up a trust fund without this being formally approved in the Board. On the other hand, if it is known that some powerful Executive Directors are likely to be antagonistic to such an initiative, it would be unwise for the management to appear to be concealing it. In this case, the issue was further complicated by the fact that Ana Palacio, the Chief Legal Counsel at the time, who would be largely responsible for making the case for the trust fund, was – as noted above – seriously compromised by her close association with the departed President Wolfowitz. For these reasons, although the trust fund was ready for signature for many months, it was – at least at the time of writing – not yet signed. Some Bank staff may be disappointed at this. 'We are not a human rights organisation and I do not think we will even have a rights-based approach', one of our interviewees told us, 'but I think that is an area where I'm very optimistic, and there's going to be lots of great work in the next couple of years, really driving this forward. ... We now have an open door to really experiment and see what difference does it make.'

Regarding the second issue, to make the case for human rights on economic grounds, it is relevant to return to the views of former Senior Advisor on human rights, Alfredo Sfeir-Younis, Although he wrote speeches for Wolfensohn, it is apparent that Sfeir-Younis' style was more theoretical-philosophical than that of his President, and of his colleagues. Perhaps the clearest statement of his position is in his essay 'Human Rights and Economic Development: Can They Be Reconciled? A View from the World Bank' (Sfeir-Younis 2003).[38] First, Sfeir-Younis argues that it is crucial to address the role that economics, and in particular economic values, play in restraining the Bank from engaging more openly with human rights issues. Economics can be characterised, he argues, as a collection of values – albeit changing with context and over time; it is impossible to view economic issues, rights and the operationalisation of policies as separate matters. What weaves them together are precisely underlying values; and a focus on values is the most important way to mainstream human rights into economic development (Sfeir-Younis 2003: 3). Some values are dominant (thus consumerism and individualism dominate economics), but it is not clear that this situation should continue; and values vary across different countries and contexts. It is crucial then to see the role played by institutions, Sfeir-Younis claims, in changing the course of humanity, in enabling change. The reconciliation between economic and human rights issues needs to occur at an institutional level, he argues, as much as at an ideological level. Sfeir-Younis addresses the ways in which new approaches in the Bank related to poverty reduction have put the Bank closer to human rights principles, such as for example the recent emphasis on empowerment or lack of 'voice'. A second important area of emphasis in Sfeir-Younis' article is the relation between rights-based development and socio-economic rights. He argues that this leads one to investigate processes of wealth creation and wealth accumulation. Unless wealth creation is linked to socio-economic rights, human rights may remain disassociated from economic planning and economic decision-making.

Sfeir-Younis' arguments were too radical for the organisation; but also too 'philosophical'. They represented not only a rather fundamental conceptual challenge;[39] equally important was the fact that it was unclear how such ideas could be 'operationalised'. What would they mean in practice for the policies and projects of a bank whose overriding purpose is to lend money? For operational purposes, those directly concerned with providing loans are the ones that matter most; and the imperative for them, as already noted, is to keep the money flowing.

Within this political and organisational context, those promoting the trust fund chose not to argue for a fundamental reassessment of economics and its underlying values, but rather to follow earlier practice – in relation to debates about good governance – and make the case for human rights in terms of the less controversial argument that this is good for economic growth (and perhaps equity).[40] This would imply, for example, undertaking studies on 'measuring justice'. A similar strategy had been adopted in relation to the World Bank's *Doing Business Report*, 2005, written by Michael Klein, Vice President of the International Finance Corporation. This presented indicators of how business-friendly different countries were, and was followed up by a strategy of 'confront and assist' in those countries which performed badly, i.e. to present the data summarising the situation in their country, and then to assist in improving the situation.

In summary, it has not proved easy to introduce discussion of human rights into the World Bank. The initiative of the former Chief Legal Counsel has been important; but for several interrelated reasons, the chosen way forward is cautious: justifying work in this field primarily on instrumental grounds – showing how it may promote economic growth – rather than seeking a link with ethics and the World Bank's moral responsibility in the global fight against poverty.

Conclusion

It is only a slight exaggeration to say that the WDR is written by economists for economists. This creates a situation which both constrains and, by a circular process of self-reinforcement, validates the outcome. Critical comments by non-economists, mainly outside the Bank, to some extent counter this tendency. But there are also other countervailing tendencies, for example the fact that an increasing number of ministers of finance in developing countries are economists trained in the same tradition as Bank staff, and thus become part of this self-reinforcing process – in which the audience is itself shaped by the organisation.

For professionals in development agencies, many types of expertise may, in principle, be of relevance; but in the Bank, as elsewhere, economics is certainly the most influential, both with regard to the macro (national policy) and the micro level (project assessment). Even if not necessarily neo-liberal, mainstream economics exerts a powerful disciplining force. And it combines very effectively with the bureaucratic imperative to 'operationalise' the contributions of researchers, thus creating a powerful economic/technocratic nexus; the cognitive values of economics fitting very well the values of policy-making (Bøås and McNeill 2004; St. Clair 2006b). Bank experts' understanding of the relationship between ethics and their work relates largely if not exclusively to the values associated with their professionalism: objectivity, technical excellence and operational relevance. As 'experts', they seek to satisfy the academic community of economists; and as Bank staff they are required to produce policy-oriented work that fits the institutional demands of that organisation.

The decision by the new Chief Economist to choose 'equity' as the topic for his first WDR may be characterised as brave or perhaps foolhardy. By contrast with, for example, 'infrastructure', this topic is clearly a challenge to the organisation, and to the discipline of economics which dominates it. The report therefore provides a revealing case study. Our examination of the process and product demonstrates, we suggest, the power of (mainstream) economics in the Bank. It shows how economic expertise is a key element in maintaining the legitimacy of the organisation, and in determining what the Bank says and does; at the same time as it constrains and even censors discussion of ethical issues.

The forces that militate against promoting a human rights agenda in the Bank are in many respects similar: resistance from many Board members, who prefer to insist on a narrow interpretation of the Bank's mandate. Those who wish to take up human rights issues therefore feel obliged to keep 'below the radar'. But, as we have shown, here too the power of economic expertise plays an important part, because a choice is made to present human rights as an economic issue – to justify it in economic terms. This is in part because this is the logic which staff of the Bank feels comfortable with, and in part because it can be argued that in this way one avoids the risk of exceeding the mandate of the Bank.

The World Bank is reluctant to address the question of its own responsibilities as a global actor. What we found was that the main focus as regards the question of responsibility was concerned with the situation within countries: governments' obligations to meet the demands of accountability and transparency proper to any contractual situation, and to meet their own responsibilities as political representatives of 'their' people. For Bank experts, their obligations are met as long as their work helps reducing poverty; and this is at the same time the guarantee of their own legitimacy and moral standing as global actors. The most 'extreme' argument we heard voiced among the staff referred to the possible co-responsibility of the Bank – together with those governments and the rest of the donor community.

> If we deliver the goods, if we help governments reduce poverty, I think we have a position of moral standing. Where we don't – we don't, and we'd better worry about it. So, it also means it's about what the outcome is. And I think what is interesting about the Bank, especially in low-income countries is that … we have to take co-responsibility for what the government does. We can't step aside and say, 'Oh, you didn't have the capacity to follow all our plans'. That's a big mind shift that's coming very slowly in the Bank.

Staff did acknowledge the important role now played by the Inspection Panel in giving a voice to the citizens of those countries affected, and permitting them to file complaints about Bank funded projects that have negatively affected them, regardless of the acceptance of the project by their government. But as World Bank funding becomes more and more about 'budget support' (often jointly with other agencies and donors) the identification of which projects are Bank-funded becomes more difficult, and the role of the Inspection Panel reduced. Another accountability mechanism of the Bank, the Independent Evaluation Group (IEG), has also very limited capacity to become a tool for transforming the Bank into a 'responsible' institution. This is especially the case when activities move outside the simple world of infrastructure projects. As one interviewee sharply put it,

> It's very interesting to read (IEG) reports because you see there's fluctuations … that the Bank didn't do its work, or the Bank did do its work, but the Government failed. Well, that you can do if you're building a highway, right … if you're financing a highway. But, if you're helping build the education system, you can't. You cannot.

Accountability mechanisms such as these may ensure that the Bank follows approved procedures and processes, but they do not render it a responsible global institution in the broader sense we have discussed. And the prospects for this situation changing through increased focus on human rights are not yet very encouraging. The Bank is the most important multilateral institution in the world with a mandate of reducing poverty. Precisely because of its power, we argue that the organisation is 'response-able' and hence also morally responsible for protecting people from poverty.

6　UNESCO

'Poverty as a violation of human rights'

Introduction

In this chapter, we analyse a UNESCO initiative – the Poverty as a Human
Rights Violation Project – which, led by Pierre Sané, Assistant Director-
General (ADG) for the Social and Human Sciences (SHS), and formerly
head of Amnesty International (AI), sought to structure UNESCO's poverty
strategy around the claim that 'poverty is a violation of human rights' and
around the idea of 'abolition'. Our aim is to trace the trajectory of the claim –
that poverty is a violation of human rights – within UNESCO, and relate the
promotion of such a view to UNESCO's mandate, organisational structure
and the role that political forces can have in promoting or preventing specific
approaches. Of particular importance is the role of powerful countries, such
as the United States, and the ways in which ideas in the multilateral system
fit or do not fit with widely spread norms and beliefs. We will argue that the
initiative's core idea proved to be too radical for UNESCO, which attempted
to tone down its controversial wording. But our analysis will take up the
broader themes we are concerned with in this book – such as the role of
UNESCO in the multilateral system, and the problems that arise when a
multilateral institution attempts to adopt ethical language and to address
matters of global justice which do not fit well with the instrumentalised,
depoliticised and allegedly value-free ideas and approaches that dominate
global policy discourse.

To assert that freedom from poverty is a human right is a controversial claim,
implying a substantial divergence from standard approaches to the challenge
of poverty. But it has acquired some currency in recent years with the
revamping of human rights discourse at the global level, as we have shown in
Chapter 3. The difference between the phrases 'freedom from' and 'violation
of', appearing in the statements of, for example, former High Commissioner
for Human Rights Mary Robinson, may to some seem not very significant.
But the term 'violation' has in fact proved controversial when explicitly used
in a global institution's strategy – raising, as it does, issues of accountability
and responsibility, and the indivisibility of socio-economic from liberty
rights, and thus proving particularly challenging to well established beliefs of

rich and powerful countries. To claim that poverty is a violation of human rights establishes poverty as a new category of political thought. The statement is value laden and thus action guiding. Not only does the language of violation convey considerations of duties and responsibilities in a more unequivocal way than the language of freedom, it also challenges dominant expert ideas about poverty that are favoured by global organisations. The language of violation implies a relational approach between wealth and poverty that is difficult to ignore, placing advanced and developing countries, developers and the developed, within a common framework. To characterise poverty as a violation of human rights can perhaps influence attitudes to poverty – moving away from the notion that poverty is the responsibility of the poor themselves, or of their states. The term 'violation' entails that poverty is not only bad, but wrong, calling for serious and immediate action and preventive measures. The claim that poverty is a violation of some globally recognised set of human rights re-politicises the global poverty debate and presents it as a question of global justice; its abolition, a question of political will, and global institutions as key actors in working towards the responsibility to protect people from poverty.

As we have seen, the characterisation of poverty as a question of human rights originates within the UN system institutions, but has also had a history within ethical and religious movements as well as among movements of struggle and contestation. For our purposes in this book it is important to situate the emergence, trajectory and evolution of the use of the term 'violation' in relation to global organisational structures and global power relations.[1] As our earlier chapters show, the fate of this approach to poverty may in part be determined by the way in which current global politics develop in the coming years, and the power and moral authority of the institutions that promote 'global ideas'. Just as other ideas, and associated policies, were in the past heavily influenced by Cold War relations, the fate of a human rights view of poverty may depend not so much on conceptual clarification as on changes in the global political situation. But ideas that challenge power relations are often denied the necessary critical and ethical space. This chapter shows how even an institution free of the constraints facing development organisations such as UNDP and the World Bank found it problematic to implement quite a modest initiative – to explore the implications of an alternative perspective on poverty and human rights – and was required to curtail it, or at best keep it 'under the radar'.

Historical background[2]

UNESCO has, from the start, had multiple functions and a rather unclear mandate, resulting from the many competing forces and different motivations involved in its creation. The main justification used for its establishment was functional; according to its constitution, 'the purpose of the Organization is to contribute to peace and security by promoting collaboration among the nations through education, science and culture' (article 1, section 2). The constitution further calls on members to 'collaborate in the work of advancing the mutual knowledge and understanding of people through all means of mass communication and to that end, recommend such international agreements as may be necessary to promote the free flow of ideas by work or image' (article 1, section 2).

The focus on peace and security as the overarching goal of UNESCO was met with criticism from two sides: those who argued that 'international scientific cooperation was an end in itself and would always be so', and it should not be considered simply a means to a higher goal (Ascher 1950: 14); and from a classical realist perspective, that UNESCO was 'in the paradoxical position of performing most useful and necessary functions in the nascent world community but of giving very implausible reasons for the performance of its functions' (Niebuhr 1950: 3).

As a result of these differing forces, UNESCO was established as an institution with built-in tensions. And it was increasingly affected by US attempts to make it an instrument for its strategy to combat communism, and by opposition from the Soviet Union and, later, Third World countries. This 'Cold War' conflict surfaced on a number of occasions. The US often, but certainly not always, got its way (Coate 1992). But over the course of the 1970s and 1980s, criticism of UNESCO increased. This had several different aspects. First, UNESCO was increasingly attacked – not only by the US government, but also by European intellectuals – for being influenced by relativist ideas about culture. Second, the US viewed UNESCO as a hotbed of left-wing thought, espousing ideas of state intervention in the press and other areas of communication. The United States characterised its attitude as 'hostility towards a free society, especially a free market and free press'.[3] Third, the US viewed UNESCO as an overly bureaucratic and inefficient organisation. As a result of these criticisms, the US withdrew from the organisation in 1984, which contributed to a slump in funding and no growth in the regular budget for two decades since the mid-1980s.[4] UNESCO suffered gravely as a result.

As Lourdes Arizpe, former Assistant Director-General (for culture), claims in her interview with the UN Intellectual History Project, 'UNESCO was so strongly hit because of some of its policies. When this was followed by a permanent campaign against UNESCO's work in the 1980s and 1990s, I think this was very deleterious to the work of the institution' (UNIHP, Arizpe 2002: 29). A downward spiral set in – similar to, but perhaps more extreme than, the experience of some other UN agencies – reducing the extent of its achievements and the calibre of its staff. Even now that the budget has increased again, the organisation is very vulnerable to the views of richer member countries – a major factor, we shall later argue, behind UNESCO's reluctance to move forward with the poverty and human rights initiative.

UNESCO had from the start a double constituency: it was created as an organisation of member states, supported by contributions voted by national parliaments from public treasuries; at the same time, it has always cooperated closely with non-governmental organisations and individuals. UNESCO national commissions were the organisational instruments permitting the collaboration of writers, thinkers and artists. According to Arizpe, one of the biggest problems for UNESCO is the disagreements among countries about the appropriate tasks for the organisation:

> European countries, as well as many other countries of the Americas and of Asia believe that UNESCO should devote itself primarily to international intellectual cooperation – that UNESCO should exercise moral and intellectual leadership in fostering the creation of ideas, and representations, and of fostering science and education to give a sense of direction to development. Countries with middle-income development needs, however, want UNESCO to produce development blueprints that they can apply in their own countries. And countries with the greatest development needs want UNESCO to be a funding agency to compensate in areas where they have no resources to apply.
>
> (UNIHP, Arizpe 2002: 32)

UNESCO has, in the last half century, both changed its role and lost considerable influence. It has never had a significant role as an 'implementing agency' that finances projects. It does have a reputation for its expertise in certain fields, most notably education; but even here it has a small budget compared to other agencies. It has a role based on its 'ethical and intellectual mandate';[5] but its influence here has declined, not only because of its own organisational decline but also because of changes in the international context, examined below.

UNESCO organisation

UNESCO is governed by its member states, operating through General Conferences where representatives from member states meet every two years to determine the policies and main lines of work of the organisation. The Executive Board meets twice a year to ensure that decisions taken by the General Conference are implemented. The present Director-General of UNESCO, who was appointed in 1999, is Koïchiro Matsuura of Japan. An important task for him was to bring the USA, and others, back into UNESCO – both in order to make it a truly international organisation, but also to increase its budget. The Director-General is the head of the Secretariat, which is composed of international civil servants based at Paris headquarters and in field offices.

UNESCO has five 'sectors', each headed by an Assistant Director-General: Education, Natural Sciences, Social and Human Sciences (SHS), Culture, Communication and Information. SHS is the weakest, in terms of budget and number of staff. These operate almost as autonomous 'kingdoms'. Part of the efforts of the current Director-General relate to the attempt to work across disciplines and try to break down the barriers between the sectors. As we shall later see, this had consequences for the ways in which the initiative was structured because although SHS has responsibility for the 'Poverty' initiative, it is dependent on approval – not least of funding – from the central administration of the organisation. Reporting on UNESCO's contribution to the Millennium Development Goals (MDGs) is the responsibility of the Director of the Bureau of Strategic Planning.

As noted above, UNESCO was for many years the site of ideological strife related to the Cold War. But it was also criticised as 'bureaucratic', 'pompous', 'wasteful', etc. This criticism was commonly expressed in terms of inefficiency and bad management, and it was this, rather than ideological reasons, that was the formal reason for the USA and some other countries (the UK, Singapore) to leave the organisation. The USA was by no means alone in criticising UNESCO's management. Even countries very favourable in principle, such as Sweden, have demanded change, and there have been a number of attempts at reorganisation and reform.

UNESCO, and perhaps SHS in particular, perceives itself as having an ethical and intellectual role within the UN system, as well as being operational (although clearly not a development agency). This results in a tension between those favouring operations and those who see the organisation as the conscience of humanity. Although it still has some formal claim to an ethical and intellectual leadership role, and devotes some efforts to contributing to ethical debates related to technology[6] and even celebrates a philosophy day, its status in this respect has declined. One of the reasons for this may perhaps be traced to changes in member state delegations within UNESCO, and changing global power relations.

The national delegations and commissions

UNESCO has 179 member states, and unlike most other multilateral organisations, UNESCO has country delegations permanently 'on the spot'. Until 1954 the members of these were elected in a personal capacity. Subsequently they were considered as representatives of member states, but many continued to be people with a 'cultural' or 'academic' background. In the 1990s, however, changes were made and the national delegations are now staffed exclusively by 'bureaucrats' – representatives of member states, and not representatives of the cultural world. In some cases, such as the USA which has a large delegation, they keep in very close touch with their home base. In addition, UNESCO also has national commissions in each country which provide an organisational link between the governmental and the non-governmental institutions of each member state. From the 1950s up to the 1970s, these were as important in UNESCO as governments. But, since cultural representatives were replaced by bureaucrats, governments have insisted that UNESCO subordinate itself to the interests of governments, national commissions have lost much of their punch. In some countries, UNESCO commissions function extremely well – in the Nordic countries, in Japan, and others. But in other countries, the commissions are appointed by the minister of culture, or some other bureaucrat.

(UNIHP, Arizpe 2002: 36)

She adds (countering the accusation of inefficiency against UNESCO bureaucrats) that she always thought that the problem was related to the interference of narrow-minded national interests; 'having the delegations in Paris, breathing down our necks, makes it impossible to work well, because there were all these narrow interests that were interfering'. The problem is, Arizpe concludes,

a governance structure in which political interests were paramount over quality, substance and fairness. I used to say that working in UNESCO was like working in a government in which all the political parties are in power at the same time. This is why the question of who the director-general is, is so important. He can deflect or allow the pursuit of narrow political or personal interests.

(UNIHP, Arizpe 2002: 31)

As this brief review indicates, UNESCO's power has been much reduced. It is nevertheless, at least in theory, well placed to promote challenging ideas, such as the view that extreme poverty is a violation of human rights. In this case, the initiative came from above, as a consequence of the increasing focus on poverty among development aid agencies, and, as elaborated in Chapter 3, because of the pressure from Kofi Annan to mainstream human rights in all UN agencies.

The Poverty as a Human Rights Violation Project

Background

After the signature of the Millennium Declaration by most heads of state, UN Secretary-General Kofi Annan requested the United Nations Development Programme (UNDP) and all UN specialised agencies and funds to streamline their programming and budgeting in an effort to meet the Millennium Development Goals (MDGs), which sought to focus attention more clearly on the central task of eradicating poverty. This was a new field for UNESCO, which responded by creating a programme for 'Eradication of Poverty, Especially Extreme Poverty'.[7] The Director-General assigned the task of developing a cross-cutting activity involving several sectors at UNESCO to the smallest of them (SHS – Sector of Social and Human Sciences). When

Pierre Sané, newly appointed Assistant Ddirector-General for the SHS, took up his post, the project already had a structure, and he was mandated to develop it and to implement it. Under Sané, the project developed in an untraditional way, taking the form of a set of sub-projects, and the involvement of an international network of philosophers, economists, lawyers and other intellectuals, exploring the claim that poverty is a violation of human rights. In the words of one of our interviewees, Sané's initiatives were

> A powerful instrument in promoting fresh thinking and questioning the traditional Human Rights Based Approaches. These projects attracted a disproportionate number of visionaries who saw them as an opportunity to do the kind of work they came to the UN system to do. It also attracted the young, the bright and the visionaries within each of the sectors because their work on these projects was not rewarded through any formal mechanism.

The 'strategy for cross-cutting theme: eradication of poverty, especially extreme poverty' was approved by the General Conference in November 2001 as part of UNESCO's Medium-Term Strategy 2002–7. (UNESCO operates with six-year strategies, divided into two-year increments.) Along with a project on information and communication technologies, this was chosen as one of two cross-cutting themes in UNESCO and allocated US$5.12 million in the regular budget approved by the Executive Board in 2003. The strategy is built up around twenty projects. Of this, a large proportion (US$2.05 million) was allocated to SHS.
   SHS argued that

> SHS has the necessary potential, experience and expertise to think through the concept of freedom from poverty as a human right and conceive an action plan; ... More specifically, with its expertise in philosophy, SHS can explore the ideological ramifications of this concept and through its work on human rights and discrimination can monitor the impact such an approach would have. It can propose a framework for action to promote human rights and link them to poverty eradication. Moreover, with its work on ethics, SHS can address the ethical dimension of this anti-poverty approach and, with its expertise in social science, will be able to identify and manage the social changes that will accompany the application of this new paradigm.
>
> (UNESCO 2004)[8]

Most UNESCO documents today refer to 'freedom from poverty as human right', 'poverty as a denial of human rights', or more broadly to a 'rights-based approach to poverty'. But the original idea of the particular project led by Sané was to centre UNESCO's contribution to the debate on the promotion of poverty as a 'violation of human rights', and around the idea that poverty is to be 'abolished' rather than 'reduced.'

Of the twenty projects involved in the UNESCO Poverty Programme, two were 'research projects',[9] and eighteen were 'pilot projects'.[10] Both types were placed under the heading of 'action research', but the two research projects were the ones where the notion of violation was more clearly stated:

> *Ethical and human rights dimensions of poverty: towards a new paradigm in the fight against poverty.*

and the

> *UNESCO Small grants programme on poverty eradication/building national capacities for research and policy analysis.*

In these two initiatives the concepts of 'violation' and 'abolition' were central in the early stages, but in the subsequent years references to 'violations of human rights' have been toned down or even excised, and 'abolition' has often been replaced by milder terms. Yet a few references to the notion of violation still survive in some documents, although scattered within the various web pages at UNESCO. For example, the text of the call for proposals to allocate the Small Grants money clearly states that

> UNESCO wishes to encourage research and policy analysis focusing on the relationship between poverty and human rights. ... In cooperation with partners, UNESCO hopes to support work that moves toward a view of poverty as a human rights violation
> (UNESCO Small Grants Programme)

The project 'Ethical and human rights dimensions of poverty: towards a new paradigm in the fight against poverty' was initiated with the same radical view – that severe poverty is a human rights violation – but currently describes its aims more cautiously: 'principally at developing an ethically and rights-based approach to poverty reduction. Poverty is not simply a matter of material deprivation. It is a matter of human dignity, justice, fundamental freedoms and basic human rights.'[11]

The project aimed primarily to support a series of workshops and academic publications to develop and promote the link between poverty and human rights. At the time of writing only one of those volumes has been published, under the editorial leadership of Thomas Pogge. In the next sections we examine the trajectory of the project, from its initial ambition to examine the claim that poverty entails a violation of human rights, and to promote the abolition of poverty, to a much more modest set of activities concerned with poverty and human rights more generally, often simply replicating what other UN system organisations are already doing. A project that could have created an important arena for debate on the pros and cons of viewing poverty as a violation of human rights, and on how to address the abolition – rather than merely the reduction – of poverty, a project that could have helped to raise awareness of the political implications and global responsibilities that would follow from such view, has been largely stifled.

We describe below the evolution of the project. As noted in Chapter 1, we obtained our data partly through our 'observant participation' in meetings organised under this project, in addition to document analysis and interviews. We acknowledge that the account of the evolution of the project we present here may be contested, and may compete with other alternative narratives.

Evolution of the project

The idea of a cross-cutting project was in part a response to a long-standing problem in UNESCO – that its five sectors operated very independently. It was also seen as desirable to encourage junior staff to propose projects, and give them more responsibility. The research project with which this chapter is especially concerned – 'Ethical and Human Rights Dimensions of Poverty: Towards a New Paradigm in the Fight Against Poverty' – was proposed by a middle-level (grade P2) staff member with a background in philosophy. Soon after it was approved, the new Assistant Director-General, Pierre Sané, took up his post. He decided to modify the overall portfolio of projects – including this one – so as to give them more of a human rights focus. The aim was to create a space for debate and contestation, to build the case for the abolition of poverty, for promoting the view of poverty as a violation of human rights by building on scientific knowledge, advocacy tools and pilot projects.

A central component of the project was therefore to organise a number of seminars worldwide, where thinkers – philosophers, economists, lawyers, social scientists – would come together to look at poverty and human rights issues from the perspective of violation and abolition.[12] While these were going to be events to debate the issues at the conceptual level, a number of pilot projects would (it was intended) be undertaken in the field, with interaction between the two. These had mixed success. The money allocated was large (by UNESCO standards); much of it was not additional but taken from other projects. Conceptually, this was seen by SHS as an opportunity to be innovative, and radical. There were numerous internal discussions, seminars, etc., in planning the programme, and contacts with a network of academics outside UNESCO who could contribute to building a conceptual understanding of poverty as a human rights question, and, it was hoped, contribute significantly with fresh ideas to the already large body of work being produced on human rights based approaches to poverty. UNESCO was a latecomer to the theme, and seen by other UN agencies as a fairly marginal player in the overall issue of poverty.

The staff involved needed to demonstrate intellectual innovation, while at the same time showing some concrete results. The leadership of Sané, coupled with the energy and entrepreneurship of some of the young staff involved in the project, gave it an intellectually powerful start. It began with the seminar at All Souls College, Oxford during March 2003 co-organised by UNESCO and Thomas Pogge.[13] Sané's team had identified Thomas Pogge as the leading philosopher analysing global poverty as a question of human rights and asked him to co-organise the meeting with UNESCO. The meeting was, to a large extent centred around the work of Pogge, in particular the then recently published book *World Poverty and Human Rights* (Pogge 2002) which many participants had read. The key idea in Pogge's work is that of conceiving a human right to be free of severe poverty as primarily *negative* and *institutional*. On a positive-interactional construal, the right would entail a correlative duty on all others to help and aid those in poverty. On the negative-institutional construal, the primary correlative duty is to not make uncompensated contributions to the design and imposition of a (national or supranational) institutional order that foreseeably and avoidably leads to massive severe poverty. Pogge's work was a philosophical argument for viewing poverty as a matter of liberty rights, and although he did not use the term 'violation' in the 2002 publication, he talked about severe poverty as crime against humanity, and thus his arguments fitted very well the goals of Sané's project.

Along with Pogge's book, participants read a draft paper which outlined the UNESCO strategy, utilising the notions of violation and the abolition of poverty. The views presented inspired lively debate and, by setting the ideas of Pogge within the context of the UN system, brought a coherence to the meeting beyond the views of the individual philosophers present. As well as provoking intense debate between competing philosophical views, the readings were also met with some scepticism among senior researchers who had long experience in studying the relations between rights and poverty. As one participant at the Oxford workshop put it: 'you will need to change the whole way development aid and its bureaucracies work if this view of poverty as a violation of human rights is ever to take root'.

Such hybrid debate – linking the activities of global development institutions with scholarly work of academics – is quite common. But in the same way that the choice of editorial groups for a World Bank report affects the outcome of the report, the choice of participants in such meetings often represents a fine balance between encouraging debate and limiting the range of views within acceptable bounds. What was new here was the combination of UNESCO, as a new player in the field of poverty, and a rather unusual group of experts; most participants at the All Souls meeting were new to the game of working with multilateral institutions. Shortly after, a meeting with lawyers was arranged in Brazil. Drawing on papers presented in both seminars, Thomas Pogge (2007) edited a volume entitled *Freedom from Poverty as a Human Right: Who Owes What to the Very Poor?* This is a collection of essays primarily discussing the notion of severe poverty as a violation of human rights. It was the pioneering publication that Sané and his team were after, but its publication was long delayed. Opening space for such debate among academics is, we suggest, indeed an important intellectual contribution consistent with the mandate of UNESCO. But it should be noted that Sané's strategy was very largely one of 'advocacy'. 'I wish to put a strong vocabulary in the hands of civil society groups to really empower the poor to claim their rights', he declared at the All Souls workshop.

Leadership: the role of Pierre Sané

The role of Pierre Sané is of utmost importance for understanding the development of this project. As mentioned earlier, he was appointed Assistant Director-General, to head SHS in the same year that the plans for this initiative were being made. He came directly from a decade of experience as Secretary-General of Amnesty International (AI) after AI had defined torture as a violation of human rights. Sané was recruited and hired by AI, in large part, due to his understanding of this field of human rights and his ability to move the agenda forward. His transitional role at Amnesty was advancing the role of social, economic and cultural rights in AI's work. This came from a series of decisions taken by International Council meetings during the 1980s, but implementation proved to be very difficult and controversial. There was resistance among both researchers as well as many established AI members. Sané had earlier, from 1977 until 1992, worked in IDRC (International Development Research Centre), Canada. Unlike most of his colleagues, therefore, he was not a 'UN bureaucrat'; he was seen as intellectual, charismatic and controversial – viewed by some with suspicion, by others as a genius. Here was a new, radical person, promoting a new, radical idea in an organisation which many felt had become rather conservative.[14] We were informed that the controversy and debate among those involved regarding the conception of poverty as a violation of HR was exhilarating, but also threatening to the status quo. Sané used semi-annual review meetings for each of the projects to challenge the human rights principles behind the work being done, to provoke debate, examination and analysis. This began to raise questions about many aspects of UNESCO's working methods, and resulted in changes both in the projects themselves and the way in which UNESCO staff, especially the younger ones, went about their work. The theoretical discussions were thus accompanied also by impacts at a practical level, affecting numerous people. Sané was quite strategic in his efforts to bring about change at UNESCO, but his probing, bordering on provocation, was challenging to the organisation. He held staff and their programmes to a high level of accountability, and, independent of the Secretary-General's office, he convened breakfast 'information sessions' about the work of SHS to which national delegations were invited. Here was presented the SHS strategy, with measurable outcomes and programmes designed to meet them. This brought Sané strong support from some key delegations at a time just before the criticism about his poverty work was beginning to mount.

In the light of subsequent events, one wonders whether UNESCO, and more specifically its Director-General, knew what they were getting in recruiting Sané. But even if the issue of 'poverty as a violation of human rights' was not directly taken up when Sané was interviewed for the job, it must have been clear from his record that he was a person who had devoted much of his life to human rights and to controversial advocacy on behalf of the disempowered; and that this was his perspective on major social issues. At Amnesty International he had dealt with human rights more from a legal perspective; while at IDRC it was more from a policy perspective. Sané was interested in the philosophical foundations of poverty and human rights.

But Sané was not acting as a mere idealist, pursuing a theoretical interest in questions of justice and ethics; he was looking for ways to push for broader social change, and have real influence on governments and the international community. He encouraged and promoted debate and seminars, with the intention also of influencing practice: to turn abstract concepts like poverty eradication, human rights and ethics into the day-to-day practice and policies of governments.

In addition to the workshops with philosophers and others, Sané asked one of UNESCO's partner organisations, CROP (the Comparative Research Programme on Poverty) to organise a consultation workshop in Bergen, Norway in June 2003, based on the draft document 'Abolishing Poverty Through the International Human Rights Framework: Towards an Integrated Strategy for the Social and Human Sciences'. This draft also mentions explicitly the choice of the term *abolition*. 'The popular phrase within the UN is *eradication* of poverty. UNESCO is proposing to campaign the term abolition of poverty on the grounds that poverty – extreme or relative – is a violation of human rights.'[15]

The report from that meeting, which is built primarily around the concluding remarks made by Sané, is very clear in promoting the notion of violation. The introductory remarks state:

> The document outlines the special role and responsibility of UNESCO, being endowed with an ethical mandate within the UN system, to address the problem of poverty as a moral responsibility and ethical necessity that must implicate the world community. The UN Community has already accepted that poverty is a denial of all human rights. UNESCO infers from this that poverty is a violation of human rights and, as such, must be considered illegal, according to international law. The insight that poverty is a denial of all human rights, though accepted both by the UN system and by the international community working with poverty reduction, still has not moved far beyond the stage of rhetoric. UNESCO therefore sees it as its special task, within the MDG process, to launch a concerted global campaign to influence the UN system, the political will of governments and NGOs to internalise the notion that poverty is a violation of human rights, and to raise

national and international awareness of the political implications of this fundamental paradigmatic shift.

(CROP 2003)

In addition, the text includes statements such as:

The theoretical basis for regarding poverty as a violation of human rights should be further substantiated and relevant knowledge must be provided for states and the international community to construct legal instruments and new policy approaches needed to achieve the ultimate goal of poverty abolition.

This raises the question of what kind of knowledge is sought. Is this leaning towards a legalistic interpretation of human rights violation, reflecting the views of lawyers? Does violation of human rights necessarily imply justiciability, or can it be interpreted as a moral claim, and, as we argue in the last section, as a political project seeking forward-looking responsibilities and duties?

But the debate never moved on. In terms of its ambitions 2003 was the high point of the project. The plans to continue building up 'substantiated and relevant knowledge' petered out, and the language used was toned down, for reasons explored in the next section. Sané and his team did indeed tap into the knowledge and expertise of some of the most radical and independent thinkers on poverty, whose views and proposals for policy change tend to be excluded in the processes of knowledge formation of other much more powerful global institutions. But this radical initiative, following a flurry of activity in 2003, soon met a series of organisational obstacles.

Resistance to the project

This initiative was not the first to meet resistance in UNESCO. On a larger scale, the Non-Aligned Movement's proposal for a 'new world information and communication order' (NWICO) in the mid-1970s, was rejected by UNESCO due to opposition from the US, and from major international news agencies mostly based in the United States (Wells 1987).

One manifestation of resistance to the initiative was pressure to tone down the language. And this had an effect; one may observe, in the texts and websites of UNESCO, the gradual replacement of the term 'violation of human rights' by terms less radical, and with less legalistic implications. In the world of activism, with which Sané was well acquainted from his work at Amnesty International, the notion of violation of human rights had always been an advocacy claim; a means to put pressure on actors and governments. But he was also well aware of the complexity of the debate – in academic, policy and activist circles. But for an inter-governmental organisation like UNESCO this is dangerous terrain. If violating human rights can lead to justiciability, rather than mere moral condemnation, the poor of the world would have a strong claim against the rich. Such ideas are anathema to the rich and powerful.[16]

A second, and more explicit, manifestation of resistance to the initiative was the cancellation of two high-profile conferences and a cut in funding. A conference to be held at Harvard in 2004 was first postponed and then cancelled. A second conference planned to be held at the London School of Economics in 2005 was also cancelled, and plans for subsequent events were dropped. The former case, of the Harvard conference, was particularly acute since the decision was taken at very short notice. It is not easy to trace the internal decision-making process within UNESCO leading to the cancellation of the Harvard conference, but this was certainly a decision taken at the highest level. In late January 2005, after many months of dealing with the US National Commission for UNESCO, a formal letter confirmed that the USA had no objection to the Harvard conference. It may be noted that the US policy on academic freedom in UNESCO is a controversial issue, as evidenced in an earlier case which led to a decision by the American Sociological Association to

> urge the President [of the United States] to direct the U.S. Delegation to UNESCO to refrain from vetting U.S. scientists duly selected by UNESCO for their expertise based upon whether the delegation views their presumed policy or political views to be consistent with current U.S. policy.[17]

Yet, soon after the letter was received from the National Commission, the participants in the seminar series were informed that 'In light of a Directorate meeting held at UNESCO Headquarters ... a decision was made to cancel all planned seminars, while keeping the planned publications as well as an international conference in Brazil in late 2005/early 2006'. Why was this decision taken? Apparently some countries were particularly sceptical about the initiative, including the USA – which is frequently resistant to claims about rights.[18] Did the US delegation convey their views directly to the Director-General? Formally, the involvement of member states in UNESCO's activities is limited to when they speak, and vote, at the General Conference, and on the Executive Board. Although the USA was in the rather special position of having a liaison officer in the Director-General's Office, according to article VI.5 of UNESCO's constitution,

> The responsibilities of the Director-General and of the staff shall be exclusively international in character. In the discharge of their duties they shall not seek or receive instructions from any government or from any authority external to the Organisation. They shall refrain from any action which might prejudice their positions as international officials. Each State Member of the Organisation undertakes to respect the

international character of the responsibilities of the Director-General and the staff, and not to seek to influence them in the discharge of their duties.

Certainly there was resistance within the organisation among those who felt that the statement 'poverty is a violation of human rights' is too radical; what might be called a political criticism.

A second source of resistance came from those within UNESCO who did not doubt the importance of the aim, but questioned whether it was feasible; 'how can a rather academic debate among philosophers and other scholars translate into real change on the ground?' This is not easy to distinguish from a third source of resistance in UNESCO – perhaps especially from those outside SHS – which may be regarded more as 'turf battles' or competition over funds. Other sections of UNESCO could, with some justification, claim that questions of human rights, or the more general topic of 'poverty', fell within their remit. It appears that this source of resistance was related in part to differences of perspective but also to concern that the new ADG was being granted a relatively large share of a very limited total budget. The internal opposition to Sané was sometimes so great that it was questioned whether he would survive, but some thought that his association with former UN Secretary-General Kofi Annan provided a level of protection.

In other international organisations, also, there may have been some sense of competition. UNESCO is certainly new to the field of poverty; and even with regard to human rights there are other organisations that have a well established stake.[19] In a meeting held in Paris during 2005, there was some scepticism among participants from other UN agencies and Human Rights organisations towards UNESCO's initiative and Sané's take on the issue. This came, not least, from those with a legal background. The language of 'violation', many lawyers would claim, moves the issue onto legal terrain, the terrain of justiciability; yet justice systems are neither used to, nor prepared to, handle such a challenge. The main disagreement presented by lawyers is that justiciability is impossible in cases where a particular violator or perpetrator cannot be identified, and thus it is *inaccurate* to talk about violations in such cases. Disagreements also came from economists; treating poverty as a violation of human rights simply does not fit the analytical perspectives, cognitive and policy instruments of economics. But the goal of the project was clearly not to conclude with a definitive philosophical, legal, economic, or any other single answer, but rather to stimulate debate among serious and respected academics and *to promote a political agenda to abolish poverty*.

The project seems now to have become simply one more rights-based approach to poverty, losing much or all of its power to promote a critical view on poverty, foster new debates on duties and responsibilities, and promote innovative actions and responses to poverty. In examining this case, our concern is not to pass judgement on any individuals but to suggest that

UNESCO has in the end stifled a potentially positive debate; and that in doing so revealed its weakness as an institution for providing global moral and intellectual leadership. As we have argued in the historical sections of this chapter, this may be traced largely to changes in member state delegations within UNESCO, and changing global power relations.

Implications of the terms 'violation' and 'abolition'

The language of abolition and violation is substantially different from the terminology used by human rights based approaches to poverty (HRBA).[20] Relating poverty to rights is currently much in vogue; but if such approaches are to be translated into effective policies, there is a need for clarification about the nature of the relation between poverty and human rights, and what responsibilities this may call for. For some, a human rights based approach to poverty may be regarded as consistent with neo-liberal economic approaches that place responsibility for poverty on the poor themselves; or on the national government, ignoring the role of global actors and the international 'rules of the game'. Behind HRB approaches are a multitude of voices, interests and perspectives that draw on very different understandings of rights and of poverty, and of the relations between them. This lack of conceptual clarity permits the widespread use of 'rights' terminology in relation to poverty without this entailing a serious commitment to obligations and responsibilities. The language of rights can be used by development agencies simply as a rhetorical tool that does not challenge the underlying assumptions of the dominant paradigm. Human rights and poverty may end up relating simply as 'ships passing in the night' (Alston and Robinson 2005); parallel discourses which never really confront one another, and thus lead to no substantial change in the way poverty is conceptualised and treated.

To use the terms 'violation' and 'abolition' is significant. Language matters. It structures, or 'frames' the way in which actors envision a particular issue, the descriptions and methodologies developed to conceptualise and map its extent. Language structures the way we think, and hence the way we act. In particular, ethical discourses can have great influence in national and international affairs. Quoting Neta Crawford's *Argument and Change in World Politics* (2002) which reviews five centuries of debates over imperial conquest, slavery and the slave trade, forced labour, colonisation, trusteeship and decolonisation, Gasper argues that such historical analysis

> shows how ethical discourses can gradually structure and restructure pre-analytical feelings and analytical attention and how they can interact with and influence other factors – by the range of comparisons that they make, by the categories and default cases that they introduce and defend, by the ways they reconstitute conceptions of 'interests' and perceptions of constraints.
>
> (Gasper 2007a)

Violation and abolition are ethical and political terms. They are political because they present the issue of poverty as a matter of power relations. To define poverty, or to prevent poverty from being defined in particular ways, is in itself a political act; language and ideas do indeed matter. Thus, to deliberately avoid the term 'abolition' is a tacit recognition of the power of this word, steeped, as it is, in history, and hence marked with a specific set of connotations. The term is, of course, related to the abolition of slavery – now widely accepted as evil and wrong. The term 'abolition' carries with it associations of a political struggle for restoring the dignity of a particular group of human beings. It refers to a set of actions at global, as well as local and national, level – of political resistance and challenging of established power structures. Using the term 'abolition of poverty' reminds us that the abolitionists' fight was not a theoretical debate about terminology, but a political battle to humanise the slaves and to raise awareness and support for their case.

Violation and abolition have an undeniable ethical charge that is difficult to distort or to ignore. These twin terms frame poverty not only as a 'bad' thing, but also as a 'wrong' thing. Even if it is impossible in a particular situation to identify the particular actor or actors who may be involved in the violation of the rights of a particular poor person or a particular group of poor people, reference to a violation of rights takes us beyond the methodological territorialism that dominates poverty research. It transforms poverty into a global as well as a local problem. Even if no one single actor or group may be capable of abolishing poverty, the use of the term abolition implies that the world community as a whole has a responsibility to terminate it. This is in direct contradiction with a widely held view that poverty is the responsibility of the poor, a private responsibility. The language of values is not only 'public', that is, it refers to what human beings do together and to one another, but also an attempt to shape how we feel about a particular issue. The language of values is about structuring our emotional as well as our rational responses (Appiah 2006). The use of the terms violation and abolition can shape the ways in which human beings feel about poverty and the poor; the emotional responses of academics and non-academics alike. An open debate on the strengths and weaknesses of the use of 'violation' and 'abolition' in relation to poverty may lead to constructing alternative futures in different ways. It may substantially affect the way in which expert knowledge on poverty is constructed and thus restructure political action. Every poverty researcher thinks poverty is bad, but not all of them have learned to view poverty as wrong.

One frequent objection to the term 'violation' is on the grounds of non-justiciability. This is commonly argued by lawyers, and shows the power of the legal discourse on poverty and human rights. But human rights need not be seen merely as legal instruments; this ignores their ethical and political content. As we have noted in Chapter 3, we subscribe to a forward looking notion of global responsibility as perhaps the most promising path towards the abolition of poverty. This may entail, as Pogge (2002) has argued, carefully designed and monitored global norms that prevent severe poverty; and international organisations are 'response-able': as they are particularly well placed to act by virtue of the powers that we, the people of the world, have given them.

In contrast to many of the widely used human rights based approaches to poverty (HRBA), the language of violation confronts the coexistence of poverty reduction strategies with the logic and the ethic of the market. The idea also forces self-reflection in affluent societies, in many of which severe poverty is on the increase despite higher average standards of living. The claim that poverty is a violation of some globally recognised set of human rights is difficult to distort and to empty of its moral and political content. It re-politicises the global poverty debate and presents it as a question of global justice. Some may argue that abolition is in fact a weaker term than eradication. Something may be abolished (that is legally prohibited) without necessarily being *eradicated*. That might be the case if a word's only meaning was that given in dictionaries and encyclopedias. But 'abolition' cannot be used without dragging with it the history of slavery and all the moral and ethical problems that it has raised, and continues to raise in modern history. It reminds us of a history of violence and abuse done by human beings to human beings. It reminds us of a history of radical inequalities, of shame. Abolition calls for immediate action, for stopping harm, for intolerance and preventive measures. It transforms the question of poverty into a 'public question'. There are indeed new forms of slavery in the world today, but these do not come from a failure of the abolition of slavery, they can be traced to severe poverty, to the structural conditions that permit the abuse of human beings by other human beings. The phrase 'eradication of poverty', on the other hand, can be part of a technocratic discourse that constructs poverty and the poor in ways that do not necessarily highlight the moral dimensions of poverty and the moral harm done to the poor. The reasons for eradicating poverty can be hidden, and so can the poor as human beings suffering. Abolition, like the term 'violation', puts into one single frame the poor and the non-poor, the privileges of the affluent and the suffering of the vulnerable. The language of violation and abolition is imbued with moral awareness, challenging people's emotions, attitudes, and sense of virtue. Violation of rights calls not only for empathy but for active solidarity; not charity but justice. It puts ethics first (Farmer 2005).

These ethico-political implications of the characterisation of poverty as a violation of human rights are indeed controversial, uncommon, and contestable. But the power of naming social phenomena in particular ways is indeed a political action; and to inhibit such naming is an act of political contestation – as this case study demonstrates.

Concluding remarks

Some might say that Sané confused his role as an activist with that of a bureaucrat in an intergovernmental organisation. But a compelling counter-argument would be that with this approach he is providing the sort of moral and intellectual leadership that was intended to characterise UNESCO. Over half a century ago, as the world recovered from the second devastating war of the century, idealistic men and women came together to create, or revitalise, organisations to secure peace and prosperity for all. The USA, personified in the figure of Eleanor Roosevelt, played a leading role in this endeavour. Artists and intellectuals, too, provided inspiration – not least through UNESCO, whose mandate was, in part, to provide leadership, both moral and intellectual.[21] Whatever the criticisms that may be brought against the project described in this chapter, it must surely be seen as very much in keeping with the early aspirations of the organisation: a bold, challenging call to academics, politicians and UN bureaucrats all over the world to address the issue of extreme poverty in a way that makes it hard to ignore how wrong it is for today's global society to accept severe poverty. And whatever the criticisms that may be levelled against Pierre Sané, the key figure behind the project, he surely exemplifies for many people the figure of the engaged intellectual: provocative in the cause of social change. It is therefore ironic that it is UNESCO itself that found it necessary to smother the project, to discourage debate and intellectual contestation. What can we learn – about UNESCO, and about today's multilateral system more generally – from this small case study?

By comparison with other international organisations, UNESCO is a good example of a multilateral organisation which has little 'clout' but at least a claim to both intellectual and moral authority. As described in Chapter 2, clout, in the multilateral system, derives primarily from the extent of an organisation's budget and technical expertise (especially in the field of economics). UNESCO has a small budget, which has long been under threat from major member states. As regards expertise it does have an established reputation in the fields of education and culture; but if measured in terms of staff numbers this is small by comparison with an agency such as the World Bank.

As regards intellectual and moral authority, many commentators would maintain that UNESCO's has diminished considerably in the last half century; but they might not agree on the reasons. Following the idealistic days of reconstruction after the Second World War, the task of securing peace and prosperity proved difficult; and it immediately became threatened by the divisions of the Cold War – which were particularly damaging for the organisation. One could argue that UNESCO has suffered as a result of changes in the international system as a whole. Over this period, also, the role of intellectuals has been reduced – replaced by some more abstract 'knowledge', of a technical kind. More generally, the ideals that led to the creation of post-war organisations, and motivated the staff of these organisations in the 1950s and 1960s, have been largely replaced by bureaucratic ideals of efficiency and good management – as remarked by Arizpe, and by several other of the numerous authoritative voices recorded by the team of the United Nations Intellectual History Project (UNIHP). And, as noted, the

UNESCO delegations have changed from being composed of individuals from the arts and academia, to being bureaucrats representing governments. In the moral sphere, the place of the intellectual/moral critic – 'the conscience of the world' – has been largely taken over by NGOs – and become more politicised in the process.[22]

UNESCO did not succeed in coping with this adverse environment. As noted in earlier sections, they were subjected to an extreme financial 'squeeze'. They also, perhaps, suffered from competition not only from existing agencies, but new ones which to some extent competed for the 'intellectual' mandate, such as UNRISD and UNU/WIDER. As Arizpe (2002: 29) claims 'this [division of labour between agencies] began breaking down in the 1980s, I believe, as UNESCO was so strongly hit because of some of its policies'.

In the Cold War era, UNESCO was to some extent associated with radical views: if not necessarily pro-communist, at least anti-American. Following the end of the Cold War, the situation has changed – with 'globalisation' the new buzzword. But the new situation still finds many who characterise the USA as the villain. To the extent that moral authority is, in this situation, derived from 'bashing the US' it is hardly surprising that that country reacts negatively.

On the development agenda, it is of course poverty that is back at the top of the list; hence the MDGs, and Kofi Annan's call for action from every UN agency. UNESCO, not being a development organisation in the usual sense of the term, was not well equipped to react. Instead of building on its mandate and comparative advantage – in terms of intellectual and moral leadership – the organisation chose to respond largely by designing projects. Is this a sign that it had moved so far from its initial role that it was no longer capable of building on its earlier strength? Or did it choose not to do so? It is ironic that the very modest project (at least in money terms) which is described in this chapter, that was so clearly in line with its intellectual/moral role, met with so little support – and was indeed actively resisted.

UNESCO is an intergovernmental bureaucracy entrusted with an intellectual and ethical role: the former (bureaucratic) personified in the position of, say, the head of strategic planning, and the latter, in the case of this initiative, Pierre Sané. It is a challenge to navigate between the two very differing imperatives that this implies. It appears that UNESCO, in this instance, chose the more cautious approach. Perhaps this is a wise, or simply pragmatic, response to the current international context. But is it also possible that the ideas and values that were once so important in the UN system, and subsequently declined, are now returning to the global arena? If so, perhaps UNESCO has an opportunity, in the international war against poverty, to play a valuable moral and intellectual role, by continuing to promote an important debate inside and outside the UN system around the concepts of violation and abolition, with all the implications this change in language has, and contribute to a 'real' conceptual shift in global poverty studies.

7   The Inter-American Development Bank
'Social capital, ethics and development'

Introduction

In this chapter we analyse the trajectory, achievements and failures of the Inter-American Development Bank's Initiative on Social Capital, Ethics and Development (the Initiative). Established at the beginning of the millennium, with the support of the Norwegian government and directly under the responsibility of the President's office, this is a particularly clear case of an institutional mechanism inside a multilateral bank specifically focused on introducing the role of ethics in development work. The goal of the Initiative was to 'contribut(e) to the strengthening and deepening of democracy, economic and social growth, and the forging of a participatory, just, and booming Latin America to which all the communities of the region aspire' (IDB website). It took off with the full support of Enrique Iglesias, its charismatic President, who was highly influential not only in the IDB but in the whole region, with a strong commitment to the social aspects of development. The Initiative seemed to be particularly timely, in view of the substantial political changes in the region – with increasing discontent with neo-liberalism and its consequences, and greater openness to debate and alternative ideas.

The Initiative was very visible – with well attended public conferences, the enrolment of key figures such as Amartya Sen as guests at events and activities, the creation of a programme for social responsibility in academia, a digital library and a web portal, and a host of projects and activities aiming to promote social capital, ethical thinking and concern for the poor and marginalised; but by the time of writing, 2008, its practical achievements are few. The new President, Luis Alberto Moreno, is in the process of restructuring the Bank and orienting it towards more private sector and infrastructure funding. Sadly, and ironically, the coordinator of the Initiative, Bernardo Kliksberg, was, in 2007, found guilty of violating the code of ethics and professional conduct of the Inter-American Development Bank. The Initiative's status was of course negatively affected by this, but it was already falling far short of its ambitions, despite the commendable efforts of the remaining staff to salvage its projects and its ideas. A unique opportunity was lost; but it may nevertheless be possible to learn from a critical analysis of the experience. This we seek to provide in the rest of this chapter.

We ourselves were to some extent involved in the Initiative, engaged by the Norwegian Ministry of Foreign Affairs: providing support in organising activities in Norway, and background papers and advice concerning the Initiative. In comparison with the other case studies, this one perhaps poses for us the most serious methodological and ethical challenges of the kind described in Chapter 1.

The IDB in brief

The agreement establishing the Inter-American Development Bank became effective on 30 December 1959. IDB is the oldest and largest regional bank in the world, and according to its website, 'the main source of multilateral financing for economic, social and institutional development in Latin America and the Caribbean' (IDB website). The purpose of the Bank is defined as contributing to the acceleration of the process of economic and social development of the regional developing member countries, both as individual countries and collectively as a region. According to its own definition, 'The Bank assists countries in formulating development policies and provides financing and technical assistance to achieve environmentally sustainable economic growth and increase competitiveness, enhance social equity and fight poverty, modernize the state, and foster free trade and regional integration' (IDB website).

By the end of 2007, the Bank had approved over $156 billion in loans and guarantees to finance projects with investments totalling $353 billion, as well as $2.4 billion in grants and technical cooperation financing; making it slightly more significant than the World Bank in the region when measured in terms of funding. The IDB has forty-seven member countries: twenty-six borrowing member countries in Latin America and the Caribbean and twenty-one lending member countries, including the United States, Canada, Japan, South Korea, sixteen European countries and Israel. The United States has approximately 30 per cent of the voting power, but the twenty-six Latin American and Caribbean borrowing members collectively control 50.02 per cent of the IDB's shares (Argentina and Brazil with 10.75 per cent, followed by Mexico with 6.9 per cent). Other major shareholders are Japan, 5 per cent and Canada, 4 per cent. As in the World Bank, the president has considerable power, in part because decisions are made by consensus. (The Board has never voted down an operation brought before them, and only the US ED has abstained, twice in 2003 [IDB website].) In addition IDB, like the World Bank, receives donor funds via trust funds established for specific topics or areas (such as the one discussed in this case).

Not least because the 'client' countries hold a majority of the shares, the IDB has greater political legitimacy in the region than the World Bank. It is overwhelmingly staffed by people from LAC (Latin America and the Caribbean), and has a long tradition of being the 'banco amigo' (friendly bank) to its borrowing countries, viewed as a 'protector' of the countries and a guiding hand in the integration of Latin America and the Caribbean's markets. On the other hand, its headquarters are located in Washington DC, very close to the White House and other powerful US public and private institutions, and critics of the IDB see this institution as being too close to the United States, its neo-liberal policies and its hegemonic role in the Americas.

IDB is in many ways similar to the World Bank; indeed it shares exactly the same mandate when it comes to being restricted to the economic – narrowly defined.[1] Although not nearly so well known or studied as the WB, internationally, it is well known in Latin America.[2] And, many would say, the culture of the IDB reflects the culture of Latin America, unequal in terms of ethnic representation in its staff (dominated by non-indigenous), with a prevailing 'male' culture, and where personal connections matter a great deal. Several of those interviewed asserted that IDB's economic ideas follow those of the World Bank; and one staff member we interviewed said that 'IDB economists are painfully aware of how their skills are not excellent in the same way as World Bank staff are aware of their excellence as economists.' (But the situation has changed over the years; under Iglesias the organisation established a position of Chief Economist and strengthened its research orientation.) Of course many of the Latin American countries – such as Brazil, Argentina and Chile – are well endowed with very able economists. Hence, although in relation to smaller and poorer countries – such as Nicaragua, Bolivia or small Caribbean islands[3] – the IDB clearly has powerful expertise, it is generally less dominant in relation to its 'clients' than is the case for the WB. But IDB staff also take pride in having a wider range of expertise than economics alone; and in emphasising their collaborative and open relationship of dialogue with their client countries.[4] Furthermore, at least during the era of Iglesias, a major part of the Bank's work has been in the social arena – with a target of 50 per cent to be allocated to social sectors.

In October 2005, Luis Alberto Moreno took over as President of the IDB. Just before taking office, he had served as Colombia's ambassador to the United States for seven years.

> In this post, his most notable achievement was the successful effort to build bipartisan support for passage in the U.S. Congress of 'Plan Colombia,' which consisted of more than $4 billion in military and economic assistance programs for Colombia. He also lobbied hard for negotiations towards a Colombia-U.S. Free Trade Agreement. This made him well known in Washington, D.C. political circles and a clear favorite of the Bush Administration for the IDB presidency.
>
> (Bank Information Center)

This marked a major break with the Iglesias presidency. At the annual meeting in April 2006 Moreno put forward proposals for a realignment and a restructuring of the Bank – under the overarching concept of 'building opportunity for the majority'. The effective implications of this concept are taking time to emerge, but it appears to mark a significant change of direction for the Bank. And the restructuring process has certainly been very radical: all staff losing their posts and having to reapply within the new structure. The initiator of the Initiative has thus been replaced with a very different President.

We believe that to understand the Initiative it is necessary to place it within the historical context of Latin America and the personal context of Enrique Iglesias; and the two are closely interconnected. By comparison with other parts of the 'South', Latin America is characterised by very high degrees of inequality, civil strife and, until recently, repressive authoritarian regimes in many countries. The region has for decades been an arena for political contestation, and radical ideas about development. Iglesias himself has been much influenced by these ideas, and by the injustice of poverty co-existing with great wealth. The political context in Latin America has changed considerably in the last two or three decades, and hence also the room for manoeuvre for himself and the IDB. The initiative may, we suggest, be seen as an attempt to make use of this space to promote ideas that had lain dormant. We shall return to this line of thinking at the end of the chapter. But we begin by critically examining the rise and fall of the Initiative.

The Initiative on Social Capital, Ethics and Development

The President of the IDB, Enrique Iglesias, visited Norway in October 1998. At a seminar at the University of Oslo[5] he gave a keynote lecture entitled 'Ethics and Development' in which he argued that '(e)thics must again become a central consideration in any reflection on daily life in general and development in particular.' Iglesias expressed particular interest in the views of the then Norwegian prime minister, Kjell Magne Bondevik and more specifically the 'Verdikommisjonen' (the Values Commission) which he had established in January 1998.[6] Iglesias used the opportunity of his visit to Norway to present the Initiative and its intellectual rationale as well as asking for economic support to realise it. He clearly stated that the idea originated with his own initiative to rethink the values of development, its goals and means, and to put ethics – broadly defined – in the front seat. If taken seriously, these and other statements Iglesias made would have had a significant impact on development practice inside IDB and in the region.

> Ethics must again become a central consideration in any reflection on daily life in general and development in particular. ... Ethics needs no justification. Values like those already mentioned: equity, respect for life, personal growth and self fulfillment, respect for culture, an affinity for cooperation, are ends in themselves.

Contrary to rather widespread notions that would relegate ethics to the realm of spiritual luxuries that are fundamentally irrelevant to the harsh realities of economics, the fact is that equity, strengthening of human capital and development of social capital are some of the essential underpinnings of genuine and sustained growth.

Ultimately development is a matter of human rights ... We have to make a leap to a new generation of human rights that ensures that every person will have the right to a healthy childhood, a proper education, a solid family. ... In short, today we must vigorously defend the human being's right to development.

He concluded that: 'At the Inter-American Development Bank, I have decided to institute a far-reaching line of action on "Ethics and Development"'.

He found support from the Norwegian Ministry of Foreign Affairs, and in particular the Secretary of State for International Development Olav Kjørven. The Initiative received direct funding from the Norwegian government in 2001, and in 2005 Norway created the Social Capital, Ethics and Development Trust Fund with the sum of US$1.5 million. In 2006 Canada joined the trust fund with US$300,000, and others also followed, including Israel and Japan. In total, the Initiative received about 3 million US dollars in seven years, with Norway remaining the largest funder. In addition to providing a substantial amount of funds, the Norwegian Ministry of Foreign Affairs supported the Initiative through attendance at conferences by Norwegian politicians, embassy officials, researchers and others.[7]

But Iglesias could not be confident of support from other members of the IDB board; not only the USA, but other powerful countries – Argentina, Brazil, Chile and Mexico – might be wary of entering into new and potentially dangerous territory. Whether one sees the Initiative as driven by Iglesias' own desire to promote a social agenda, or his response to a groundswell in the region which others on the IDB Board did not recognise, he was necessarily constrained by the willingness of the Board to give approval.

The Initiative was placed under the direct supervision of the President's Office, coordinated through the Secretary's Office. Bernardo Kliksberg was appointed the General Coordinator. He had already worked for several years at the IDB; and before that, as an economist and academic, he had spent twenty-five years heading a United Nations anti-poverty programme in Latin America, a job which he retained – as chief advisor to the UNDP's Latin America Bureau. Among his publications are: 'The Role of Social and Cultural Capital in the Development Process', and 'Facing the Inequalities of Development: Some lessons from Judaism and Christianity'. In his writing one finds powerful criticism of the extreme inequality in Latin America, combined with an optimistic view of the potential of democratisation and of participation by civil society; also, in places, a rejection of 'a profoundly economistic and reductionistic approach to development' (Kliksberg 2004: 663).

An engaged economist with long-term commitments with religious groups in the region,[8] Kliksberg led the work of the Initiative until 2007 when he was dismissed for violating IDB's code of ethics and professional integrity. His scope for action was limited by the same political constraints from member countries that faced Iglesias; and his strategy may be interpreted as seeking to build on pressure 'from below', within the region, to bring about change. Kliksberg was very active in organising high-profile events, which attracted public and media attention, and in involving key names in his activities, both academics and politicians. Amartya Sen, who was on the board of the Initiative, has been at various times the keynote speaker of the IDB's Ethics Day, an annual symposium organised at IDB's headquarters, together with politicians and other scholars from Latin America and the Caribbean.

The official website of the Initiative sets out in detail its vision, direction and goals.[9] In summary, its aims were:

- to be a catalyst in awakening an interest to propel the themes of ethics, development, and social capital in government, political parties, business entities, trade unions, universities, religious communities, non-governmental organisations and all the organisations that work for the collective wellbeing of the continent's societies.
- A mobilisation on a wide front of joint action in these crucial areas, allows the Initiative to improve the quality of the debate on development, enrich the framework for the adoption of such policies, increase the possibility for actionable agreements, and contribute to the rise of codes and conduct based on desirable ethical criteria by those who are principally responsible for development.
- In short, the Initiative is collectively contributing to the strengthening and deepening of democracy, economic and social growth, and the forging of a participatory, just, and booming Latin America to which all the communities of the region aspire.

Its key areas of work were: social responsibility of public policies; corporate social responsibility; strengthening of volunteerism; citizen participation; empowerment of marginalised communities; and insertion of the concepts of 'ethics and social capital' in university academic programmes.

What the initiative did achieve was a considerable number of events – seminars, fora, etc. – mostly in Latin America, but beginning in December 2000 in Washington DC, with an event on 'Ethics and Development'. Some of the others may be briefly described. The forum in Tegucigalpa, Honduras in 2001 was entitled 'Ethics and Development: The New Challenges'. The meeting in Santiago, Chile, in 2003 – 'Mobilizing Social Capital and Volunteer Action in Latin America' – was attended by over 5,000 people. The Second International Seminar 'Social Capital, Ethics and Sustainable Development' was held in Belo Horizonte, Brazil. The initiative established a network of partners in many countries in the region to collaborate in the organisation of these events, and maintained a very active website which included a digital library; in early 2004, this was the second most popular homepage on the IDB site (Marshall and Keough 2004: 70).

The Initiative came about because of a charismatic leader with the requisite political power – President Enrique Iglesias. Also important was the work of the well connected and energetic coordinator, Bernardo Kliksberg, who was responsible for its implementation. Another important factor was the support – especially in financial terms – of Norway, whose Prime Minister at the time, Kjell Magne Bondevik, came from the Christian Party and was himself an ordained priest with a network of contacts in the religious world. He had a personal commitment to the issue of ethics and development, but also saw that the Initiative might yield valuable high-level contacts in major countries of the region. Another crucial reason why the Initiative 'took off' was what Kliksberg described as Latin America's 'thirst for ethics'[10] and the need to raise awareness about the appalling inequalities in the region, and the immorality of severe poverty amidst riches. One could summarise by saying that in Latin America the time was ripe for such an initiative; and the combination of Iglesias' commitment and Norway's support made it possible to take advantage of this opportunity.

The Initiative succeeded in raising considerable interest among various constituencies in the region. The series of conferences organised by the Initiative (recorded on its website), were often attended by thousands of people, including important scholars and politicians, and were quite well covered in the media. This may be the result of well planned events and powerful supporters (also in economic terms), but undeniably also the result of a real 'thirst for ethics' in the region. Kliksberg's efforts did indeed raise awareness of the ethical challenges involved in development work.

In summary, its success (in Latin America) appears to be due to a very real desire for debate about basic issues of justice in a continent with the highest levels of inequality in the world that had tasted the negative consequences of neo-liberal policies affecting a broad range of social sectors – as, for example, in Argentina. Latin America is a region with a long tradition of social movements, contestation and collective action, but many of those were suppressed or altogether stopped in earlier decades. During the repressive years of the 1970s and 1980s, debate about social justice was in many countries stifled. But alternative development paradigms centred on the relationships between the poor and the non-poor, such as the dependista school, are the fruit of this region's intellectual heritage. The Initiative did provide an opportunity for public fora to debate and discuss questions about 'maldevelopment', as Denis Goulet had called it, although this was often at a rather superficial level.

It should be noted that the primary focus of the Initiative was, initially, in the region; it was largely as a result of pressure from Norway that the objective was introduced of achieving change within the IDB itself. In this respect it was generally unsuccessful. It did not stimulate the interest and involvement of staff, or make a significant impact on the policies and practice of the organisation. Bringing ethics to the centre stage of the daily considerations of a development bank official is not an easy task.[11] The IDB was established with a specific financial purpose: to provide funding for development projects in the region by acting as a financial intermediary in capital markets and channelling concessional funds from donors. As such, it has to relate to many different stakeholders – including donors, investors and investment banks, rating agencies and borrowing governments – not all of whom are accustomed to placing values such as equity and the strengthening of human rights as priorities above economic considerations. Moreover, over the course of the years, the Bank has added a number of other issues to its 'economic' agenda: environmental protection, gender equity, and concern for excluded groups, such as indigenous peoples. In addition, a major emphasis has been placed on improving the development effectiveness of the Bank. Thus, IDB officials already had a 'tall order' of demands – some of them perhaps contradictory.

There are several reasons for the failure – or at best very limited success – of the Initiative. We present them here not necessarily in order of importance. One was the lack of an adequate conceptual base. The Initiative did not draw on the well established work of development ethics, dating back to the groundbreaking work of Denis Goulet. The idea of development as liberation that Denis Goulet built up, inspired by the work of Joseph Louis Lebret and liberation theologians, was by the time of the Initiative an important inspiration for new scholarship in the region, clearly apparent in the work of the well known Mexican philosopher, Enrique Dussel. As we summarised in Chapter 3, liberation theology was also one of the key inspirations for Goulet, and it is surprising, especially considering Kliksberg's religious orientation, that the Initiative did not actively involve the many and world-renowned theologians in the region working on liberation theology and poverty. And despite invoking the name of Amartya Sen, the Initiative did not substantially engage with the capabilities approach and the substantial body of scholarship flowing from the work of Sen. For example, the Initiative had no presence at the annual Human Development and Capability Association (HDCA) meetings.

The second pillar of the Initiative, social capital, also provided little support. The concept, developed by the World Bank, based on the work of the political scientist Robert Putnam, was concerned with the role that social networks can play in enhancing economic performance. This approach has been widely criticised for being unduly economistic – ignoring the well established work of anthropologists and sociologists on the study of social relations, and seeking to apply it in a technocratic form, which serves to exclude the important political dimension of the role of civil society in development and social change (McNeill 2004). In the context of Latin America this is an especially significant weakness.

There appears to have been an unwillingness on the part of the coordinator to connect the Initiative too closely to a political/activist agenda – whether related to liberation theology or to new social movements in the region. The choice of social capital as the second conceptual pillar may be seen as further evidence of this. But the literature on social capital does open for a more 'politicised' use of the term. There is some disagreement among researchers about the extent to which more politically oriented groups such as social movements aimed at a profound transformation of society also are to be considered beneficial for the accumulation of social capital. In the earlier works on the significance of civic associations for the functioning of democracy, Putnam focused partly on their roles in advocacy and the expression of interests of local groups towards the state (Putnam 1993). However, he later became more concerned about the internal functioning of the organisations, and emphasised the importance of groups such as choirs and bowling clubs rather than more political organisations such as unions and social movements, that he argued also could produce divisions in society (Putnam 2000). Yet, recent research points to the importance of social movements and political organisations in explaining the high level of social capital found in some areas (Wollebæk and Selle 2002). Social movements vary very widely in scale and type; and they are often seen as a threat, in political terms. However, many also constitute important 'schools of democracy' and provide important networks for the people involved. These could be regarded as manifestations of social capital – without their being a priori classified as either 'good' or 'bad' social capital. Indeed, increased participation and representation may lead to the establishment of socially inclusive political projects and new channels for social mobility. However, the extent to which they do so depends on the nature of the social movements and civil organisations, the responsiveness and institutional strength of the state to which they place their demands (or eventually take control), and the set of policies available to them (Bull 2006). In order to be useful in the Latin American context, the work on social capital would, we suggest, have had to be defined broadly to include all activities that contribute to enhancing networks between people, social dialogue and understanding.[12] The Initiative could have expanded the notion of social capital by generating scholarly work on the role of social movements in the region and produced work in collaboration with Latin American scholars and activists on the ways in which social movements operate as actors for global social justice in the region. Latin America has been the pioneer of social movement action in the world, and the Initiative could have contributed to its also becoming a leader in new theories and practical approaches in this area. We regard this as a missed opportunity for the Initiative.

In examining the conceptual basis of the Initiative, one may add that the two pillars – ethics and social capital – did not appear to combine in any effective sense. Also, in examining the 'ideas' sustaining the Initiative, we should note the absence of linkages with the then strongly emerging global concerns with human rights and human rights based approaches to development. It is surprising that the Initiative did not engage with this powerful global discourse, the global ethic of our secular age, as we have called it in Chapter 3, and the very strong Latin American tradition which led to the region's active role in promoting the Universal Declaration and the UN charter (Carozza 2003; Helleiner 2007).

The limitations that we have just outlined may, we suggest, be attributed largely to an unwillingness on the part of Kliksberg (and perhaps also Iglesias) to connect the Initiative too closely to a political/activist agenda, whether related to liberation theology or to new social movements in the region. If the 'thirst for ethics' is to be used as a source of energy and inspiration for the rethinking of what is and what ought to be development and the work of a regional multilateral bank, then, we would argue, the coordinator missed a substantial opportunity to use his position and delegated power (as well as funds) to promote such a debate in the region and within the organisation. But it must also be recognised that the IDB is not an ideal base for such an approach. Indeed, another reason why the Initiative had very limited success was resistance (either actual or anticipated) from the countries of Latin America: within the region and, perhaps more importantly, in the Board. The region includes governments spread extremely widely across the political spectrum. The Initiative could not risk entering too manifestly into the realm of politics and ideology, since this might appear threatening to those who actually controlled the organisation.

Another problem confronting the Initiative was that it was very difficult to 'operationalise' in the IDB. As noted above, this was an objective which was important for Norway, but not particularly interesting for the IDB itself (perhaps even including the coordinator). For an organisation such as this, the major purpose, and measure of success, is the implementation of projects and programmes. A new idea – to overstate the case somewhat – is successful only to the extent that it leads to a change in the operations of the organisation which produces better results. But the new idea of 'ethics', as we have also seen in the chapter on the World Bank, does not really fit the approaches, methodologies and epistemologies dominant in multilateral banks.

Certainly we encountered quite negative responses in our interviews with IDB staff about the Initiative, and ethics more generally. There were some who dismissed the suggestion that this was anything new: 'we already do it'. As one of our informants put it,

> IDB cannot have a unique ethical position, there are many different ways to address ethics in development. Furthermore, concerns for ethical dilemmas are already part of our projects and work. ... ethics is already incorporated and people who work with us are already conscious of ethical problems.

Of those who agreed with the implicit importance of ethics in their work, many related this mainly or solely to the question of integrity in public service. Just as in the World Bank, staff related ethics to questions of corruption and transparent public management, which became key issues at IDB at the same time as the Initiative was formed (sometimes expressed in terms of promoting 'the modernisation of the state'). In the words of one of our informants, 'ethics relates to the well functioning of states, the legitimacy of states and the participation of citizens in political processes'. In addition to the common understanding that ethics is more relevant to their work when poverty and inequality are viewed as key goals of development, we found a majority of informants asserting that the main identity of IDB is to be a mediator between government and civil society through the organisation's mandate and its technical expertise. In the words of another: 'civil society is the metric of fairness in our work'. But this raises questions about the Bank's role in relation to government: 'We can never put in doubt the legitimacy of the governments', a senior staff member told us, 'but we can put pressure via our technical work'. Such views are similar to those of staff in the World Bank, but the strong political legitimacy of IDB in the region, the 'banco amigo', was seen by many as a disadvantage in relation to promoting 'technical work' with too much explicit reference to ethical issues of the questions of justice and fairness.[13] To quote one informant,

> The downside of this is – without getting into a detailed analysis of the quality of democracy in the region ... the quality of the decision making in the region is very bad, and our ability to do something about that is very much intertwined in this notion of being in their side. Yes we have legitimacy, yes we get through the door ... but we are constrained in our willingness to push the countries into a direction that may lead to doing things better.

Those who were more positive nevertheless thought that adding concerns for ethics to an already crowded set of requirements for development projects would be like adding 'another ball on the Christmas tree' of development work. Like gender or empowerment or participation, adding ethical issues to development work was perceived by several of the staff interviewed as one more 'obstacle' in their assisting their client countries with economic planning and projects.[14] Others referred to the inclusion of ethics as leading to inefficiency, while others thought it necessary to demonstrate what is the 'value added' of an ethical analysis, vis-à-vis say other perspectives, such as good governance.

Many of these views are similar to those we encountered in the World Bank. Staff in IDB, like those in most global development institutions, tend to perceive the role of ethics not only as 'alien' to their work, but also as a possible intrusion in the political processes of their client countries and thus affecting negatively the institution's political legitimacy. This is of particular importance at IDB, an institution whose identity is primarily defined as being the 'friendly bank', there to consult and to help, not to intrude into a country's own business. The Initiative was never clear as to how its work could be 'operationalised' in the IDB. What, specifically, might the Bank do – in terms of changing its policies, procedures or programmes – in response to the initiative? Here, the contrast with the UNESCO case is relevant, because UNESCO is not a development agency, with projects and programmes; and – unlike the IDB – part of its purpose is precisely to stimulate debate and discussion.

Clearly it is no easy task to 'operationalise' ethics in a multilateral institution such as the IDB; nor was this the major aim of the Initiative at the start. Perhaps more could have been achieved if Iglesias himself had more actively supported this aspect of the Initiative, but what happened in practice was that, within the IDB, the Initiative was some sort of a side event, a 'project' parallel to the work of IDB's main departments but never really integrated, embedded, in the organisational structure.

This was further exacerbated by the marginal position of the coordinator, Bernardo Kliksberg, within the organisation. He was not on the permanent staff of IDB; at the time of his appointment as coordinator he was acting as an external consultant, and he built up this section only with administrative personnel or young temporary staff. Although it had impressive names among its advisors, the Initiative was in practice a very small hierarchical group dominated by Kliksberg. The themes and content of the Initiative were very much determined by him, and did not necessarily fit the needs and opportunities of IDB's organisational culture, thematic areas, and areas of expertise. He failed to create a successful dialogue inside the institution or negotiate for effective implementation and collaboration with specific departments. Indeed, the high-profile and personality-driven activities (like famous keynote speakers in conferences or the personalising of development ethical issues) may even have been counter-productive as regards relations with others in the IDB. Kliksberg and his ethics and development agenda were seen by most of our informants as either irrelevant or at worse, moralising.

After the retirement of Iglesias and the creation of a special trust fund for this theme, the Initiative was moved from its very privileged position at the President's Secretary's Office to one more project under the Sustainable Development Department. Once the new President was clear in his attempt to initiate a total reorganisation of IDB, the Initiative was put under pressure to justify its role within the organisation. Attempts were made to link the role of ethics and social capital with 'development effectiveness'. But, shortly after, Kliksberg was accused of violating the ethics code and professional standards of IDB. The Initiative was hard hit, and attempts of the remaining administrative staff did not have the necessary political support to succeed in promoting the ideas they were trying to feed into the reorganisation of IDB. The Initiative was placed by Moreno under the 'gender and diversity section', one of the departments under Social Development. At the time of writing this chapter, we understand that the Initiative is likely to be 'dissolved' once the funds allocated for 2008 expire.[15] But why and how come did such an initiative come to exist in the first place?

The Initiative in personal and historical context

In brief, our argument in this chapter is that the Initiative emerged in IDB because of a combination of factors: the power of Enrique Iglesias to promote what was an unusual agenda of action for a regional multilateral bank; the efforts of an experienced and motivated networker, Bernardo Kliksberg, whose work we have just outlined; and the moral and material support of a donor country. But we also argue that a very real 'thirst for ethics' in Latin America was crucial. The recent desire for change in the region, which made the Initiative attractive, was manifested in the new political developments in Latin America and rejection of neo-liberal economic adjustment. It is primarily within this context that we can understand the welcome that the Initiative received among many groups. In this section we will therefore seek to place the initiative within the modern historical context of Latin America, and within the personal history of Enrique Iglesias himself – a charismatic figure who was formed and constrained by this context, but also exerted some influence over it, in his various roles. In tracing Iglesias' own career, one may understand something about the place of IDB in the political context of Latin America, as well as why he chose to support the Initiative. We will here draw on the very rich material available from the interview with Iglesias conducted under the United Nations Intellectual History Project (while recognising that we thereby risk exaggerating the importance of Iglesias in our account).

Iglesias was president of IDB for 17 years (1988–2005) and a towering figure in the organisation. From 1972 to 1985 he was Executive Secretary of ECLAC (The United Nations Economic Commission for Latin America and the Caribbean[16]). ECLAC was established by the UN in 1948, and was heavily influenced by the ideas of Raul Prebisch, its executive secretary from 1950 to 1963. According to the organisation itself (ECLAC website), the intellectual trajectory of ECLAC began with the drafting by Prebisch, in 1949 and 1950, of three documents that contained the basic elements that would figure as the great ideological and analytical references for Latin American and Caribbean developmentalists. For ECLAC, the 1950s were the high point of creativity, when the organisation was both daring and influential. Prebisch and intellectual courage are synonymous in Latin America. In terms of being historically appropriate, ECLAC's ideology was well suited to the political projects of several Latin American governments at that time. The notion of 'dependency' was central to ECLAC's perspective and its associated policy prescriptions recommending the protection of local and national markets via, amongst others, policy tools such as the fostering of 'import substitution'. More radical versions of 'dependency' theory than those of ECLAC – linking the 'underdevelopment of the South' with the historical processes of accumulation in the North – were also developed, and these survive today in critical perspectives such as 'world systems theory' defended by Immanuel Wallerstein and others. They remain central in many of the underlying discourses and ideas we see coming from new social movements and critical globalisation studies. But the economic and political crises in the mid-1970s put such radical views very much on the defensive, and in the 1980s 'the main intellectual effort would shift to the historically imposed area of opposition to the adjustment modality required by the creditor banks and IMF'. Prebisch, however, had by then become head of the new organisation, UNCTAD, where he found a different multilateral arena for his views.

Iglesias was, according to his own account, very much influenced by Prebisch. To quote from his introduction to a book on Prebisch: 'He stands astride the region as a giant of thought and action' (Iglesias 2006 : 5), and he was much influenced also by ECLAC:

> I cannot exaggerate ECLAC's impact on my generation. … Under Prebisch's direction, ECLAC became the leading intellectual center of Latin America, dominating intellectual debates throughout the region. … As the founding Secretary General of UNCTAD, Prebisch moved to the global level. … Collectively the principles Prebisch elaborated in UNCTAD came to be known as the New International Economic Order (NIEO).
>
> (Iglesias 2006: 6)

Iglesias assisted Prebisch on an assignment commissioned by the IDB in 1968, culminating in a report, 'The Challenge of Development', published in 1971.

As part of the United Nations Intellectual History Project, Iglesias was interviewed at length by Louis Emmerij, co-Director of the UNIHP study, but also – from 1993 to 1999 – very close to Iglesias, whom he served as special advisor at IDB.[17] Emmerij notes that ECLAC had become very famous in the 1950s. 'It had an economic philosophy. But, when you came in 1972 you came to a kind of transitional period, from the glorious days of ECLAC into a more pacific period. It must have been a difficult period.' (Note: ECLAC was based in Chile.) According to Iglesias, this was indeed 'Very difficult, because one had to survive internally. When the coup d'état happens in Chile, the situation became complicated with a new dimension: Human Rights' (UNIHP, Iglesias, 2001: 43). Emmerij continues:

> [T]he Pinochet government that wanted really to do away with CEPAL. You had to fight on three, four fronts simultaneously. And then, of course, the substantial thing, the old guard of CEPAL, with their model that was getting out of date and resisting new thinking.
>
> (UNIHP, Iglesias, 2001: 45)

'It was difficult', Iglesias answers, and acknowledges that the New International Economic Order (NIEO), had less importance than it deserved, but argues that in the end its ideas permeated ECLAC, for example represented in the figure of Osvaldo Sunkel.

> Prebisch was above all an intellectual, a thinker, with a wonderful eloquence and colloquial style, that I like very much and that I use in my own presentations. ... he was a man of profound convictions formed along his life, who worked on a theme for a long, long time, and moving from one theme to another along the years.
>
> (UNIHP, Iglesias 2001: 47)

Prebisch's legacy is immense, Iglesias claims, and even though he had no confidence in the dynamism and rationality of the private sector, he was not an extremist, his main suspicions were against foreign corporations and foreign investment, a common issue at the time; 'our generation shared those beliefs', Iglesias clearly says.

> I think his main contribution was on economic growth and competition. He is the first one to speak openly about the need to introduce modern technology. He is also the first one to speak about the key role of institutions, even back into the 1950s. Later this will become an element emphasized all over the world.
>
> (UNIHP, Iglesias 2001: 50)

But according to Iglesias, concern with social development was not part of ECLAC in the 1950s. Prebisch does not mention social issues, nor does he mention political aspects in his report; he could not as a United Nations functionary at the time. But Prebisch did open the door to sociologists in ECLAC in the 1960s. 'That was a very important step especially when he introduced José Medina Echevarria, the father of Latin American sociology. In the end, Prebisch's creation of UNCTAD was his way to continue his ideas and thinking' (UNIHP, Iglesias 2001: 51).

Iglesias replaced Prebisch as leader of ECLAC, and, by his own account, attempted to maintain his legacy while adapting to the new winds in the region. According to ECLAC's website:

> The action of the Executive Secretary Enrique Iglesias during the session of the Commission in Lima in 1984 symbolizes the ECLAC position during that period. Iglesias countered the idea with dark and accurate projections of a 'lost decade' for the region – an expression which ECLAC would later use to describe that period. ... The text presented at that meeting ... shows how close the ECLAC position was to the cream of the Latin American heterodoxy which was then debating such questions.

In 1995, Iglesias left ECLAC and was for three years Uruguay's Foreign Minister until being appointed IDB President on 1 April 1988, in which position he remained for seventeen years. He was only the third person to hold this position. The IDB has a history of long-lasting presidents, his predecessors being Felipe Herrera of Chile (1960–71) and Antonio Ortiz Mena of Mexico (1971–88).

When asked by Emmerij what happens when someone moves from a place of independence, such as an academic or a research institute to a political position, Iglesias answers that is very important to respect the need for confronting real problems and to beware of anachronistic criticisms. 'It is not that one has to renounce one's principles, it is that the limits of power and reality are there' (UNIHP, Iglesias 2001: 54).

His successors at the IDB walked a cautious path. To quote ECLA again:

> The ECLAC of the 1990s managed with great dexterity to take up a position between the two extremes. It did not oppose the tide of reforms, but based its judgement on the criterion of the existence of a 'reformist strategy' which could maximize the benefits and minimize shortcomings in the medium and long term.

And,

> In recent years, since the end of the 1990s, ECLAC has brought into relief the profound asymmetries in the global order, showing the way in which the conditions for integration of Latin America and the Caribbean in this order affect the region negatively in productive and financial terms, and cause a significant degree of macroeconomic instability, a low level of economic growth and very adverse social effects.

In brief, during the most challenging period in its history, ECLAC adopted a low profile – or, some would argue, became largely marginalised in policy debate; but as the political/ideological tide turned, it began again to voice some more critical – albeit not very radical – positions. At the IDB, Iglesias was confronted with the same situation. This was a much more powerful organisation than ECLAC, but both its Board members and its policies were anything but radical. Iglesias did not explicitly challenge this conservatism, but followed a 'middle of the road' line, which he sets out quite clearly in the book he wrote in 1992, reviewing the Latin American experience:

> When the emphasis has been solely on the economic aspect, neglecting the equity of the system, the result has been an economy without a society, fueling social conflict and political instability. When efforts have concentrated on resolving social problems spurred by the region's grave economic disequilibria and the ethical demand for social justice, macro-economic equilibria have been neglected; in most cases, the result has been a growth in populism and rampant inflation, stifling economic growth. In these cases, we have had society without economy.
>
> (Iglesias 1992: 143)

But, on the other hand, he did try to emphasise the social aspects of the Bank's work:

> During the Iglesias administration the Bank expanded into nontraditional areas of operations, such as the promotion of governance and transparency, modernization of the state, reduction of violence and crime and prevention and relief from natural disasters. More than 50 percent of the volume of financing was directed at social and poverty reduction programs.[18]

In his interview with Emmerij, Iglesias presents himself as something of a pragmatist. We quote this part of the interview at length, because we think it summarizes both Iglesias' view of the ECLAC ideology as well as giving valuable insights into his ideas today.

'It is very difficult to formulate new universal paradigms ... '

'So you do not believe in them?' Emmerij asks.

> No, because the big paradigms have failed over time, yet we have had what I call 'incremental paradigms' that is learning based in praxis, to take the good and to build upon it. In the globalized world we live in it is very difficult to propose the formulation of a general scheme of things. I do believe in common sense, in pragmatism. We must maintain in sight three great objectives – competition, social justice and the internationalization of economies. In the pursuit of these three objectives we are learning issues that Prebisch did say in his time and that are important contributions of Prebisch intellectual legacy and ECLAC. Prebisch was the first to propose the importance of the relations between centre and periphery; the first that incorporated questions of technology; the first that spoke of interdependence between the national and the international. He did not enter into the social, into the political; he did so at the end of his life in a very theoretical form. But I keep thinking that one must look at things with pragmatism, because reality is cruel. And one has no capacity to 'twist' reality, like the big leaders that push big movements in their time. Only the great (charismatic), can and they are very few. The intellectual must live with the restrictions imposed by reality.
>
> (UNIHP, Iglesias 2001: 55)

Iglesias appears here as admiring personality and charisma, but also defining himself as a pragmatic person – implying that he has kept his ideas but has had to adjust to the restrictions imposed by the realities in Latin America and his own position. Thus, a little later in the interview he says, speaking again of paradigms: 'If it is about maintaining certain central objectives, I agree. I am profoundly convinced of the relevance of the social, around which one can reconcile all the other objectives' (UNIHP, Iglesias 2001: 56).

In the whole interview, Iglesias makes only one reference to ethics. This is in response to Emmerij's remark: 'I heard that the Bank is working on culture?'[19] Iglesias replies: 'It is not easy to defend it. But we have a modest action in the development of culture, and ultimately in ethics and development' (UNIHP, Iglesias 2001: 57).

Iglesias expresses admiration for James Wolfensohn, and also for Camdessus, 'one of my best personal friends' (respectively president of the World Bank and of the International Monetary Fund at the time of the interview). He appears to see Wolfensohn facing a similar challenge to his own: 'Wolfensohn is a man of good intentions. He wants to change the Bank, and has given it a social orientation that is very important; he has opened the doors to a dialogue with civil society. He has a great sensibility for the problems of humanity' (UNIHP, Iglesias 2001: 77).

All in all, Iglesias places himself in the middle ground politically and ideologically. 'I believe that the Washington Consensus was a necessary reaction and a healthy one in order to get out of economic malfunctioning in the 1980s.' And again: '[But] the original paradigm, with its objective of putting the house in order, stability, openness ... was correct' (UNIHP, Iglesias 2001: 79). To this Iglesias adds,

> Now why did austere countries fail? I think we exceeded too much in ideology. Europe knows this very well, one cannot open the financial sector from one day to the other. Stability is a public function, it can be managed by the private sector, but it is a public function nevertheless.
>
> (UNIHP, Iglesias 2001: 79)

Iglesias' personal vision for the IDB is clearly expressed:

> The first priority is the social. Second, is that this is a Bank committed to integration. Integration is a very important ideological force. Third is the modernization of the state. But all these are macro objectives. The Bank was also a pioneer of micro objectives.
>
> (UNIHP, Iglesias 2001: 79)

But Iglesias also expresses his views about the moral and political legitimacy of IDB in a very revealing passage. Emmerij says, 'If you are a loved organisation, you achieve a lot more than if you are merely respected.' To which Iglesias replies

> Exactly. Because from respect one passes to fear; whereas from affection one moves on to cooperation. In that sense, I think that is much better to have a 'banco amigo'. We try to maintain that sense. I always tell my people: the international public servant is a person that generates a certain resistance. A person that is well paid, travels, and has all the facilities of the world.
>
> (UNIHP, Iglesias 2001: 97–98)

'So how was this fight of trying to introduce a part of your soul into the bureaucracy? That is very difficult', suggests Emmerij. 'Yes', replies Iglesias, 'difficult, but there is one thing Luis, that one must also discover; the majority of people are good people' (UNIHP, Iglesias 2001: 98).

In summary, it appears that Iglesias himself occupies a pragmatic, middle ground between two extremes – the radicals of the dependency school and the conservatives of the IMF and World Bank. The image that flows from the interview of the UNIHP is of a man with strong moral convictions: a believer in God, and a man with strong convictions regarding the role of multilateral organisations in representing as well as working for the materialisation of the global common good. In his interview, Iglesias emphasises the role of 'the social' across his long career in national and multilateral institutions; for him, this was crucial for bringing about good development in the region.

Against this background, one can interpret the Ethics and Social Capital Initiative as an attempt by a charismatic, influential and powerful leader to bring about change, and a new ethical perspective on extreme poverty and inequality, in a region of the world where these two issues are blatantly evident. It is significant that this attempt to draw insights from ethics did not come from someone with very politically radical ideas, but one who was simply attempting to 'introduce a part of his soul into the bureaucracy'.[20] Iglesias is a good example of a leader using 'sailor's skills' (Cox 1969) to negotiate in the sometimes very choppy waters of a multilateral organisation. It is all the more regrettable that, for reasons outlined above, the success of the Initiative was so limited.

Concluding remarks

The experience of the Initiative outlined above may be briefly compared to the cases discussed in earlier chapters. The contrast with the UNESCO initiative is perhaps the most stark. The IDB initiative was started by the head of the organisation, a powerful and charismatic man. But it was built on weak conceptual foundations, and avoided risky engagement with politically controversial issues; exactly the opposite of the circumstances in the UNESCO case. A comparison with the World Bank and UNDP is also revealing. The economic expertise of the IDB may be less than that of the World Bank, but its financial clout – in the region – is just as strong. Unlike the World Bank, it was not faced with the need to respond to powerful criticism from NGOs: no '50 Years Is Enough' campaign, so that the Initiative was more of a positive action by a motivated leader than a defensive tactic by an organisation under attack. However, like the UNDP, the IDB has relatively strong legitimacy in the 'client' countries of the region; it is therefore very reluctant to appear to be imposing its views, especially in what could be presented as a controversial area.

8 Conclusion

The extreme and pervasive poverty that exists in the world today is an affront to social justice. It violates fundamental principles of secular and religious beliefs in most if not all societies; and in a globalised world that possesses immense wealth and resources, this is one of the greatest moral challenges facing our generation. But there seem to be both political and practical impediments to the situation being improved. The former is a reluctance on the part of the rich (in both advanced and developing economies) to make any substantial sacrifice; the latter is the inefficacy of the aid system. Unfortunately the latter compounds the former: the willingness of the rich to give is severely reduced by their observation that the funds that are provided through the aid system are not well used. But why is the sheer moral force of the injustice not sufficient to overcome these barriers? What, more specifically, hinders global organisations which are charged with reducing world poverty from making a better job of it?

To adequately describe how outrageous the situation is, two points should be emphasised. The first is to underline the extent of asymmetry that exists in the world in terms of economic well-being; the richest 5 per cent of people receive as much of the world's income as the poorest 80 per cent; and according to Milanovic (2005) the situation has been getting worse.[1] The second is to point out that while the numbers living in extreme poverty are enormous (about 1 billion people on incomes of under one dollar a day), the scale of the required transfer of funds from the rich is very modest – only about 1 per cent of their incomes (Pogge 2008). This is not an excessively high target; indeed, it has already been reached by the Scandinavian countries.[2] To claim that the rich cannot afford the sacrifice is therefore absurd. But experience over several decades of development assistance has shown that even where there is a willingness to provide aid, it is difficult to do this in an effective way. And it appears that a major hindrance to the redistribution of resources is the role played by sovereign states.

The situation is now very different than it was a century ago. At that time, people in rich countries did not, in general, consider that they had a moral responsibility to the poor beyond their borders – but at most towards their own compatriots. Today, many people in rich countries do consider that they have a moral responsibility towards the poor of the world. But in the absence of some sort of global government this is merely rhetorical; there is no effective means of bringing about global justice.

The existence of sovereign states acts as an impediment to effective remedial action, because while rich countries rail against the inequality within poor countries, the governments of poor countries can respond by railing against the inequality between rich and poor countries. A sort of moral stalemate is reached. (To make things more complicated, global elites in the South and the North align their interests, protecting the 'system' at the expense of the poor.)

As noted in Chapter 2, under the 'grand bargain' of the post-war international economic system of 'embedded liberalism', 'societies were asked to embrace the change and dislocation attending international liberalization, but the state promised to cushion those effects by means of its newly acquired domestic economic and social policy roles' (Ruggie 1997: 5). But this system manifestly fails; the poorest nations of the world have become increasingly ill-equipped to 'cushion these effects'.

In the continuing conversation between rich and poor countries, one observes a continuous 'passing of the buck', in moral terms: rich countries are accused of imposing international rules of the game that favour their own interests, while poor countries are accused of incompetence and corruption in the management of their affairs. In order to break out of this impasse, we argue, it is necessary to think through the implications of accepting a cosmopolitan world order; to accept the consequences of all people being 'citizens of the world' in a moral, if not a political sense.

A major claim that we have made in this book is that the existing multilateral development institutions could play a central role in making this cosmopolitan world order a reality. So far, however, they are falling far short of the mark. In this book, we have examined what some selected multilateral agencies are saying and doing in the face of this situation – and the gap between word and action.

It is revealing here to refer to the controversial initiative examined in Chapter 6 – the 'Poverty as a Violation of Human Rights' project of UNESCO. The initiative was resisted by powerful interests that sought to stifle it. Why are such ideas regarded as so dangerous? And what does such an example tell us about the multilateral system itself?

One conclusion from our case studies is that staff of international organisations are often more radical than are the organisations themselves; more willing, or even eager, to reveal and seek to counter what they see as global injustice. They can, and often do, achieve something by operating by stealth – 'under the radar'. But could more progress be made if ethical debate was actively encouraged within these institutions? A major contribution that could be made by ethical analysis and the language of human rights is to provide the basis for an alternative knowledge for development centred on the equal moral worth and dignity of all human beings, thereby also influencing the goals and policies of multilateral institutions. Ethicists could interact with other experts in the same way that experts in medical ethics work with medical doctors; and a human rights approach could lead to fundamental changes in the ways multilateral agencies see their role, their expertise and their responsibilities – and hence in the ways in which they use their power.

In international organisations, and bureaucracies in general, ideas are meant to bring enhanced intellectual understanding. But we would argue that ideas can also motivate; ideas can be powerful if they link up to fundamental ethical concerns. The language of human rights and global justice promises much in this regard; but our case studies cast a damper on such hopes. The language of responsibility seems to be absent – bypassed, or simply avoided. This book arises in part out of a frustration with this experience; with the failure of the rhetoric of global justice surrounding the Millennium Goals and the mainstreaming of human rights in the UN system to be matched by requisite action. But this frustration is shared by many who work in these international organisations, and one can hope that it will encourage them to challenge rather than accept the unspoken, unwritten constraints that so powerfully limit their freedom of thought and action. For that reason, although we are quite critical of the organisations we have examined, we are heartened by the views expressed by many of the staff that we have spoken to in connection with our study. If global justice is to be achieved, it will ultimately be as the result of people such as these; and despite, perhaps, the governments that created and now sustain the global organisations in which they work.

Notes

1 Introduction

1 Not charity; to quote Mary Wollstonecraft's *A Vindication of the Rights of Woman*: 'It is justice, not charity, that is wanting in the world.'

2 It is true that, in practice, it is often not the poor who benefit from foreign aid; and the taxpayers in rich countries are not all rich – though all are rich relative to the vast majority in poor countries. But this does not affect the main argument.

3 It is also the case that direct transfers from rich to poor, on a person-to-person basis, are possible, and they do take place to some extent; but the fact remains that in order for rich people to give to poor people some system has to be in place. (We are here ignoring remittances, from poor migrants working in rich countries, the amount of which is in fact very large.)

4 A notable case is that of the anthropologist David Mosse (2005), whose book *Cultivating Development: An Ethnography of Aid Policy and Practice* was based on his experience working on a British (DfID) aid project in India. He was heavily criticised by some of those working on the same project, but, following an open discussion, was supported by the ethics committee of the Royal Anthropological Society.

5 We should make it clear that the views expressed in this book in no way reflect those of the Norwegian Ministry of Foreign Affairs.

2 International organisations and the challenge of global poverty

1 To quote Lourdes Arizpe, formerly assistant director-general in UNESCO:

> Someone once said that the United Nations is a dream managed by bureaucrats. I would correct that by saying that it has become a bureaucracy managed by dreamers. Certainly you have to be a dreamer to work in the United Nations with conviction. It is only if you have this sense of mission that you can withstand the constant battering by governments who are afraid that the United Nations will become a world government.
>
> (UNIHP, Arizpe 2002: 44)

2 For example, Barnett and Finnemore, whom we quote below. They also refer to 'moral standing' (Barnett and Finnemore 2004: 20), and 'moral claims' (Barnett and Finnemore 2004: 18)

3 Hall asserts that: 'Moral authority acquires utility as a power resource when it become socially embedded in a system of actors whose social identities and interests impel them to recognize it as a power resource' (Hall 1997: 594).

4 Associated with writers such as E. H. Carr, Kenneth Waltz and Hedley Bull.
5 Represented by theorists such as Alexander Wendt (1999), Stephen Gill, Robert Cox and Thomas Risse.
6 This section draws on Bull and McNeill (2007).
7 For example, Cox (1983), while agreeing with much of Ruggie's argument, takes a more critical view of the new world order, and the role of the multilateral organisations.
8 Nye, with his concept of 'soft power', is a rare example. He notes:

> though it is true that America's size creates a necessity to lead and makes it a target for resentment as well as admiration, both the substance and style of our foreign policy can make a difference to our image of legitimacy, and thus our soft power.
>
> (Nye 2004: 68)

9 The distinction between power, legitimacy and authority is rather blurred in our presentation here; and, we would claim, in Barnett and Finnemore also. (They certainly concede in the work cited that the distinction is somewhat unclear.) Although their categories match quite closely those that we have identified, it may be important to note that they employ them in order to examine the *degree of autonomy* of international organisations (Barnett and Finnemore 2004: 25).
10 Risse distinguishes between different forms of legitimacy: 'output legitimacy' (which we suggest roughly corresponds to substantive legitimacy); and 'input legitimacy' (which relates more to procedural legitimacy). Regarding the latter, he distinguishes between external accountability (to stakeholders) and internal accountability (to owners).
11 Hall chooses the term 'moral authority' following Durkheim. He refers to Durkheim's *Sociology and Philosophy* (1974: 45). He does not discuss this choice at any length, simply conceding that it is 'more difficult to specify' (Hall 1997: 595).
12 Moral authority is emphasised as a source of legitimacy of non-governmental organisations in global politics (Hall and Biersteker 2002). Their emancipatory and normatively progressive social agendas, and their ostensible objectivity or neutrality as non-state actors, it is claimed, make them legitimate participants in global governance in spite of their having weak formal authority. Such a view of NGOs is, however, highly contested (e.g. Scholte 2004).
13 This is a slightly more 'moral' interpretation than Barnett and Finnemore's (2004) 'representing the world community's interest as opposed to national interests'.
14 The IMF is one of the organisations studied in the book by Barnett and Finnemore. Concerning Amnesty International, an excellent recent account may be found in Hopgood, S. (2006) *Keepers of the Flame: Understanding Amnesty International*.
15 In recent years, and especially after the financial crises of the late 1990s, the expertise of IMF staff has been seriously called into question. But it still retains power by virtue of its reputation, and the formal qualifications of its staff.
16 The IMF's mandate is to ensure the smooth running of the international finance system. Some believe that it thereby reduces poverty, others the reverse; but poverty reduction is not its stated purpose.
17 Ref. debate in the World Bank in the early 1990s on 'structural adjustment and good governance'.
18 This is not to ignore claims by its leadership, including Paul Wolfowitz, quoted above. For further detail see McNeill 2007b.
19 Nye refers to what he calls the 'fungibility' of different sources of power.

> Power resources are not as fungible as money. ... Converting resources into realized power in the sense of obtaining desired outcomes requires well-designed

strategies and skillful leadership. ... But it is equally important to understand what game you are playing. Which resources provide the best basis for power behaviour in a particular context?

(Nye 2004: 3)

And 'The agenda of world politics has become like a three-dimensional chess game in which one can win only by playing vertically as well as horizontally': military and economic power are on the top board, while 'on the bottom board ... power is widely distributed ... In the long term ... obtaining favourable outcomes on the bottom transnational board often requires the use of soft power assets' (Nye 2004: 5).

20 They can be subject to criticism also from 'their own'. See, for example, the recent review of the World Bank's economic research by an independent group (Banerjee *et al.* 2006).

21 This issue arose frequently in the interviews we conducted with senior UNDP staff, debating the differences between neutrality, objectivity, impartiality, etc.

22 We are grateful to Rosalind Eyben, former social development adviser to DfID, for this observation.

23 We refer particularly to the United Nations Commission on Human Rights, which clearly has the primary mandate within this field. And one may also mention that when it comes to projects and activities on the ground, other UN agencies, most notably UNICEF, are better placed to put human rights-based approaches into practice.

3 Ethics, human rights and global justice

1 See McNeill 1981; Martinussen and Engberg-Pedersen 2003; Riddel 2007.

2 Criticisms of the limitations of Rawls' justice as fairness, and arguments for a 'global scope', evolve later, in the 1990s, and acquire influence through the work of Thomas Pogge.

3 See Aiken and LaFollete (1995).

4 'The Project of International Development: Where Did It Come From?', unpublished paper, Helleiner (2007).

5 Helleiner notes also the support from India, and from Chiang Kai-shek: 'Hardly surprising since his mentor, Sun Yat-sen, was one of the first policy-makers ever to press for the project of "international development" (Helleiner 2007: 22).

6 From India, Gandhi has already been mentioned. From North Africa, Franz Fanon's classic *The Wretched of the Earth* (1961), is not only an attempt to wrestle with the marginalisation of politically suppressed peoples during the colonial era, but also a reflection of the power relations entailed by the project of development and development aid that emerged after World War II. Fanon addresses the dominance and greed of emerging African upper classes, arguing that they benefited from a development project which perpetuated imperialism disguised as nation-building while ignoring the pleas and needs of the poor, who constituted the majority.

7 More radical scholars from Latin America include Enso Falleto, Fernando Henrique Cardoso and Andre Gunder Frank.

8 Together with Hans Singer, Prebisch is famous for the hypothesis of declining international terms of trade for primary producing countries.

9 This was also seen in the field of pedagogy, primarily represented by the work of Brazilian Paulo Freire.

10 'If one asks why Paul VI should set out to subvert "sound Catholic social doctrine", Novak's answer is that Paul brought together to write it "intellectuals who specialized in Third World Development. ... Louis Lebret, Barbara Ward and George Jarlot"' (Hebblethwaite 1994: 484).

11 Unfortunately much of the work by Lebret has never been translated into English, and most secondary literature on his life, work and legacy is in French and Spanish.

12 In addition, Lebret produced valuable empirical work in the region and developed methodological tools to apply his ideas to the real world. For example, he developed an innovative methodology to establish the needs of people living in favelas in Rio de Janeiro and directed the first ever survey among marginalised groups of housing conditions in Brazil (Valladares 2005).

13 He is also the forerunner of the more contemporary notion of 'relational poverty' (Mosse 2007). He warned that poor and marginalised groups, not only in poor countries but also elsewhere in the world, are unlikely to catch up with the more fortunate.

14 Goulet's legacy includes also a parallel of alternative economics inspiring the work of those also following the path of Louis-Joseph Lebret bringing explicitly religious values and ethics to the discipline of economics. According to Charles Wilber,

> The issue of ethical value judgments in economics is at least as old as the John Neville Keynes argument [father of John Maynard Keynes] which divided economics into three areas: positive (economic theory), normative (welfare economics), and practical (economic policy). The first deals with 'what is', the second with 'what ought to be', and the third with how to get from one to the other. Although the majority of economists admit that ethical values permeate welfare economics and economic policy, they proceed with some confidence in the belief that their work in pure and applied economic theory is ethically neutral. Methodologists studying the question are more cautious.
>
> (www.nd.edu/~cwilber/pub/recent/ethichbk.html [accessed 10 June 2008])

15 We take the phrase from Des Gasper's book *The Ethics of Development: From Economism to Human Development* (Gasper 2004).

16 There is by now an extensive bibliography building on the capabilities approach. The HD-CA maintains an updated list of publications.

17 Kung's first publication on these issues does not use the term global ethic, but rather world ethic, and most importantly for our later analysis, the emphasis is on global responsibilities. See Kung (1991).

18 Centre for Global Ethics, University of Birmingham, www.globalethics.bham.ac.uk/aboutglobalethics.shtml (accessed 15 June 2008). This centre also pioneered a new journal, *Journal of Global Ethics*.

19 www.luiss.it/ricerca/centri/ethics/index.html (accessed 25 July 2008). Centre of Global Ethics and Politics at LUISS University, Rome, Italy.

20 Centre for Value Inquiry, University of Ghent, Belgium, www.cevi-globalethics.be/index.php?LAN = E

21 The full title of Mary Wollstonecraft's pioneer work is *A Vindication of the Rights of Woman: With Strictures on Political and Moral Subjects* (1792).

22 http://www2.ohchr.org/english/law/millennium.htm (accessed 25 July 2008).

23 See Patomaki 2006.

24 Pogge's more recent work centres on the elaboration of practical schemes and global reforms that may help solve several of the urgent problems associated with severe poverty. Pogge is also engaged in doing extensive editing work soliciting and compiling new scholarly work to promote research on global justice (Barry and Pogge 2005; Pogge and Føllesdal 2005; see also Caney 2005; Wenar 2006). Of importance for our case study is Pogge's work for UNESCO (see Chapter 6).

25 In this section we quote extensively the work of the late Iris Marion Young in her article 'Responsibility and Global Labor Justice' (Young 2004).

26 'Structural injustice occurs as a consequence of many individuals and institutions acting in pursuit of their particular goals and interests, within given institutional rules and accepted norms. All the persons who participate by their actions in the ongoing schemes of cooperation that constitute these structures are responsible for them, in the sense that they are part of the process that causes them. They are not responsible, however, in the sense of having directed the process or intended its outcomes.'

27 'This phenomenology of agency and the conception of responsibility it supports, Scheffler argues, does not correspond well to the issues that face moral agents because of the density of communication, economic exchange, technological effects, migration, and political interaction among the world's people. Because the common sense conception of responsibility, which corresponds in significant ways to what I call the liability model, has little to say in relation to such massive global issues, Scheffler suggests, we are in danger of losing a sense of individuals as bearers of responsibility altogether' (Young 2006: 374).

4   UNDP: the human development paradigm

1 It is an interesting curiosity that the same person, Bruce Ross-Larson, has been editor of both WDRs and HDRs; but this is certainly not to suggest that this in any way explains any similarity in content.

2 'Independent studies have hitherto paid relatively little attention to UNDP and the debate on its reform. Apart from showing some interest in the Human Development Report, most donor countries, research institutes and groups engaged in the debate on development policy have failed to consider UNDP in any depth' (Klingebiel 1999: 12).

3 The report was to assess the capacity of the United Nations system to handle the resources made available by the UNDP first, at their present level and second, if doubled over the next five years. The study originated with the UNDP's Inter-Agency Consultative Board.

4 Annual report 2007, available at www.undp.org/publications/annualreport2007/resources.shtml (accessed 25 July 2008).

5 Co-directors Louis Emmerij, Richard Jolly and Thomas G. Weiss. See: www.unhistory.org (accessed 25 July 2008).

6 Inge Kaul was director of the Office of Development Studies from 1995 until 2005, and subsequently, until her retirement, a special policy advisor.

7 Kaul *et al.* (1999, 2003); Kaul and Conceicao (2006).

8 www.earthsummit2002.org/es/issues/GPG/gpg.pdf (accessed 25 July 2008).

9 The BDP, we were informed, is 'owned by the Japanese'. (Ref. also Murphy's account referred to above.) Some believe the work on global public goods might more naturally have been located here.

10 This section draws heavily on McNeill (2007a).

11 The first (written) explicit mention of 'human development' in this process was apparently in 1986, in a publication co-edited by ul Haq's wife, Kirdar (Haq and Kirdar 1986) based on the Islamabad North–South Roundtable in September 1985 (St. Clair 2004).

12 Jolly was Principal Coordinator of HDR for several years from 1996, and played a key role in earlier very relevant activities: in the RwG debate (while at IDS Sussex), and at UNICEF.

13 The report, *Adjustment with a Human Face*, edited by G. Cornia, R. Jolly, and F. Stewart, was published in 1987.

14 For further elaboration of the 'economic-technocratic nexus' see Bøås and McNeill (2004).

15 Cf. 'Like all *Human Development Reports* this is an independent study ... not a statement of United Nations or UNDP policy. *However*, by taking up an issue often neglected by development economists ... it presents important arguments for UNDP and its partners' (UNDP 2004) (emphasis added).
And UNDP now refers to this – for example in the Annual Report 2006 – as its 'flagship report'.

16 To quote its founder:

> The impact of the *Human Development Report* on the global policy dialogue has exceeded expectations. More than 100,000 copies of the report now circulate in 13 languages. ... This response is rather unusual for a report from the UN system.
>
> (Haq 1995: 43)

In addition to the HDR, nearly 500 National Human Development Reports have been produced. In his history of UNDP, Craig Murphy notes that on 29 November 2005, the Google search engine found 2 million pages that mention at least one Human Development Report – an indicator of its extraordinary success. (Of these, 108,000 were on the UNDP site, and 82,000 on the World Bank site.) In recent years, special efforts have been made – with some success – to attract more attention in countries in the South.

17 It may be relevant to record that Sen wrote *Development as Freedom* at the invitation of the World Bank.

18 'His [Malloch Brown's] efforts included a major push to expand UN support to developing countries in areas such as democratic governance, a new advocacy dimension as reflected in pioneering publications including the Arab Human Development Reports, and strengthened UNDP operational leadership in natural disasters and post-conflict situations' (www.undp.org/about/mmb-bio.shtml [accessed 25 July 2008]).

19 www.rbf.org/resources/resources_show.htm?doc_id = 502803 (accessed 25 July 2008). Rockefeller Bros Fund.

20 http://content.undp.org/go/newsroom/2007/september/dervis-statement-executiveb oard-20070911.en?categoryID = 593043&lang = en (accessed 25 July 2008).

21 Earlier based in Oslo, Norway, but recently moved to headquarters in New York.

22 We refer particularly to the United Nations Commission on Human Rights, which clearly has the primary mandate within this field. And one may also mention that when it comes to projects and activities on the ground, other UN agencies, most notably UNICEF, are better placed to 'put human rights based approaches into practice'.

23 Statement by Kemal Derviş, Administrator of the United Nations Development Programme on the occasion of the second regular session of the UNDP/UNFPA executive board, 10 September 2007.

24 Statement by Ad Melkert, Associate Administrator, United Nations Development Programme, on item 4: UNDP Strategic Plan, 2008–11. Executive Board of UNDP/UNFPA, annual session, 19 June 2007, New York.

5   The World Bank: the internal dynamics of a complex organisation

1 We make references to some of this work in this chapter, but we do not provide an extensive bibliography of work on the World Bank; our focus is mainly on the issue of expertise.

2 See: http://web.worldbank.org/WBSITE/EXTERNAL/EXTABOUTUS/PARTNE RS/EXTRAD/0,contentMDK:20298492~pagePK:64168445~piPK:64168309~the SitePK:551955,00.html (accessed 25 July 2008).

3 The WDR 2000/1 'Attacking Poverty' is used worldwide as a key reference on poverty studies; and the World Bank Institute (WBI) organises courses in client countries teaching the ideas of WDR 2000/1.
4 www.gdnet.org/ (accessed 25 July 2008).
5 www.capacity.undp.org/index.cfm?module = Networks&page = Network&Networ kID = 8 (accessed 25 July 2008).
6 See Circi (2006).
7 www.saprin.org/SAPRIN_Findings.pdf
8 Announced in 2000 and considered by the Board in 2004, the review was undertaken 'in response to concerns expressed by a variety of stakeholders, primarily environmental and human rights organizations'. www.ifc.org/eir (accessed 25 July 2008).
9 Arising out of discussions between World Bank and the IUCN (World Conservation Union) this was an independent international commission, established in May 1998, which presented its findings on 16 November 2000. www.dams.org/ (accessed 25 July 2008).
10 A multi-country research study undertaken to inform the bank's Activities and the *World Development Report 2000/01: Attacking Poverty.*
11 This is not to say that the staff is uninterested in discussion of ethical issues. The Bank has for many years had an informal gathering called the 'Friday morning group' where a few staff members meet to discuss issues relevant to values and ethics in development. www.dgroups.org/groups/worldbank/FMG/index.cfm? CookieTested = TRUE (accessed 25 July 2008).
12 Formal title: Advisor to the Managing Directors of the World Bank and the Institutional Focal Point on Human Rights.
13 Writing about his experience in this position, Sfeir-Younis describes how he developed a new framework for understanding human rights and responsibilities, but experienced 'institutional resistance'. www.kosmosjournal.org/kjo/backissue/ f2005/peace-abundance.shtml (accessed 25 July 2008).
14 For a useful analysis of WDRs over the years, see Mawdsley and Rigg 2002, 2003.
15 The Human Development Report (see Chapter 4) is often seen as its major rival for international attention.
16 McNeill's first involvement was in fact his attendance at a meeting in Oslo in summer 2004, at which the initial outline of the report was presented in the Ministry of Foreign Affairs.
17 The World Bank website recorded summaries of the numerous consultations held during the preparation of the WDR. The outline of the report was completed in mid-2004, and the draft of the report in March 2005. http://econ.worldbank.org/ WBSITE/EXTERNAL/EXTDEC/EXTRESEARCH/EXTWDRS/EXTWDR200 6/0,contentMDK:20232854~menuPK:477653~pagePK:64167689~piPK:6416767 3~theSitePK:477642,00.html (accessed 25 July 2008).
18 This section draws heavily on 'Equity and Development: Is There a Place for Ethics?', a paper presented at the World Bank Legal Forum in December 2005, and subsequently published by the World Bank (McNeill 2007b).
19 The following quote from former director of the Bank's Economic Research Group, Paul Collier is also relevant: 'Economists are trained to high standards of precision in thought, especially causal arguments. The mindset which gives you econometrics is the mental hygiene of disentangling causation' (Bøås and McNeill 2004: 116).
20 Sometimes, changes in the structure of the report may also reveal tensions between differing positions. In 2000/2001 there was much debate about the order in which chapters were presented – apparently of sufficient importance for this to be a factor in the resignation of the author.

21 The very definition of the term equity, which was adopted in the report at an early stage, represents a compromise, although not necessarily an incoherent position. The report states that 'By equity we mean that individuals should have equal opportunities to pursue a life of their choosing and be spared from extreme deprivation in outcomes' (p. 2). This is a concept of equity as 'equal opportunity', but not irrespective of final outcome.

22 The *Journal of Experimental Economics*, established as recently as 1998, states that it: 'uses experimental methods to evaluate theoretical predictions of economic behaviour'.

23 An online discussion of the report's outline, available in French, English and Spanish, was held from 12 October to 19 November 2004. The discussion on this point was summarised as follows:

> 1. Should this WDR address intrinsic reasons why people care about various inequalities, or restrict its attention to instrumental reasons, such as their effect on the growth elasticity of poverty reduction?
>
> Participants indicated that inequalities matter both because they violate basic human rights and because they hinder growth and poverty reduction and agreed that the WDR should address both reasons. ...

24 In the outline of the report, produced at an earlier stage, these two are given equal weight. 'Inequalities of opportunities or of outcomes may matter for both intrinsic and instrumental reasons' (p. 10).

25 In his review essay, Roemer (2006), usually quite a critical commentator, commends the WDR:

> The Report marks a major step forward in the discussion of poverty and development. Economists have, far too frequently, lauded themselves on their discipline's being 'value free', and eschewed any justice talk in favor of efficiency talk. This is, I believe, a mistake, and the publication in question makes a strong case against that narrow view.

We suggest, however, that the step taken by the Bank could have been a much bigger 'leap.'

26 de Ferranti *et al.* (2004). http://www-wds.worldbank.org/external/default/main? pagePK = 64193027&piPK = 64187937&theSitePK = 523679&menuPK = 64187510&searchMenuPK = 64187283&theSitePK = 523679&entityID = 000160016_20040622141728&searchMenuPK = 64187283&theSitePK = 523679 (accessed 25 July 2008).

27 Of these, two (Sir Tony Atkinson at Oxford and Angus Deaton, now President of the American Economic Association, at Princeton) are very highly reputed academic economists; one (Martin Ravallion) is among the most senior research economists in the Bank (currently director of the Development Research Group), one (Naila Kabeer) is a professor at the Institute of Development Studies, Sussex, and describes herself as a social economist.

28 DEC 'seeks to increase understanding of development policies and programs by providing intellectual leadership and analytical services to the bank and the development community'. http://econ.worldbank.org/WBSITE/EXTERNAL/EXTDEC/0,contentMDK:202 79993~menuPK:477172~pagePK:64165401~piPK:64165026~theSitePK:469372,0 0.html (accessed 25 July 2008).

29 The article does not deal explicitly with the WDR, but gives clear evidence, based on numerous interviews, of the processes by which dissonant voices are silenced –

being characterised as 'idiosyncratic', 'iconoclastic' or 'disaffected' (p. 407). Ellerman, one of the few internal critics, is quoted as referring to pressures for 'bureaucratic conformity' from the 'thought police to the black sheep in the organization who are "not on message" (p. 407). Stern, former Chief Economist, expresses the situation in DEC more cautiously: 'there is the strong hierarchy and an atmosphere much more deferential than would be found in universities' (Stern and Ferreira 1997: 594).

30 An increasingly high proportion of such ministers were trained in economics in the US or the UK, and/or attended short courses organised by the World Bank Institute.

31 As noted, it has become practice that drafts of the report are made available to a wider audience for comment at various stages during its preparation. For the 2000/1 report this was a very major exercise, with posting on the internet and considerable interaction with NGOs and other commentators. Perhaps because of the problems that arose with this WDR 2000/1, a rather less demanding approach has been followed subsequently.

32 There are political scientists among Bank staff, but usually with close links to economics (rational choice theory, new institutional economics, etc., as was evident in the 1990s debate about 'structural adjustment and good governance'). In this regard, it is interesting that in their sources of evidence for equity, the WDR 2006 editorial team did not make linkages with the social democratic theories and traditions in Scandinavia and the work of sociologists such as Stein Rokkan or, more recently, Stein Kuhnle (Kuhnle *et al.* 2003).

33 When what are seen as radical ideas are promoted in an organisation such as the World Bank, it is a matter of fine judgement as to how much one can 'get away with'. The resulting self-censorship can be as effective as, and in some ways more pernicious than, censorship by others.

34 This would be the case if human rights were included as part of the bank's safeguard policy. Middle-income countries were already concerned at the stringency of the bank's environmental requirements.

35 He was interested in promoting the 'rule of law', which could easily become confused with 'governance' and by extension human rights. This is a good example of the slippery nature of the terms used, and the danger that political support for an agenda may be gained at the expense of savagely distorting that agenda.

36 Ref. her article in the World Bank Institute's magazine *Development Outreach*, drafted in the time of Dañino. http://www1.worldbank.org/devoutreach/october0 6/article.asp?id = 386 (accessed 25 July 2008).

37 McNeill chaired the Reference Group for this fund from 2002 to 2008.

38 Sfeir-Younis notes that the text expresses his own opinions, and not those of the bank as an institution.

39 As noted, the Social Department saw the human rights agenda as an opportunity, but potentially also risky. Among those who emphasise the importance of human rights, there is still some discussion as to whether this is qualitatively different or whether it can best be integrated with concepts that have already been advanced in recent years: empowerment and participation, or a more expansive use of Sen's capabilities approach. While the Social Development Strategy argues, for example, that accountability is a very important element, this does not necessarily mean that this can or should be operationalised through explicit reference to human rights.

40 Ref. the work of Daniel Kaufmann, from the World Bank Institute, making the economic case for good governance, including the series of 'Governance Matters' reports, e.g. Kaufmann *et al.* (2007).

6   UNESCO: 'poverty as a violation of human rights'

1 See Special Rapporteur on Human Rights and Extreme Poverty Leandro Despouy's final report (E/CN.4/Sub.2/1996/13).
2 This section draws heavily on Bull and McNeill (2007)
3 Assistant Secretary of State for International Organizations Gregory Newell, 'The United States and the Withdrawal from UNESCO', *Time*, 9 January 1984, p. 17.
4 Its total budget has been between US$550 and 600 million biannually, of which the USA now contributes roughly one tenth.
5 SHS emphasises this role, e.g. 'UNESCO's ethical and intellectual mandate and its role in standard setting and policy promotion, places it in a key position to contribute to achieving the first of the United Nations' Millennium Development Goals, that of eradicating poverty, especially extreme poverty and hunger' (http://portal.unesco.org/shs/en/ev.php-URL_ID = 1396&URL_DO = DO_TOPIC&URL_SECTION = 201.html (accessed 25 July 2008). But so too does the director-general. E.g. Message of 21 November 2002. Koichiro Matsuura: 'Many people ask: why philosophy at UNESCO? My reply is: how could UNESCO, as the intellectual and ethical arm of the United Nations, function without promoting philosophical reflection as the basis for democracy, human rights and a just society?' (*SHS Newsletter* no. 1: p. 14).
6 See for example the sub-commission on the ethics of the information society (COMEST) http://portal.unesco.org/shs/en/ev.php-URL_ID = 1957&URL_DO = DO_TOPIC&URL_SECTION = 201.html (accessed 25 July 2008).
7 http://unesdoc.unesco.org/images/0014/001415/141598E.pdf (accessed 25 July 2008).
8 A description of the research project: 'Ethical and Human Rights Dimensions of Poverty: Towards a New Paradigm in the Fight Against Poverty' was accessed in 2004. Today it is no longer available at UNESCO's website. A French version with links to some of the papers presented in the workshops organised by this team can be found at http://portal.unesco.org/shs/fr/ev.php-URL_ID = 3557&URL_DO = DO_TOPIC&URL_SECTION = 201.html (accessed 25 July 2008).
9 http://portal.unesco.org/shs/en/ev.php-URL_ID = 4677&URL_DO = DO_TOPIC&URL_SECTION = -477.html (accessed in 2004 and 25 July 2008).
10 http://portal.unesco.org/shs/en/ev.php-URL_ID = 4678&URL_DO = DO_TOPIC&URL_SECTION = -477.html (accessed in 2004 and 25 July 2008).
11 http://portal.unesco.org/shs/en/ev.php-URL_ID = 4677&URL_DO = DO_TOPIC&URL_SECTION = -477.html (accessed in 2004 and 25 July 2008).
12 The project was launched in 2002 with two brainstorming sessions at UNESCO Paris. Then followed four seminars on the philosophical aspects of promoting poverty as a human rights violation: at All Souls College, Oxford, February 2003; UNESCO Paris, April 2003; Sao Paulo University, Brazil, May 2003; and New Delhi, September 2003. In addition, there was one seminar of jurists/legal scholars in Sao Paulo University, Brazil, May 2003; and one of economists, in New Delhi, India, September 2003.
13 Asunción Lera St. Clair participated in the Oxford Workshop.
14 To give a flavour of his style, and views, we may cite his keynote address at the World Federalist Movement Congress, 13 July 2002, London.

> Combating massive human rights violations means also combating the violations of the masses who live in poverty where all human rights are being indiscriminately abused. ... Clearly the international human rights regime has not turned its attention urgently to economic and trade relations. Away from aid assistance to human rights obligations. Away from compassion to

global justice. ... Yes, the Berlin Wall may have come down. But other walls have been erected and they need to be brought down. The wall of poverty. The wall of intolerance. The wall of indifference. The wall of hypocrisy of governments who conference after conference promise to protect our common heritage and protect human rights.

(www.wfm.org/congress/sanespeech.html
[accessed 21 December 2004])

15 The original draft entitled 'Abolishing Poverty Through the International Human Rights Framework: Towards an Integrated Strategy for the Social and Human Sciences' is no longer available. However, a summary of this meeting, which includes suggestions for modification of the original text presented by UNESCO, and which was drafted building primarily on the closing comments made by Sané, is available at www.crop.org/publications/files/report/CROP_UNESCO_consultation_report.pdf (accessed 25 July 2008).

16 But the Director-General of UNESCO, Mr Matsuura, said in his message on Human Rights Day 2002,

> extreme poverty constitutes a denial of human rights and a flagrant violation of human rights. The fact that almost one-third of the worlds population lives in conditions of poverty is incompatible with the United Nations Charter, in which the States proclaimed their common determination to promote social progress and better standards of life in the ambit of broader freedom. The eradication of poverty is the clear priority on the international agenda, thereby confirming that freedom from want should be guaranteed for all.
> (Message by Director-General of UNESCO on Human Rights Day,
> UNESCO Media Services, 10 December 2002)

And on 5 February 2003, the High Commissioner for Human Rights and UNESCO's Director-General signed a memorandum of understanding in which the text states 'that extreme poverty is a flagrant violation of human rights and a denial of human dignity'.

17 See: Statement of the American Sociological Association on the U.S. Government Vetting of Scientists to Serve on International Advisory Bodies, 18 August 2004.

18 For example, it formally opposed a General Assembly resolution on the right to food, in the 57th session (September – December 2002). To quote the International Service for Human Rights (http://ishr.ch/About%20UN/Reports%20and%20Analysis/GA/GA-57thSession.pdf [accessed 1 February 2007]),

> Another controversy arose in the context of voting on the resolution of the right to food, with the US pushing what is called its 'more conservative view' on the right to food and economic and social rights in general. ... The US refused to join the consensus on the resolution as a whole, voting against it. The resolution was adopted by a vote of 176 in favour, one against (US), with seven abstentions (Australia, Canada, Fiji, Israel, Marshall Islands, Federated States of Micronesia, Palau).

19 There are always turf battles and unclear divisions of labour and expertise within the UN system. But it may be relevant here to refer to the UN General Assembly Draft Resolution IX, Human Rights and Extreme Poverty, which, in calling for action by United Nations bodies, specifies 'in particular the Office of the United Nations High Commissioner for Human Rights and the United Nations Development Programme'. (It is also worth noting the specific language used:

Recalling its resolution 47/134 of 18 December 1992, in which it reaffirmed that extreme poverty and exclusion from society constituted a violation of human dignity ...

1. Reaffirms that extreme poverty and exclusion from society constitute a violation of human dignity and that urgent national and international action is therefore required to eliminate them.

(A/57/556/add.2 ...)

20 By HRBA we refer also to the now accepted references to poverty as 'a denial of human rights', or 'freedom from poverty is a human right'.

21 Lourdes Arizpe states in this regard,

I was very impressed with many of the people of UNESCO, because of their commitment, their conviction, and their sense of mission. Many of them I had met in the 1970s and 1980s, so there was this whole generation, including my generation of 1968, that, paraphrasing Virginia Woolf, I would say, 'We galloped through life behind ideals.'

(UNIHP, Arizpe 2002: 30)

22 Cf. Arizpe:

I think the United Nations, in terms of ideas, is the conscience of the world. ... And I think the United Nations has an extremely important role, because even though it brings out resolution after resolution, so that you can paper the whole building with them, as I've heard it said, these resolutions place a mirror in front of governments and people.

(UNIHP, Arizpe 2002: 34)

7   The Inter-American Development Bank: 'social capital, ethics and development'

1 To quote the Articles of Agreement: 'The Bank and its officers shall not interfere in the political affairs of any member country. ... Only economic considerations shall be relevant to their decisions'.

2 To quote Louis Emmerij, formerly Special Advisor to President Iglesias, in his UNIHP interview with Iglesias:

What always struck me ... was that the Bank is really seen as Latin American – their bank. The Latin American Bank. Not only at the level of governments. Taxi-drivers! I would take a taxi to the local office of the BID, and I didn't have to give an address. The driver would start talking to me about what the BID should do. I think that is a sign of success.

3 Note: there is also a Caribbean Development Bank. See: www.caribank.org (accessed 25 July 2008).

4 This point was made by several interviewees. For example: 'IDB is prepared differently than WB people, when we go on a mission ... you can see that the dynamics of interactions are different in sociological terms because we have a wider range of skills'.

5 The seminar was organised by SUM (the Centre for Development and the Environment), of which Desmond McNeill was then Director. This was the start of the Centre's involvement in the Initiative, an involvement which continued for several years, with financial support from the Ministry of Foreign Affairs.

6 The Values Commission was widely criticised by the media, academics and others in Norway and had no lasting impact. For a representative and well articulated view see, for example, Siri Meyer in the Norwegian government's own *Maktu-tredning* ('report on power'). She criticises the Norwegian 'godhetsdiskurs' ('discourse of goodness'): 'The Values Commission was for example, against war, violence and traffic accidents, and for welfare and care. ... Thereby the recipient is placed in a specific position in the dialogue: as uncritical (klakør) or powerless. For who can be against the good?' (our translation).

7 We are included in this group, having received funds to prepare background papers, as noted above.

8 According to an interviewer in the *Washington Diplomat* in 2004, 'Kliksberg, 64, heads up the Bank's Inter-American Initiative on Social Capital, Ethics and Development. And his Orthodox Jewish faith has given him an unusual air of respectability in an organization dominated by Spanish- and Portuguese-speaking Catholics and Protestants.'

9 www.iadb.org/etica/ (accessed 25 July 2008). Cf. text on the current website – see endnote XX.

10 'There is a profound thirst for ethics in Latin America; there is a call for ethical values to shape the development process, the behavior of leaders, and to confront poverty and inequality.' Website: brochure.

11 Ref. McNeill (2007b). 'Es necesario integrar plenamente a la reflexion y a la practica de los esfuerzos por el desarrollo une dimension etica.' Iglesias International Seminar, 26 November 2002, La Paz, Bolivia.

12 The concept of 'social dialogue' has been developed and tested by staff associated with the Initiative (Piazze and Flaño Calderon 2005).

13 On the other hand, we also heard complaints about decisions being taken at headquarters in Washington DC and passed on to the country offices.

14 But according to one our interviewees, there was a substantial difference between the Ethics and Social Capital Initiative and, say, the issue of gender: that the former had the very strong personal support of President Iglesias.

15 The Norwegian government has redirected its financing to another trust fund.

16 In Spanish, La Comisión Económica para América Latina (CEPAL). Established as ECLA in 1948, it added the Caribbean to its name in 1984, to become ECLAC. We shall refer to 'ECLAC', except when quoting others.

17 The interview is almost in bilingual form with Emmerij speaking in English and Iglesias mainly responding in Spanish. The translation to English is ours.

18 http://66.102.9.104/search?q = cache:DArYA2fOFXQJ:www.iadb.org/exr/prensa/ biographies/evi97e.htm+enrique+iglesias+IDB&hl = no&ct = clnk&cd = 1&gl = no (accessed 21 April 2008). As one of our interviewees put it: 'Iglesias could do this – and other things – to a large extent because he worked masterfully through consensus and was careful not to go hard against the major shareholder.'

19 This appears to be a loaded comment in the light of Emmerij's follow-up remark, which represents a rather common view among IDB staff: 'Don't disperse yourself too much' (UNIHP, Iglesias 2001: 76).

20 In our conversations and interviews with diverse IDB staff, we found echoes of Iglesias' views. When describing the role of ethics or social justice in the IDB (outside the Initiative) we were repeatedly told that this was the background to IDB's strong focus on providing support and guidance for better public management, for the modernisation of the state, for focusing on poverty and inequality where ethical concerns arise; that social issues were much more important than in the World Bank, in the sense of being much more included and respected in standard economic work and analysis. Even if we did not explicitly refer to Iglesias, his charisma and his long-term engagement both in the region and in IDB came naturally into the conversation. At the time of our interviews, Moreno had

already taken over, and this was perhaps a period of doubt among the staff as regards the role of ethics and human rights.

8 Conclusion

1 Although there are members of the 'global elite' in the South, the overwhelming concentration of wealth is still in the North.
2 It is also worth noting that the social welfare societies in Scandinavian countries combine very low levels of poverty and inequality with very high levels of labour productivity.

Bibliography

Aiken, W. and LaFollette, H. (eds) (1995) *World Hunger and Morality*, Chicago IL: Prentice Hall.

Alkire, S. (2002) *Valuing Freedoms: Sen's Capability Approach and Poverty Reduction*, Oxford: Oxford University Press.

Alkire, S. and Ritchie, A. (2008) 'Winning Ideas: Lessons from Free-Market Economics', Oxford Poverty and Human Development Initiative, OPHI, Working Paper no. 6, www.ophi.org.uk/subindex.php?id = people101#publicationsSA

Alston, P. and Robinson, M. (2005) *Human Rights and Development: Towards Mutual Reinforcement*, Oxford and New York: Oxford University Press.

Aman, K. (ed.) (1991) *Ethical Principles for Development: Needs, Capacities or Rights*, Institute for Critical Thinking, Montclair State University, Montclair NJ.

Anderson, E. (1993) *Value in Ethics and in Economics*, Cambridge MA: Harvard University Press.

Appadurai, A. (ed.) (2002) *Globalization*, Durham NC: Duke University Press.

Appiah, K. A. (2006) *Cosmopolitanism: Ethics in a World of Strangers*, New York: Norton.

Apthorpe, R. (1997) 'Human Development Reporting and Social Anthropology', *Social Anthropology* 5:1, 21–34.

Arndt, H. W. (1987) *Economic Development: The History of an Idea*, Chicago IL: University of Chicago Press.

Ascher, C. S. (1950) 'The Development of UNESCO's Program', *International Organization* 4:1, 12–26.

Banerjee, A., Deaton, A., Lustig, N. and Rogoff, K. (2006) *An Evaluation of World Bank Research, 1998–2005*, http://siteresources.worldbank.org/DEC/Resources/84797-1109362238001/726454-1164121166494/RESEARCH-EVALUATION-2006-Main-Report.pdf

Barnett, M. and Finnemore, M. (2004) *Rules for the World: International Organizations in Global Politics*, Ithaca NY and London: Cornell University Press.

Barry, C. and Pogge, T. (eds) (2005) *Global Institutions and Responsibilities: Achieving Global Justice*, Oxford: Blackwell.

Bebbington, A., Woolcock, M., Guggenheim, S. and Olson, E. (eds) (2005) *The Search for Empowerment: Social Capital as Idea and Practice at the World Bank*, Bloomfield CT: Kumarian Press.

Berle, Adolph (1941) 'The Economic Interests of the United States in Inter-American Relations', *Department of State Bulletin* (June 28) 4:105, 756–760.

Broad, B. (2006) 'Research, Knowledge, and the Art of "Paradigm Maintenance": The World Bank's Development Economics Vice-Presidency (DEC)', *Review of International Political Economy* 13:3, 387–419.

Bull, B. (2005) *Aid, Power and Privatization: The Politics of Telecommunication Reform in Central America*, Cheltenham and Northampton MA: Edward Elgar.

—— (2006) Paper presented at the International Social Capital, Ethics and Development Day, 24 February, IDB.

Bull, B. and McNeill, D. (2007) *Development Issues in Global Governance: Public-Private Partnerships and Market Multilateralism*, London: Routledge.

Bøås, M. and McNeill, D. (2003) *Multilateral Institutions: A Critical Introduction*, London: Pluto Press.

Bøås, M. and McNeill, D. (eds) (2004) *Global Institutions and Development: Framing the World?*, London: Routledge.

Caney, S. (2005) *Justice Beyond Borders: A Global Political Theory*, London: Oxford University Press.

Carozza, P. G. (2003) 'From Conquest to Constitutions: Retrieving a Latin American Tradition of the Idea of Human Rights', *Human Rights Quarterly* 25, 281–313.

Cernea, M. (1995) 'Social Organization and Development Anthropology', *Human Organization* 54:3, 340–352.

Chatterjee, D. and McLean, D. (eds) (2004) *Ethics of Assistance: Morality and the Distant Needy*, Cambridge MA: Cambridge University Press.

Chiappero-Martinetti, E. (ed.) (forthcoming) *Debating Global Society. Reach and Limits of the Capability Approach*, Milan: Feltrinelli.

Circi, M. (2006) 'The World Bank Inspection Panel: Is It Really Effective?', *Global Jurist Advances* 6:3.

Coate, R. (1992) 'Changing Patterns of Conflict: The United States and UNESCO', in M. P. Karns and K. A. Mingst (eds) *The United States and Multilateral Institutions*. Merson Center Series on International Security and Foreign Policy, Volume V, London and New York: Routledge.

Cohen, D. (1993) 'Forgotten Actors', *PAS News and Events*, Evanston IL: Northwestern University Program of African Studies.

Comim, F., Qizilbash, M. and Alkire, S. (2008) *The Capability Approach: Concepts, Measures and Applications*, Cambridge: Cambridge University Press.

Commers, R., Vandekerckhove, W. and Verlinden, A. (eds) (2008) *Ethics in an Era of Globalization*, London: Ashgate.

Cornia, G., Jolly, R. and Stewart, F. (1987) *Adjustment with a Human Face*, Oxford: Clarendon Press.

Cox, R. W. (1969) 'The Executive Head: An Essay on Leadership in International Organization', reprinted in R. W. Cox with T. J. Sinclair (1996) *Approaches to World Order*, Cambridge: Cambridge University Press.

—— (1983) 'Gramsci, Hegemony and International Relations: An Essay in Method', *Journal of International Studies* 12:2, 162–175.

—— (1986) 'Social Forces, States and World Orders: Beyond International Relations Theory' in Keohane, R. O. (ed.) *Neorealism and its Critics*, New York: Columbia University Press, 204–254.

Crawford, N. (2002) *Argument and Change in World Politics: Ethics, Decolonization, and Humanitarian Intervention*, Cambridge MA: Cambridge University Press.

Crocker, D. (1991) 'Toward Development Ethics,' *World Development* 19:5, 457–483.

—— (2006a) 'Development Ethics, Globalization, and Stiglitz', in M. Krausz and D. Chatterjee (eds) *Globalization, Development, and Democracy: Philosophical Perspectives*, Lanham MD: Rowman & Littlefield.

—— (2006b) 'Foreword', in D. Goulet, *Development Ethics at Work: Explorations 1960–2002*, New York and London: Routledge.

—— (2008) *Ethics of Global Development: Agency, Capability, and Deliberative Democracy*, Oxford: Oxford University Press.

Crocker, D. A. and Schwenke, S. (2005) *The Relevance of Development Ethics for USAID*, Washington DC: United States Agency for International Development.

CROP (Comparative Research on Poverty Programme) (2003) 'Abolishing Poverty Through the International Human Rights Framework: Towards an Integrated Strategy for the Social and Human Sciences', Consultation Bergen, Norway, 5–6 June 2003. Organised by CROP for UNESCO, Sector for the Social and Human Sciences. Online. Available at www.crop.org/publications/files/report/CROP_UNES CO_consultation_report.pdf (accessed 24 July 2008).

Dañino, R. (2006) 'The Legal Aspects of the World Bank's Work on Human Rights', in C. Sage and M. Woolcock (eds) *The World Bank Legal Review: Law, Equity, and Development Volume 2*, Washington DC: World Bank and Martinus Nijhoff Publishers.

Darrow, M. (2003) *Between Light and Shadow: The World Bank, the International Monetary Fund and International Human Rights Law*, Portland OR and Oxford: Hart Publishing.

De Ferranti, D., Perry, G., Ferreira, F. and Walton, M. (2004) *Inequality in Latin America: Breaking with History? World Bank Latin American and Caribbean Studies 28989*, Washington DC: World Bank.

De Martino, G. F. (2000) *Global Economy, Global Justice*, London and New York: Routledge.

De Sousa Santos, B. (2008) *Conocer desde el Sur: Para una Cultura Política Emancipatoria*, La Paz, Bolivia: Plural editores.

De Sousa Santos, B. (ed.) (2007) *Another Knowledge is Possible: Beyond Northern Epistemologies*, London: Verso.

Deacon, B. (2007) *Global Social Policy and Governance*, London: Sage.

Deneulin, S. (2006) *The Capability Approach and the Praxis of Development*, Basingstoke: Palgrave Macmillan.

Derviş, K. and Ozer, C. (2005) *A Better Globalization: Legitimacy, Governance and Reform*, Washington DC: Brookings Institution Press.

Dower, N. (1988) 'What is Development? A Philosopher's Answer,' Centre for Development Studies, Occasional Paper Series 3, Glasgow: University of Glasgow.

—— (1998) *World Ethics: The New Agenda*, Edinburgh: Edinburgh University Press.

—— (2003) *An Introduction to Global Citizenship*, Edinburgh: Edinburgh University Press.

Doyal, L. and Gough, I. (1991) *A Theory of Need*, London: Macmillan.

Drydyk, J. (2005) 'When is Development More Democratic?' *Journal of Human Development* 6:2, 247–267.

Drydyk, J., Rukooko, B., Schwenke, S. and St. Clair, A. L. (2008) 'Introduction: Accountability, Responsibility and Integrity in Development', special issue of *Journal of Global Ethics*, 4:3, 231–245.

Durkheim, E. (1974) *Sociology and Philosophy*, New York: Free Press.

Dussel, E. (1978) *Ethics and the Theology of Liberation*, trans. Bernard McWilliams, hyperlink http://bibliotecavirtual.clacso.org.ar/ar/libros/dussel/camino21/camino21.html

—— (2007) *Política de la Liberación: Historia Mundial y Crítica*, Madrid: Editorial Trotta.

Easterly, W. (2006) *The White Man's Burden: Why the West's Efforts to Aid the Rest Have Done So Much Ill and So Little Good*, New York: The Penguin Press.

Erskine, T. (ed.) (2003) *Can Institutions Have Responsibilities: Collective Moral Agency and International Relations*, London: Palgrave.

Fanon, F. (1961–1963) *The Wretched of the Earth*, trans. C. Farrington, New York: Grove Press.

Farmer, P. (2003) *Pathologies of Power: Health, Human Rights, and the New War on the Poor*, California Series in Public Anthropology, Berkeley CA: University of California Press.

—— (2005) 'Never Again? Reflections on Human Values and Human Rights', the Tanner Lectures on Human Values, University of Utah, 30 March 2005. Online. Available at www.pih.org/inforesources/news/Farmer-Tanner-Lecture2005.pdf (accessed 24 July 2008).

Ferguson, J. (1994) *The Anti-Politics Machine: "Development", Depoliticization and Bureaucratic Power in Lesotho*, Minneapolis MN: University of Minnesota Press.

—— (2006) *Global Shadows: Africa in the Neoliberal World Order*, Durham NC and London: Duke University Press.

Frazer, N. (2005) 'Reframing Justice in a Globalizing World,' *New Left Review* 36, November–December.

Frazer, N. and Honneth, A. (2003) *Redistribution or Recognition? A Political-Philosophical Exchange*, London: Verso.

French, P. (1991) *The Spectrum of Responsibility*, New York: St Martin's Press.

—— (1992) *Responsibility Matters*, Lawrence KS: University Press of Kansas.

Fukuda-Parr, S. (2003) 'The Human Development Paradigm: Operationalizing Sen's Ideas on Capabilities', *Feminist Economics* 9:2–3, 301–317.

Gasper, D. (1997) 'Sen's Capability Approach and Nussbaum's Capabilities Ethic', *Journal of International Development* 9:2, 281–302.

—— (2002) 'Is Sen's Capability Approach Adequate?', *Review of Political Economy* 14:4, 435–461.

—— (2004) *The Ethics of Development: From Economism to Human Development*, Edinburgh: Edinburgh University Press.

—— (2006) 'What is the Point of Development Ethics?' in D. Gasper (ed.) 'Everything for Sale? Ethics of National and International Development', special issue of *Ethics and Economics / La revue Éthique et Économique* (University of Versailles) http://ethics-economics.com/IMG/pdf/GASPER-Intro-2.pdf

—— (2007a) 'Human Rights, Human Needs, Human Development, Human Security', *Forum for Development Studies*, 2007/1, 9–43.

—— (2007b) 'What is the Capability Approach? Its Core, Rationale, Partners and Dangers', *Journal of Socio-Economics* (Elsevier) 36:3, 335–359.

—— (2007c) 'Conceptualising Human Needs and Wellbeing', in I. Gough and J. A. MacGregor (eds) *Wellbeing in Developing Countries: New Approaches and Research Strategies*, Cambridge: Cambridge University Press, 47–70.

—— (2008a) 'From "Hume's Law" to Problem- and Policy-Analysis for Human Development: Sen after Dewey, Myrdal, Streeten, Stretton and Haq', *Review of Political Economy* 20:2, 233–256.

—— (2008b) 'Denis Goulet and the Project of Development Ethics: Choices in Methodology, Focus and Organizations,' Institute of Social Studies (ISS) Working Paper no. 456, hyperlink http://biblio.iss.nl/opac/uploads/wp/wp456.pdf (the paper is forthcoming in the *Journal of Human Development*).

Gills, B. K. (2006) 'The Global Politics of Justice',*Globalizations*, special issue, 3:2, June, 95–98.

Globalizations (2006) 3:2, June, special issue.

Glover, J. (2001) *Humanity: A Moral History of the Twentieth Century*, New Haven CT: Yale University Press.

Goldman, M. (2005) *Imperial Nature: The World Bank and Struggles for Social Justice in the Age of Globalization*, New Haven CT: Yale University Press.

Goodin, R. (1985) *Protecting the Vulnerable*, Chicago IL: University of Chicago Press.

Goulet, D. (1960) 'Pour une éthique moderne du développement', *Développement et Civilisations* 3, September, 10–23. (Translated into English in Goulet [2006a]).

—— (1969) 'The Disappointing Decade of Development,' *The Center Magazine*, Santa Barbara CA: Center for the Study of Democratic Institutions.

—— (1971a) *The Cruel Choice: A New Concept in the Theory of Development*, New York: Macmillan.

—— (1971b) 'An Ethical Model for the Study of Values', *Harvard Educational Review* 41:2, 205–227.

—— (1977) *The Uncertain Promise: Value Conflicts in Technology Transfer*, New York: IDOC.

—— (1980) 'Development Experts: The One-Eyed Giants', *World Development* 8, 481–489.

—— (1992) 'Interdisciplinary Learning in the United States: Old Problems, New Approaches', *American Studies* XII, 7–20.

—— (1995) *Development Ethics: A Guide to Theory and Practice*, London: Zed Books.

—— (1997) 'Development Ethics: A New Discipline', *International Journal of Social Economics* 24:11, 1160–1171.

—— (2000) 'The Evolving Nature of Development in the Light of Globalization', in *Proceedings of the Workshop on: The Social Dimensions of Globalization*, 21–22 February 2000, Vatican City: Pontifical Academy of Social Sciences, 27–46.

—— (2005) 'On Culture, Religion, and Development,' in Marguerite Mendell (ed.) *Recaiming Democracy: The Social Justice and Political Economy of Gregory Baum and Kari Polanyi Levitt*, Quebec: McGill–Queen University Press.

—— (2006a) *Development Ethics at Work: Explorations 1960–2002*, New York and London: Routledge.

—— (2006b) 'Development Ethics', 'Preface', 'Introduction', and 'Part I; Development Ethics,' in D. A. Clark (ed.) *The Elgar Companion to Development Studies*, Cheltenham: Edward Elgar, 115–121.

Green, M. (2005) 'Institutional Responsibility for Moral Problems', in A. Kuper (ed.) *Global Responsibilities: Who Must Deliver on Human Rights?*, London and New York: Routledge, Kindle edition, 117–135.

Griffiths, P. (2003) *The Economist's Tale: A Consultant Encounters Hunger and the World Bank*, London: Zed Books.

Haas, E. (1990) *When Knowledge Is Power: Three Models of Change in International Organizations*, Berkeley CA: University of California Press.

Haas, P. (1989) 'Do Regimes Matter: Epistemic Communities and Mediterranean Pollution Control', *International Organization* 43, 377–403.

Haas, P. (ed.) (1992) *Knowledge, Power and International Policy Coordination*, Columbia NC: University of South Carolina Press.

Hall, R. B. (1997) 'Moral Authority as a Power Resource', *International Organization* 51:4, 591–622.

Hall, R. B. and Biersteker, T. (2002) *The Emergence of Private Authority in Global Governance*, Cambridge: Cambridge University Press.

Haq, M. (1963) *The Strategy of Economic Planning*, Oxford: Oxford University Press.

—— (1976) *The Poverty Curtain: Choices for the Third World*, New York: Columbia University Press.

—— (1995) *Reflections on Human Development*, Oxford: Oxford University Press.

Haq, M. and Streeten, P. (eds) (1982) *First Things First*, Oxford: Oxford University Press.

Haq, K. and Kirdar, U. (1986) *Human Development: the Neglected Dimension*, Islamabad, Pakistan: North South Roundtable.

Hardin, G. (1974) 'Life Boat Ethics: The Case Against the Poor', www.garretthardin society.org/articles/art_lifeboat_ethics_case_against_helping_poor.html

Harper, R. (2000) 'The Social Organization of the IMF's Mission Work: An Examination of International Auditing', in M. Strathern (ed.) *Audit Cultures: Anthropological Studies in Accountability, Ethics and the Academy*, London: Routledge, 21–53.

Harvey, D. (2005) *A Brief History of Neoliberalism*, Oxford: Oxford University Press.

Hebblethwaite, P. (1994) *Paul VI: The First Modern Pope*, London: Fount Paperbacks.

Helleiner, E. (2007) 'The Project of International Development: Where Did it Come From?' Working paper presented at workshop on 'Global Governance, Poverty and Inequality', June 6–9, Centre for International Governance Innovation, Waterloo, Ontario.

Hickey, A. and Bracking, S. (2005) 'Exploring the Politics of Poverty Reduction: from Representation to a Politics of Justice?' *World Development* 33:6.

Hollis, M. (1991) *The Philosophy of Social Science: an Introduction*, Cambridge: Cambridge University Press.

Hopgood, S. (2006) *Keepers of the Flame: Understanding Amnesty International*, Ithaca NY: Cornell University Press.

Iglesias, E. (1992) *Reflections on Economic Development: Toward a New Latin American Consensus*, Washington DC: Inter-American Development Bank/Johns Hopkins University Press.

—— (2006) 'Raul Prebisch and David Pollock: The Cause of Development,' and 'Conclusion', in E. Dosman (ed.) *Raul Prebisch: Power, Principle and the Ethics of Development*, Washington DC: Inter-American Development Bank, 5–10, 121–124.

Ignatieff, M. (ed.) (2001) *Human Rights as Politics and Idolatry*, with an introduction by Amy Gutmann, Princeton NJ: Princeton University Press.

International Council on Human Rights Policy (ICHRP) (2003) *Duties sans Frontières: Human Rights and Global Social Justice*, Geneva: ICHRP.

International Labour Organization (ILO) (1976) *Employment, Growth, and Basic Needs: A One World Problem*, Geneva: ILO.

Jolly, R. (2003) 'Human Development and Neo-liberalism, Paradigms Compared', in S. Fukuda-Parr and A. K. Shiva Kumar (eds) *Readings in Human Development: Concepts, Measures and Policies for a Development Paradigm*, New Delhi: Oxford University Press.

—— (2005) 'The UN and Development Thinking and Practice', *Forum for Development Studies* 32:1, 49–74.

Jönsson, C. (1995) 'An Interorganization Approach to the Study of Multilateral Institutions: Lessons from Previous Research of International Cooperation', Development and Multilateral Institutions Programme, Working Paper no.1, Oslo: Fridtjof Nansen Institute/ECON.

Kahler, M. and Lake, D. A. (eds) (2003) *Governance in a Global Economy: political authority in transition*, Princeton NJ and Oxford: Princeton University Press.

Kanbur, R. (2001) 'Economic Policy, Distribution and Poverty: The Nature of Disagreements', *World Development* 29, 1083–1094.

Kaufmann, D., Kraay, A. and Mastruzzi, M. (2007) *Governance Matters: Governance Indicators for 1996–2006*. World Bank Policy Research Working Paper no. 4280.

Kaul, I. and Conceicao, P. (2006) *The New Public Finance; Responding to Global Challenges*, New York: Oxford University Press.

Kaul, I., Conceicao, P., Le Goulven, K. and Mendoza, R. U. (2003) *Providing Global Public Goods; Managing Globalization*, New York: Oxford University Press.

Kaul, I., Grunberg, I. and Stern, M. (1999) *Global Public Goods: International Cooperation in the 21st Century*, Oxford: Oxford University Press.

Keeley, J. and Scoones, I. (2003) *Understanding Environmental Policy Processes: Cases from Africa*, London: Earthscan Publishers.

Kiely, R. (2005) 'Globalization and Poverty, and the Poverty of Globalization Theory', *Current Sociology* 53:6, 895–914.

Killick, T., Gunatilaka, R. and Marr, A. (1998) *Aid and the Political Economy of Policy Change*, London and New York: Routledge.

King, K. and McGrath, S. (2004) *Knowledge for Development? Comparing British, Japanese, Swedish and World Bank Aid*, London: Zed Books.

Kliksberg, B. (2004) 'Examining Myths and Truths in Public Social Policy: The Latin American Case', *International Review of Administrative Sciences* 70.

Klingebiel, S. (1999) *Effectiveness and Reform of the United Nations Development Programme (UNDP)*, London and Portland OR: Frank Cass.

Kuhnle, S., Hatland, A. and Hort, S. (2003) 'A Work-Friendly Welfare State: Lessons from Europe', in K. Marshall and O. Butzbach (eds) *New Social Policy Agendas for Europe and Asia*, Washington DC: World Bank.

Kung, H. (1991) *Global Responsibility: In Search of a New World Ethic*, trans. J. Bowden, London: SCM Press.

—— (1998) *A Global Ethic for Global Politics and Economics*, Oxford: Oxford University Press.

Kuper, A. (ed.) (2005) *Global Responsibilities: Who Must Deliver on Human Rights?*, London and New York: Routledge, Kindle edition.

Mallaby, S. (2004) *The World's Banker: A Story of Failed States, Financial Crises, and the Wealth and Poverty of Nations*, New York: Penguin Press.

Marshall, K. and Keough, L. (eds) (2004) *Mind, Heart and Soul in the Fight Against Poverty*, Washington DC: World Bank.

Martinussen, J. D. and Engberg-Pedersen, P. (2003) *Understanding Development Cooperation*, London: Zed Books.

Mawdsley, E. and Rigg, J. (2002) 'A Survey of the World Development Reports I: Discursive Strategies', *Progress in Development Studies* 2:2, 93–111.

—— (2003) 'The World Development Report II: Continuity and Change in Development Orthodoxies', *Progress in Development Studies* 3:4, 271–286.

McNeill, D. (1981) *The Contradictions of Foreign Aid*, London: Croom Helm.

—— (2004) 'Social Capital and the World Bank', in M. Bøås and D. McNeill (eds) *Global Institutions and Development: Framing the World?*, London: Routledge.

—— (2005) 'Power and Ideas: Economics and Global Development Policy', in D. Stone and S. Maxwell (eds) *The Challenge of Transnational Knowledge Networks: Bridging Research and Policy in a Globalising World*, London: Routledge.

—— (2006) 'The Spread of Ideas in Development Theory and Policy: A Bibliometric Analysis', *Global Social Policy* 6:3, 334–354.

—— (2007a) '"Human Development": The Power of the Idea', *Journal of Human Development* 8:1, 5–22.

—— (2007b) 'Equity and Development: Is There a Place for Ethics?', in C. Sage and M. Woolcock (eds) *The World Bank Legal Review: Law, Equity, and Development Volume 2*, Washington DC: World Bank and Martinus Nijhoff, 419–440.

McNeill, D. and St. Clair, A. L. (2006) 'Development Ethics and Human Rights as the Basis for Poverty Reduction: the Case of the World Bank', in D. Stone and C. Wright (eds) *The World Bank and Governance: A Decade of Reform and Reaction*, London: Routledge.

—— (forthcoming) 'The World Bank's Expertise: Observant Participation in WDR 2006 Equity and Development', in D. Mosse (ed.) *The Anthropology of Expert Knowledge and Professionals in International Development*, Oxford and New York: Berghahn Books.

Milanovic, B. (2005) *Worlds Apart: Global and International Inequality 1950–2000*, Princeton NJ: Princeton University Press.

Miller-Adams, M. (1999) *The World Bank: New Agendas in a Changing World*, London: Routledge.

Moene, K. and Wallerstein, M. (2006) 'The Scandinavian Model and Economic Development', *Development Outreach*, Washington DC: World Bank Institute, 18–35.

Mosley, P., Harrigan, J. and Toye, J. (1991) *Aid and Power: The World Bank and Policy-Based Lending*, London: Routledge.

Mosse, D. (2005) *Cultivating Development: An Ethnography of Aid Policy and Practice*, London and Ann Arbor MI: Pluto Press.

—— (2007) 'Power and the Durability of Poverty: A Critical Exploration of the Links Between Culture, Marginality and Chronic Poverty', Chronic Poverty Centre Working Paper no. 107, hyperlink www.chronicpoverty.org/p/499/publication-details.php

—— (forthcoming a) 'Introduction', in D. Mosse (ed.) *Terms of Reference: The Anthropology of Expert Knowledge and Professionals in International Development*, Oxford and New York: Berghahn Books.

—— (forthcoming b) in D. Mosse (ed.) *Terms of Reference: The Anthropology of Expert Knowledge and Professionals in International Development*, Oxford and New York: Berghahn Books.

Murphy, C. (2006) *The UN Development Programme: A Better Way?*, Cambridge: Cambridge University Press.

Mutua, M. (2002) *Human Rights: A Political and Cultural Critique*, Philadelphia PA: University of Pennsylvania Press.

Nickel, J. W. (1987) *Making Sense of Human Rights*, Berkeley CA: University of California Press.

Niebuhr, R. (1950) 'The Theory and Practice of UNESCO', *International Organization* 4:1, 3–11.

Nordic UN Project (1991) *The United Nations in Development, Reform Issues in the Economic and Social Fields, Final Report by the Nordic UN Project*, Stockholm: Almqvist and Wicksell International.

Novak, M. (1984) *The Development of Catholic Social Thought*, New York: Harper and Row, 134–140.

Nussbaum, M. (2001) *Women and Human Development: The Capabilities Approach*, Cambridge: Cambridge University Press.

Nye, J. S. Jr (2004) *Soft Power: The Means to Success in World Politics*, New York: Public Affairs.

OHCHR (2002) *Draft Guidelines: A Human Rights Approach to Poverty Reduction Strategies*, Office of the High Commissioner for Human Rights, www.unhchr.ch/development/povertyfinal.html

O'Neill, O. (1986) *Faces of Hunger: Essay on Poverty, Justice and Development, Studies in Applied Philosophy*, New York: HarperCollins.

—— (1996) *Towards Justice and Virtue: A Constructive Account of Practical Reasoning*, Cambridge: Cambridge University Press.

—— (2000) *Bounds of Justice*, Cambridge: Cambridge University Press.

Osmani, S. (2005) 'Poverty and Human Rights: Building on the Capability Approach', *Journal of Human Development* 6:2, 205–219.

Patomaki, H. (2006) 'Global Justice: A Democratic Perspective', *Globalizations* 3:2, 99–120.

Patomaki, H. and Teivanen, T. (2004) *A Possible World: Democratic Transformations of Global Institutions*, London: Zed Books.

Paul VI (1967) 'Encyclical of Pope Paul VI: Populorum Progressio, 26 March 1967', hyperlink www.vatican.va/holy_father/paul_vi/encyclicals/documents/hf_p-vi_enc_2 6031967_populorum_en.html

Penz, P. (1991) 'The Priority of Basic Needs: Toward a Consensus in Development Ethics for a Political Engagement', in K. Aman (ed.) *Ethical Principles for Development: Needs, Capacities or Rights*, Montclair NJ: Institute for Critical Thinking, Montclair State University.

Piazze, A. and Flaño Calderon, N. (2005) *Diálogo social en América Latina. Un camino hacia la democracia ciudadana*, Washington DC: Inter-American Development Bank.

Pogge, T. (2002) *World Poverty and Human Rights: Cosmopolitan Responsibilities and Reform*, London and Cambridge: Polity Press.

—— (2004a) 'Can the Capability Approach be Justified?', *Philosophical Topics* 30:2, 167–228.

—— (2004b) '"Assisting" the Global Poor', in D. Chatterjee (ed.) *The Ethics of Assistance: Morality and the Distant Needy*, Cambridge: Cambridge University Press, 260–288.

—— (2005) 'What is Global Justice?', in T. Pogge and A. Føllesdal (eds) *Real World Justice*, Berlin: Springer, 2–11.

—— (2007) 'Severe Poverty as a Human Rights Violation', in T. Pogge (ed.) *Freedom from Poverty as a Human Right*, Oxford: Oxford University Press.

—— (2008) 'Pharmaceutical Innovation: Must We Exclude the Poor?', in T. Pogge, *World Poverty and Human Rights: Cosmopolitan Responsibilities and Reforms*, 2nd expanded edn, Cambridge: Polity Press.

Pogge, T. (ed.) (2007) *Freedom from Poverty as a Human Right: Who Owes What to the Very Poor?*, Oxford: Oxford University Press.

Pogge, T. and Føllesdal, A. (eds) (2005) *Real World Justice*, Berlin: Springer.

Polanyi, K. (1944) *The Great Transformation*, Boston MA: Beacon Press.

Putnam, R. (1993) 'The Prosperous Community', *The American Prospect* 4.

—— (2000) *Bowling Alone: The Collapse and Revival of American Community*, New York: Simon & Schuster.

Rajagopal, B. (2003) *International Law from Below: Development, Social Movements and Third World Resistance*, Cambridge: Cambridge University Press.

Rawls, J. (1993) *Political Liberalism*, New York: Columbia University Press.

—— (1999) *The Law of Peoples*, Cambridge MA: Harvard University Press.

Riddel, R. (2007) *Does Foreign Aid Really Work?*, New York: Oxford University Press.

Risse, T. (2004) 'Transnational Governance and Legitimacy', paper presented at the ECPR Steering Group on International Relations Conference, The Hague, 9–12 September 2004.

Robeyns, I. (2006) 'The Capability Approach in Practice', *Journal of Political Philosophy* 17:3, 351–376.

Robinson, W. I. (2002) 'Remapping Development in Light of Globalization: From a Territorial to a Social Cartography', *Third World Quarterly* 23:6.

Roemer, J. (2006) 'The 2006 World Development Report: Equity and Development', *Journal of Economic Inequality* 4: 233–244.

Roosevelt, F. D. (1941) 'The "Four Freedoms"', address to Congress, 6 January 1941.

Ruggie, J. G. (1982) 'International Regimes, Transactions, and Change: Embedded Liberalism in the Postwar Economic Order', *International Organization* 36:2, 379–415.

—— (1993) 'Territoriality and Beyond: Problematizing Modernity in International Relations', *International Organization* 47:1, 139–174.

—— (1997) 'Globalization and the Embedded Liberalism Compromise: The End of an Era?', Max Planck Institute for the Study of Societies, Working Paper 97/1, January. Available at www.ciaonet.org/wps/ruj01

Scholte, J. A. (2004) 'Democratizing the Global Economy: The Role of Civil Society', Coventry: CSGR, online, available at http://www2.warwick.ac.uk/fac/soc/pais/staff/scholte/publications/

Segal, J. (2002) 'What Is Development?', in V. Gehring and W. A. Galston (eds) *Philosophical Dimensions in Public Policy*, New Brunswick NJ: Transaction Publications.

Sen, A. K. (1981) *Poverty and Famines: An Essay on Entitlement and Deprivation*, Oxford: Oxford University Press.

—— (1985) 'Well-being, Agency and Freedom: The Dewey Lectures 1984', *Journal of Philosophy* 82, 169–221.

—— (1989) 'Development as Capabilities Expansion', *Journal of Development Planning* 19, 41–58.

—— (1999) *Development as Freedom*, New York: Knopf.

—— (2000) 'A Decade of Human Development', *Journal of Human Development* 1:1, 17–23.

—— (2002) 'Global Inequality and Human Security', Lecture 2, Ishizaka Lectures, Tokyo, 18 February. Online. Available at www.ksg.harvard.edu/gei (accessed 2 September 2003).

—— (2005a) 'Human Rights and Capabilities', *Journal of Human Development* 6:2, 151–166.

—— (2005b) *The Argumentative Indian: Writings on Indian History, Culture and Identity*, New York: Farrar, Straus and Giroux.

—— (2006) 'The Human Development Index', in D. A. Clark (ed.) *The Elgar Companion to Development Studies*, Cheltenham: Edward Elgar.

Sengupta, A. (2000) 'Realizing the Right to Development', *Development and Change* 31:3, 553–578.

—— (2002) 'On The Theory and Practice of the Right to Development', *Human Rights Quarterly* 24:4, 837–889.

—— (2007a) 'Poverty Eradication and Human Rights', in T. Pogge (ed.) *Freedom from Poverty as a Human Right: Who Owes What to the Very Poor?*, Oxford: Oxford University Press, 323–344.

—— (2007b) 'Extreme Poverty and Human Rights – A Mission Report on the United States' (6 January), http://papers.ssrn.com/sol3/papers.cfm?abstract_id = 961230

Sfeir-Younis, A. (2003) 'Human Rights and Economic Development: Can They Be Reconciled? A View from the World Bank', in W. Van Genugten, P. Hunt and S. Matthews, *World Bank, IMF and Human Rights*, Nijmegen, The Netherlands: Wolf Legal Publishers.

Shue, H. (1980) *Basic Rights: Subsistence, Affluence and U.S. Foreign Policy*, Princeton NJ: Princeton University Press.

Sindzingre, A. (2004) 'The Evolution of the Concept of Poverty in Multilateral Financial Institutions: the Case of the World Bank, in M. Bøås and D. McNeill (eds) *Global Institutions and Development: Framing the World?*, London: Routledge, 164–177.

Singer, P. (1972) 'Famine, Affluence and Morality', *Philosophy and Public Affairs* 1:1, 229–243.

—— (2002) *One World: The Ethics of Globalization*, New Haven CT: Yale University Press.

Skogly, S. (2001) *The Human Rights Obligations of the World Bank and the International Monetary Fund*, London: Cavendish Publishing.

Sridhar, D. (2007) 'Economic Ideology and Politics in the World Bank: Defining Hunger', *New Political Economy* 12:4.

St. Clair, A. L. (2003) 'Poverty Conceptions in the United Nations Development Programme and the World Bank: Knowledge, Politics and Ethics', Dr. Polit thesis, University of Bergen, Norway.

—— (2004) 'The Role of Ideas in the United Nations Development Programme', in M. Bøås and D. McNeill (eds) *Global Institutions and Development: Framing the World?*, London: Routledge.

—— (2006a) 'Global Poverty: the Co-production of Knowledge and Politics', *Global Social Policy* 6:1, 57–77.

—— (2006b) 'The World Bank as a Transnational Expertised Institution', *Global Governance* 12:1, 77–95.

—— (2006c) 'How Can Human Rights Work for Poverty Reduction? An Assessment of the Human Development Report 2000', in L. Williams (ed.) *International Poverty Law: An Emerging Discourse*, CROP International Studies in Poverty Research, London: Zed Books.

—— (2006d) 'Global Poverty: Development Ethics Meets Global Justice', *Globalizations* 3:2, 139–157.

—— (2006e) 'Development Ethics: Towards Open-ended and Inclusive Ethical Reflection for Global Development', in D. Banik (ed.) *Poverty, Politics and Development: Interdisciplinary Perspectives*, Bergen, Norway: Fagbokforlaget.

—— (2007) 'A Methodologically Pragmatist Approach to Development Ethics', *Journal of Global Ethics* 3:2, 143–164.

Stern, N. and Ferreira, F. (1997) 'The World Bank as an Intellectual Actor', in D. Kapur, J. P. Lewis and R. Webb (eds) *The World Bank: Its First Half Century*, vol 2, Washington DC: Brookings Institution Press, 523–609.

Stiglitz, J. (2002a) 'Ethics, Economic Advice, and Economic Policy', presentation at the Inter-American Development Bank. Online. Available at www.iadb.org/etica/documentos/dc_sti_ethic-i.htm (accessed 24 July 2008).

—— (2002b) *Globalisation and Its Discontents*, London: Penguin Press.

Stone, D. (2000) *Banking on Knowledge: The Genesis of the Global Development Network* (Warwick Studies in Globalisation), London: Routledge.

Stone, D. and Maxwell, S. (2004) *Global Knowledge Networks and International Development: Bridges Across Boundaries*, London: Routledge.

Stone, D. and Wright, C. (eds) (2006) *The World Bank and Governance: A Decade of Reform and Reaction*, London: Routledge.

Streeten, P. (1995) 'Foreword', in M. Haq, *Reflections on Human Development*, Oxford: Oxford University Press.

Streeten, P., Burki, S. J., ul Haq, M., Hicks, N. and Stewart, F. (1981) *First Things First: Meeting Basic Human Needs in the Developing Countries*, Oxford: Oxford University Press for the World Bank.

Summer, A. (2004) 'Epistemology and Evidence in Development Studies: A Review of Dollar and Kray', *Third World Quarterly* 25:6, 1167–1177.

Taylor, C. (2007) *A Secular Age*, Cambridge MA: Harvard University Press.

Turner, S. (2004) *Liberal Democracy 3.0*, London: Sage.

UN (1969) *Study of the Capacity of the UN Development System*, DP/5, vol I. New York: United Nations.

UNDP (1990–2007) *Human Development Reports*, New York: Oxford University Press.

—— (1998) *Human Development and Human Rights: Report of the Oslo Symposium*, Copenhagen: UNDP.

—— (2003) *Making Global Trade Work for People*, London and Sterling VA: Earthscan Publications.

—— (2004) The Arab Human Development Report 2004, 'Towards Freedom in the Arab World', www.pogar.org/publications/other/ahdr/ahdr2004e.pdf

—— (2005) The Arab Human Development Report 2005, 'Towards the Rise of Women in the Arab World', www.pogar.org/publications/other/ahdr/ahdr2005e.pdf

UNDP Annual Meeting, http://content.undp.org/go/newsroom/2007/june/ad-melkert-on-the-undp-strategic-plan-2008-2011.en

UNESCO (1995) *Our Creative Diversity: Report of the World Commission on Culture and Development*, Paris: UNESCO.

—— (2004) '*UNESCO Programme for "Eradication of Poverty Specially Extreme Poverty"*', Online. Available at http://unesdoc.unesco.org/images/0014/001415/141598E.pdf (accessed 24 July 2008).

UNIHP, Anstee, Margaret Joan (2000) The Oral History Interview of 14 December 2000, in *Oral History Collection of the United Nations Intellectual History Project*, The Graduate Center, The City University of New York. Interviewed by Tom Weiss.

UNIHP, Inglesias, E. (2001) The Oral History Interview of 3 and 6 November 2001, in *Oral History Collection of the United Nations Intellectual History Project*, The Graduate Center, The City University of New York. Interviewed by Louis Emmerij, in Washington DC.

UNIHP, Streeten, P. (2001) The Oral History Interview of 28–29 May 2001, in *Oral History Collection of the United Nations Intellectual History Project*, The Graduate Center, The City University of New York. Interviewed by Richard Jolly.

UNIHP, Arizpe, Lourdes (2002) The Oral History Interview of 9 May 2002, in *Oral History Collection of the United Nations Intellectual History Project*, The Graduate Center, The City University of New York. Interviewed by Tom Weiss.

Valladares, L. (2005) 'Louis-Joseph Lebret et les favelas de Rio de Janeiro (1957–1959): enquêter pour l'action', *Genèses* (Paris) 60, 31–56.

Vandekerckhove, W., Ronald Commers, M. S. and Verlinden, A. (2008) *Ethics in an Era of Globalization*, London: Ashgate.

Van Genugten, W. (2003) 'Introduction', in W. Van Genugten, P. Hunt and S. Mathews (eds) *World Bank, the IMF and Human Rights*, Nijmegen, The Netherlands: Wolf Legal Publishers.

Van Genugten, W., Hunt, P. and Mathews, S. (eds) (2003) *World Bank, the IMF and Human Rights*, Nijmegen, The Netherlands: Wolf Legal Publishers.

Van Genugten, W. and Perez-Bustillo, C. (eds) (2001) *The Poverty of Rights: Human Rights and the Eradication of Poverty*, CROP International Studies in Poverty Research, London: Zed Books. Online. Available at www.crop.org/publications/files/cisprserie/CROPZED2001GENUGTENBUSTILLO.pdf (accessed 24 July 2008).

Wade, R. H. (1996) 'Japan, the World Bank, and the Art of Paradigm Maintenance: The East Asian Miracle in Perspective', *New Left Review* 217.

—— (2002) 'US Hegemony and the World Bank: The Fight over People and Ideas', *Review of International Political Economy* 9:2, 215–243.

—— (2004) 'On the Causes of Increasing World Poverty and Inequality, or Why the Matthew Effect Prevails', *New Political Economy* 9:2, 163–188.

Wamala, E. (2008) 'Status to Contract Society: Africa's Integrity Crises', *Journal of Global Ethics* 4:3, 195–205.

Weiss, T. and Caryannis, T. (2005) 'Ideas Matter: Voices from the United Nations', *Forum for Development Studies* 132:1, 243–274.

Wells, C. (1987) *The UN, UNESCO and the Politics of Knowledge*, New York: St. Martins Press.

Wenar, L. (2006) 'Accountability in International Development Aid', *Ethics and International Affairs* 20:1, 1–20.

Wendt, A. (1999) *Social Theory of International Politics*, Cambridge: Cambridge University Press.

Willetts, P. (ed.) (1996) *The Conscience of the World: The Influence of Non-Governmental Organizations in the UN System*, Washington DC: Brookings Institution Press.

Wolfowitz, P. (2005) 'Charting the Way Ahead: The Results Agenda', address at the Annual Meeting of the World Bank and IMF, 24 September 2005, Washington DC. Online. Available at http://web.worldbank.org/WBSITE/EXTERNAL/NEWS/0,contentMDK:20659654~menuPK:34472~pagePK:34370~piPK:34424~theSitePK:4607,00.html (accessed 24 July, 2008).

Wollebæk, D. and Selle, P. (2002) 'The Voluntary Sector in Norway: Composition, Changes and Causes', Oslo: ISF-report 2.

Woods, N. (2006) *The Globalizers: The IMF, the World Bank, and Their Borrowers*, Ithaca NY: Cornell University Press.

World Bank (1981) *The World Bank, Accelerated Development in Sub-Saharan Africa: An Agenda for Action*, Washington DC: World Bank.

—— (1989) *Sub-Saharan Africa from Crisis to Sustainable growth*, Washington DC: World bank.

—— (2001) *World Development Report 2000/2001: Attacking Poverty*, Oxford: Oxford University Press.

—— (2006) *World Development Report 2006: Equity and Development*, New York, Oxford University Press (Outline 2004).

Young, I. (2004) 'Responsibility and Global Labor Justice', *Journal of Political Philosophy* 12:4, 365–388.

—— (2006) 'Responsibility and Global Justice: A Social Connection Model', *Social Philosophy and Policy* 23, 102–130.

Index

abolition: of poverty 28, 113, 120–5, 128–32 *see* poverty

Accountability 3, 34, 50, 123; mechanisms of 23, 112; *see* responsibility

activism 31–6, 46, 52, 125; *see* social movements

Adjustment with a human face 79, *see* UNDP

Africa 37, 66, 79, 94; and moral systems 54

Aid: development aid 38, 41–4, 122, 157, 130, 134, 164; foreign aid 3–6

Alienation 71

Alkire, S. 41–2

Allende, S. 66

Amnesty International 12, 18, 28, 52, 124

Annan, K. 47, 49, 69, 107, 118, 127, 132

Anti-globalisation 22

Arab States 74, 84

Arendt, H. 59

Arizpe, L. 115–18, 131–32

audiences: and expertise 91, 103–5

authority: delegated authority 11, 17, 21 26; moral authority 3–5, 11–12, 14–19, 21–29, 63, 85, 89–90, 114, 131–2; *see* political legitimacy

basic needs 34, 49, 77–9, 175

Berlin Wall 30, 165 note 14

Bondevik, K.M. 136, 139

Bourguignon, F. 103

Bretton Woods Institutions 4, 22, 47, 49, 65, 70–2, 79, 89

Brown, M.M. 65–9, 71, 84

bureaucracy 27–8, 98, 132, 151

capability 32–3, 50; functioning and 33–4; *see* poverty

Carozza, P.G. 46, 142

Catholic theology 37, 45

charismatic leader 93, 123, 132, 139, 145, 149, 15

charity 59, 130, 155 note 1

conditionality 5, 29, 65, 70, 87–8, 93

Chile 66, 135–8, 146, 148

China 21, 71, 85

Christianity 137

climate change 31–2, 43, 58, 62, 82

civic virtues 28; engagement 88; culture 42

clout 5, 11, 16–20; and World Bank 26; and UNDP 89; and UNESCO 131; and IDB 151

collective action 59, 60–1, 75, 139

common good 12, 15, 17, 26, 19 75, 151

communism 115

Comparative Research Programme on Poverty CROP 124–5

conditionality 5, 29, 65, 70, 87–88, 93

consensus 19, 33, 67, 72, 92; resolution 64; Washington 72, 81, 150

contestation 45, 91, 114, 121, 130, 139; intellectual 131; political 136

cosmopolitanism 4, 31, 34, 42–3

credibility 3, 23, 92, 94, 103

crime against humanity: poverty as 122

critical globalization studies 31, 41, 57, 146

critical legal theory 53

Crocker, D. 32, 34, 38

Dañino, R. 95, 105–6, 108

De las Casas, B. 45

De Sousa Santos, B. 51

democracy 25, 46, 133, 141, 143;
  economic and social growth and 133,
  138
development: research 2,30, 32, 38, 81,
  95, 103, 123; effectiveness 88, 140,
  144; ethics 32–4, 37–40, 140; *see* aid
duties 7, 47, 50, 53, 62, 107, 114, 125,
  126–8; *see* obligations

Economic Commission for Latin
  America and the Caribbean
  (ECLAC) 145–9
elite capture 53, 97
embedded liberalism 13, 153
empowerment 50, 97, 109–10, 138, 143
entitlement theory of justice 59
environmental protection 140
equity: development and 5, 27, 91, 95,
  97, 108; global 100;
ethics: analysis and 9, 33–4, 143, 156;
  globalization and 39, 44; language
  and 2, 27, 113; *see* development
experimental economics 98–9
expertise: economic 3, 5, 16, 18, 20,
  24–27, 91, 111, 151; knowledge 15,
  41, 129

famine 32–4
Ferreira, F.H.G. 104
food aid 34
Freedom: fundamental 46, 48, 120;
  from want 40, 44, 49, 165 note 16;
  negative 45; personal 45; positive 49;
  see poverty
Fukuda Parr, S. 82

Gandhi, M. 33
Gasper, D 32, 34, 37–40, 49, 86, 128
global justice: moral order 7, 44, 45;
  global responsibilities 44, 51,54, 56;
  see poverty; *see* responsibility
global norms 31, 45, 55, 130
global policy 76, 113, 160 note 16
global public goods 35, 63, 75–6, 89
Goulet, D. 39–41, 45, 140–1, 139
Gramscian hegemony 16

Hall, R. 11–12, 15, 22
Helleiner, E. 35, 142
human development: paradigm 3, 11,
  27–8, 63–4, 72–7, 83–90; index 24,
  80, 83
Human Development Report Office 21,
  23, 27, 33, 37, 73–76, *see* UNDP

human rights violations 52–3; denial of
  52, 86, 119, 124; justiciability 125–9;
  language and 129–32; see *poverty*
human security 34, 40, 49
HURITALK (human rights talk) 28,
  87, see *UNDP*

Iglesias, E. 28, 133–5, 136–9, 142–46,
  150–1
Independent Evaluation Group 26, 112;
  see World Bank
India 21, 102
Indigenous peoples 38, 45, 140
inequality 13, 34, 52, 136, 142 151–3
Inspection Panel 26, 95, 112, *see* World
  Bank
Institutional identity 11, 81
integrity 18, 82, 142; territorial integrity
  48; intellectual integrity 82
Inter-American Development Bank
  (IDB): Initiative on Social Capital,
  Ethics and Development 136–150; *see*
  Iglesias, E. and social capital
intercultural dialogue 11, 81
international collective action 75
international law 53, 107, 124

Jolly, R. 72, 79, 82
Justice between nations 7; *see* global
  justice

Kliksberg, B. 7, 137–9, 149–2, 144–5

Latin America 28, 35–7, 45, 66, 74, 103,
  133–151
Lebret, L.J. 37, 41, 140
liberal rights 45
Liberation theology 36–7, 45, 140–2

Marshall, K. 94–5, 139; *see* World Bank
Marx, K. 32; Marxist interpretations
  36–37
Matsuura, K. 116
Methodological territorialism 55, 129
MacNamara, R. 72, 93
Mexico 134, 137, 148
Milanovic, B. 152
Millennium Declaration 2, 31, 47–9,
  118; Millennium Development Goals
  (MDGs) 7, 31, 49, 72, 117–8, 132
minimum standard of living 53
moral agents; institutions as 9, 58, 61–2
morality 3, 5, 12, 14, 27, 29, 49, 57, 61,
  81, 139; accountability and 22;

discourse 3, 54–5; global 31;
  leadership 132; political 45; *see*
  authority and expertise
Moreno, L.A. 132, 135, 144
Murphy, G. 21, 61–72, 83–4; *see* UNDP

Narayan, D. 94
national sovereignty 5
neoliberal 24
neutrality 3, 14, 76, 92
New Deal 35
New International Economic Order
  (NIEO) 146
Non Governmental Organizations
  (NGOs) 4, 5, 12, 15, 22–3; World
  Bank and 26, 94, 99, 107; UNESCO
  and 132, 124, 151
Nordic countries 8, 50; World Bank and
  96, 106–7; UNESCO and 118
Norwegian ministry of foreign affairs 8,
  134, 137
Nussbaum, M. 32–3, 39, 41

obligation: justice of 57–60; legal 107–9,
  111–12; moral 4, 7, 43; positive 107;
  professionals and 99; well-being and
  58; *see* duties
observant participation 7–9–121
Office of Development Studies
organizational culture 92, 114
OXFAM 77

Palacio, A. 108–9; see *World Bank*
paradigm maintenance 92; *see* World
  Bank
Parliament of the Worlds Religions 42
participation in policymaking: citizens
  and 143; poor people and 47
peace 1, 34, 48; solidarity and 71;
  security and 87, 114–5–131–2
political legitimacy 4, 5, 9, 17–19, 25,
  32, 134, 143, 151
political philosophy 33, 36, 42, 55
political struggle 52, 129
Pope Paul VI 37
Pogge, T. 4, 55–6, 101, 129, 152;
  UNESCO and 121–2
Polanyi, K. 13
poverty: capability 33, 50; eradication
  of 120, 119, 124; freedom from 113,
  120–22; human rights and 47, 54,
  55, 114–15, 120–24, 128, 130;
  extreme 6, 8, 10, 31, 46–7, 62, 118–9,
  131, 151–2; pervasive 152; violation

of human rights as 28, 51, 114, 120–
  2, 124–5, 128, 130, 153; *see* abolition
Poverty Reduction Strategy Papers
  (PRSPs) 50
poverty studies 28, 132
power: moral 82, 46; political 51, 139;
  relations 3, 52, 114, 117, 128–9; soft
  15, 156 note 8; sources of 11, 14, 16,
  19, 23; struggle 54; *see* clout
Prebisch, R. 36, 145–50
Public opinion 23, 35

Ranis, G. 78
Rawls, J. 4, 34, 55–6
Realist school 12
Religion: values and 28,44; movements
  42, 114, 138
Response-able 9–10, 32, 57, 62, 112,
  130, 138
Responsibility: backward looking 57–8;
  forward looking 32, 58–9, 125, 130;
  moral 5, 9, 29, 55, 62, 86, 110, 124,
  152; liability model of 57, 159 note
  27 political 59, 61; protect to 114;
  restrictive conception of 4, 34, 55–6;
  shared 48, 59; *see* accountability
right: development to 34, 46–9, 137;
  education to 101; health to 51–2, 101;
  women of 45
rights-based approaches 34, 68, 86,
  96, 101
Robinson, M. 47, 50–1, 107, 113
Rodrik, D. 85
Roosevelt, F. D. 35, 44–5
Roosevelt, E. 44
Rwanda 57

Sané, P. 28, 113, 119, 121–7, 130–2
Scheffler, S. 59, 61–2
Secular beliefs 6, 43–4, 54, 98, 101, 142
Sen, A.K. 2, 4, 24, 33, 38; UNDP and
  75, 77, 80; World bank and 101; IDB
  and 133, 138, 140
Sengupta, A. 47–8, 51
Sfeir-Younis, A. 95, 109–10
social capital 28, 50, 99, 130, 137–8,
  140–2
social institutions 55–6
social movements 45, 51, 56, 139,
  141–2, 146
socio-economic and cultural rights 49,
  52, 108
solidarity 1, 28, 31, 35, 48, 52, 71, 130
Stewart, F. 78

Stiglitz, J. 24, 75
Streeten, P. 34, 77–8, 80
structural social injustice 57
structural violence 48, 52–4, 130, 149
sustainable development 63, 95, 105,
   109, 138, 143

Taylor, C. 44
tolerance 45, 130
trust funds 108–110 World Bank 134,
   137, 141 IDB

ul Haq, M. 37, 39, 77–83
United Nations Charter 1, 44, 85, 142
United Nations Children's Fund
   (UNICEF) 79
United Nations Development
   Programme (UNDP): administrator
   68–9; advocacy 71,7; ethics and
   human rights 83–9; governance
   and budget 66; global policies and
   76–7; history 64–66; in-country
   operations 69, 71; internal
   orgnisation 73–76; Office of
   development Studies 73–6; relations
   to other agencies 723; staff and
   expertise 66–68; *see* human
   development paradigm; see Human
   Development Report Office
United Nations Educational, Scientific
   and Cultural Organization
   (UNESCO): history 114–16;
   organization 116–18; poverty as a
   human rights violation project 118–
   128; Small Grants Programme 120;
   see poverty and human rights
   violations
United Nations Office of the High
   Commissioner for Human Rights
   (OHCHR) 47, 50–1
United Nations Intellectual History
   Project 74, 131, 145–6

United States 13, 45, 51–2; UNDP and
   66, 71; UNESCO and 113, 115, 125,
   126; IDB and 134–6

values; cognitive 101, 111; ethical 95,
   158 note 14, 167 note 10;
   fundamental 48, 105; intrinsic 99–
   101; instrumental 100; religious 28,
   44; shared 43;

Walton, M. 104
Weber, M. 14; Weberian 17
wellbeing 22, 138
Wolfensohn, J. 16, 22, 24, 26–7, 50,
   93–6, 103, 106–7, 109, 150; *see* World
   Bank
Wolfowitz, P. 22, 26, 93, 97, 103, 108–9;
   see World Bank
Wollstonecraft, M. 45
World Bank: 50 Years is Enough
   Campaign 94; Department for
   International Development UK
   (DfID) 100, 105, 1008; ethics and
   human rights agenda 94–95; financial
   power 92; international law 107–8;
   Legal Department 105; Legal Forum
   108; Nordic Baltic Office 106;
   Norway-Finland Trust Fund 108–9;
   World Development Report 2006 95,
   105; *see* response-able
World Development Report (WDR) 5,
   8, 23, 27, 91, 95–7; *see* World Bank
World Social Forum (WSF) 4, 56
World Trade Organisation (WTO) 10,
   12, 22, 85, 94
World War II 10, 30, 32, 35, 44, 53, 77,
   131

Young, I. 22, 57–61

Zimbabwe, 25
Zoellick, R. 93